THE UNIVERSITY OF WINCHESTER

Martial Rose Library
Tel: 01962 827306

‾ 6 OCT 2008

3 0 OCT 2008

To be returned on or before the day marked above, subject to recall.

D1393891

Socialism, Sex, and the Culture of Aestheticism in Britain, 1880–1914

Socialism, Sex, and the Culture of Aestheticism in Britain, 1880–1914

by
Ruth Livesey

A British Academy
Postdoctoral Fellowship Monograph

Published for THE BRITISH ACADEMY
by OXFORD UNIVERSITY PRESS

Oxford University Press, Great Clarendon Street, Oxford OX2 6DP

Oxford New York

Auckland Cape Town Dar es Salaam Hong Kong Karachi
Kuala Lumpur Madrid Melbourne Mexico City Nairobi
New Delhi Shanghai Taipei Toronto

With offices in
Argentina Austria Brazil Chile Czech Republic France Greece
Guatemala Hungary Italy Japan Poland Portugal Singapore
South Korea Switzerland Thailand Turkey Ukraine Vietnam

Published in the United States
by Oxford University Press Inc., New York

British Library Cataloguing in Publication Data
Data available

Library of Congress Cataloging in Publication Data
Data available

Typeset by J&L Composition, Filey, North Yorkshire
Printed in Great Britain
on acid-free paper by
The Cromwell Press Limited
Trowbridge, Wilts

ISBN 978–0–19–726398–3

Contents

List of Illustrations

Acknowledgements

A book that takes five years to complete runs up considerable intellectual, practical and moral debts in the passage from tentative idea to publication and I am glad to be able to tally up some of this account here. The work would not have taken shape without the continued support of the staff and Fellows of the British Academy. The award of a three-year postdoctoral fellowship enabled me to spend two years developing this work in the Centre for Nineteenth Century Studies at Birkbeck College; the selection of the book proposal by the Academy Publications Committee cushioned the completion of the manuscript whilst in my current post at Royal Holloway. Several lively centres for interdisciplinary thought have played a major part in shaping this book. The Centre for the Study of Women and Gender and the Challenging History Group at the University of Warwick helped me to learn how to talk to historians and to know when to stop; the Centre for Nineteenth Century Studies, Birkbeck College, remains an outstanding site for the exchange of ideas (and sociable nights out); most recently the Humanities and Arts Research Centre at Royal Holloway has acted as a constant reminder of the possibilities of work that pushes through disciplinary and academic boundaries. I owe particular thanks to the following individuals for their interest in, and comments on, the manuscript: Diana Maltz, Tonya Blowers, Carolyn Steedman, Emma Francis, Jo McDonagh, Nicola Bown, Sonny Kandola, Ana Vadillo, Marion Thain, Laurel Brake, Regenia Gagnier, Angelique Richardson, Stefan Collini, Carolyn Burdett, Peter Faulkner, John Batchelor, Simon Dentith, Peter Widdowson, Roger Ebbatson, Adam Roberts, Robert Hampson, Redell Olsen, and Isobel Armstrong.

The award of a Clark Library Fellowship by UCLA in 2002 enabled me to study the material covered in Chapter 5: my thanks to the Centre for Seventeenth and Eighteenth Century Studies and for the kind assistance of the staff of the William Andrews Clark Memorial Library itself during my month there. The archivists of the Special Collections, University College London, Sheffield City Libraries, the London School of Economics and the manuscripts department of the British Library have given much assistance to my research and permission to quote from manuscript sources where necessary. I thank Cambridge University Press for permission to reproduce Chapter 5 and some material from Chapters 1 and 4 which appeared respectively as 'Dollie Radford and the Ethical Aesthetics of Fin-de-Siècle Poetry' and in 'Morris, Carpenter, Wilde and the Political Aesthetics of Labor', *Victorian Literature and Culture*, 36 (2006), 495–517, and 34 (2004), 601–16. Part of Chapter 7 was published in 'Socialism in Bloomsbury: Virginia Woolf and the Political Aesthetics of the 1880s', *Yearbook of English Studies*, 37 (2007), 221–53. Permission to reproduce this material has been granted by the Modern Humanities Research Association. I would like to thank the following organizations for permission to reproduce visual material: the British Library (Radford frontispiece); The People's History Museum, Manchester (Hammersmith Socialist League photograph); The National Portrait Gallery (Fry portrait; Radford portrait; photograph of Woolf); City of Westminster Archives Centre (Shaw in Jaeger clothing); the Head of Sheffield Libraries, Archives and Information (photograph of Carpenter).

I owe two special debts (of rather different kinds) to two individuals who have shown continuous interest in the book from its germination to completion. First, Sally Ledger, whose advice and comments on the work have remained a constant source of support and intellectual stimulus, from her enthusiastic reply to my first query when framing the project, to her latter role as academic editor of the final manuscript. And second, but certainly not last, Paul Smith, who has never known me without this book being part of the household, but who, with the rest of my family, has always believed in its completion and taught me much along the way about the irreducibility of art.

List of Abbreviations

BL	British Library
BLPES	British Library of Political and Economic Science, London School of Economics
CL	*The Collected Letters of William Morris*, ed. Norman Kelvin, 4 vols. (Princeton: Princeton University Press, 1984–96).
CW	*The Collected Works of William Morris,* ed. May Morris, 25 vols. (London: Longmans, 1912–15).
FNL	Fellowship of the New Life
ILP	Independent Labour Party
LVW	*The Letters of Virginia Woolf*, ed. Nigel Nicolson, 6 vols. (London: Hogarth, 1975–80).
NUWSS	National Union of Women's Suffrage Societies
SCL	Sheffield City Library
SDF	Social Democratic Federation
Shaw: CL	*Bernard Shaw: Collected Letters*, ed. Dan H. Laurence, 4 vols. (London: Max Reinhardt, 1965–88).
SL	Socialist League
UCL	University College London
UCLA	University of California at Los Angeles
WPPL	Women's Protective and Provident League
WTUA	Women's Trade Union Association
WTUL	Women's Trade Union League

Introduction

> What Art gains from contemporary events is always a fascinating problem,
> and a problem that is not easy to solve. It is, however, certain that Socialism
> starts well equipped. She has her poets and her painters, her art-lecturers and
> her cunning designers, her powerful orators and her clever writers. If she fails
> it will not be for lack of expression. If she succeeds, her triumph will not be
> a triumph of mere brute force.[1]

In 1889 Oscar Wilde suggested to the readers of the *Pall Mall Gazette* that
the growth of socialist activism over the previous decade had been nurtured
by the arts. The rousing verse in the book he was reviewing at the time,
Edward Carpenter's collection, *Chants of Labour*, when added to the lectures of William Morris, the engravings of Walter Crane, and endless
debates on the future of the arts after the revolution in drawing-rooms and
meeting-halls across the country persuaded Wilde that socialism was
inescapably intertwined with aesthetics during the 1880s. This relationship
between revolutionary politics and the sensuous pleasure of the arts was at
odds with the aestheticism through which Wilde defined his own work at the
time. By the last decades of the nineteenth century, the critical movement of
aestheticism had come to be associated with an insistence on the freedom of
art from the ethical claims of the world: the individual artist could revel
in the pleasure of art for the sake of that art alone, assured that a higher
truth than that of daily life lay in the autonomous sphere of the aesthetic.[2]
This study explores how the artists and writers involved in the socialist
movement during this period evolved a distinct socialist aesthetic in creative
tension with such aestheticism. Whilst aestheticism tended towards individualism, the sensuous pleasures of taste and consumption, and insisted on

---

[1] Oscar Wilde, 'Poetical Socialists', *Pall Mall Gazette* (13 Feb. 1889), 3.
[2] The term 'aestheticism' remains as open to broader definitions now, however, as does its
complex intellectual history in the 19th cent. traced in Ch. 1 of this work. For two recent studies that work with a more inclusive definition see Diana Maltz, *British Aestheticism and the
Urban Working Classes, 1870–1900: Beauty for the People* (Basingstoke: Palgrave, 2005) and
Ana Parejo Vadillo, *Women Poets and Urban Aestheticism: Passengers of Modernity*
(Basingstoke: Palgrave, 2005).

the absolute autonomy of the aesthetic, socialist writers tried to frame an alternative in which art was by its very nature a communal product of labour and will, with only relative freedom from the material determination of capitalism.

Writing in 1889 Wilde could safely (and misguidedly) separate socialism in the metropolis from 'brute force'. Two years had passed since the events of 'Bloody Sunday' on 13 November 1887 when the brutal repression of a mass socialist demonstration in Trafalgar Square had resulted in the deaths of demonstrators and the arrest of William Morris. Only a few months after the publication of Wilde's article the remarkable upsurge in labour activism and unionization that surrounded the great dock strike renewed fears (and hopes) that a mass proletarian uprising might bring on the revolution before the end of the decade. In the relative calm of early 1889, however, Wilde could play with the relations between politics and aesthetics, 'brute force' and art. Subversively, paradoxically, typically, Wilde's article is structured by a trope of seduction that hints at unforeseen offspring from this flirtation of Art with 'fascinating' Socialism in the drawing-room, whilst crude, burly, brute force is relegated safely to the servants' quarters. Socialism, for Wilde, has a sex, and 'she has the attraction of a wonderful personality . . . and draws in this man by his hatred of injustice, and his neighbour by his faith in the future, and a third, it may be, by his love of art, or by his wild worship of a lost and buried past'.[3] It might not be simply the case that Art will '[gain] from the contemporary events' of Socialism, but rather that it will be seduced by a political mistress who makes all ends secondary to her own revolutionary hopes.

In this book I pursue Wilde's fleeting (but characteristically incisive) allusion to the sex of socialism and its relationship with aesthetics by examining the lives and works of socialist writers and activists in late nineteenth- and early twentieth-century Britain. The focus of the work falls on a disparate group of writers, all of whom met in London during the early 1880s in search of a new life.[4] That this new life was characterized as socialism or the solution to the labour question distinguishes these writers from the familiar mid-nineteenth-century narrative of the young hopeful moving to the city.[5] The metropolis, in this book, is never merely a backdrop to the writer's *Bildung* but a political subject in its own right that shapes that

---

[3] Wilde, 'Poetical Socialists', p. 3.

[4] Stephen Yeo uses the term 'new life' to characterize the millenarian spirit of late 19th-cent. socialism, although his study focuses on the non-metropolitan roots of the ILP: see 'A New Life: The Religion of Socialism in Britain, 1883–1896', *History Workshop Journal*, 4 (1977), 5–56.

[5] See Franco Moretti, *The Way of the World: The Bildungsroman in European Culture* (London: Verso, 1987).

journey of development. Writing to her husband in 1908, the South African writer Olive Schreiner recalled her time in London and asserted that 'no one who did not *live* through it can ever know the joy, and hope, and passion of enthusiasm with which we worked [for the socialist movement] in those years in the eighties'.

> I was talking about it with Keir Hardie and tears came into both our eyes when we spoke of it. But it was not for nothing. The solid, stolid (call it sordid if you will), but *real* advance in the condition of the working classes in England is the result of that movement, begun and carried on almost entirely by a small handful of men and women mostly of the 'upper' classes and all of ability. It was the brilliant sunrise, without which there could not have been any day.[6]

For Schreiner, London in the 1880s was memorialized as a time of hope; a time and place in which the beliefs of a few writers, artists, and campaigners led to the wider mobilization of the twentieth-century labour movement. The advance in the condition of the working classes that resulted from such activism may have disappointed Schreiner, like so many of the other writers studied here, because of its unaesthetic and, she feared, 'sordid' qualities. But despite the divergence between her hope that socialism would lead to a new life of beauty and fellowship, and the actual pragmatic development of labour representation and 'real' state welfare provision, Schreiner still laid claim to her place in history as a worker of that bright dawn.[7]

Schreiner's contribution to the movement was certainly rather different from that of her visitor in 1908, James Keir Hardie, the founding chairman of the Independent Labour Party (ILP). Although Schreiner's writings from the 1880s and 1890s were undoubtedly engaged with the question of labour (and also, unusually for the time, colonialism), it would be a stretch to characterize her as a socialist activist during the period within current understandings of the term. Schreiner's ability to conceive of herself as a fellow worker in the great cause stemmed rather from the peculiarly idealist and aesthetic nature of British socialism in the late nineteenth century. In this belief system, which Stephen Yeo has characterized as the 'religion of socialism', a writer or an artist—even a woman writer or artist—could conceive of herself as crafting the new life of socialism through her effortful aesthetic

---

[6] Olive Schreiner to S. C. Cronwright-Schreiner, 8 May 1908 in *The Letters of Olive Schreiner, 1876–1920*, ed. S. C. Cronwright-Schreiner (London: T. Fisher Unwin, 1924), pp. 278–9.

[7] On the transition from the ethical socialism of the 1880s and 1890s to the formation of the Labour Representation Committee and Parliamentary Labour Party see Stanley Pierson, *British Socialists: The Journey from Fantasy to Politics* (Cambridge, Mass.: Harvard University Press, 1979), pp. 45–80, 125–57.

labour.[8] Socialist lecturers such as Edward Carpenter and William Morris worked with a distinctive, politicized aesthetic during the 1880s in which both the manual labourer and the artist stood on the same aesthetic continuum. Both were struggling to bring forth the new life by producing objects that united all in a communal desire for the still greater beauty that could only exist under socialism. Whilst some of the writers studied here—for example, William Morris, George Bernard Shaw, and Clementina Black—are well known (if not best known) for their political activism and labour organization, others, such as Schreiner and Dollie Radford, made a contribution through their writings alone. These aesthetic contributions were considered an important part of the work of the movement from the early 1880s and the chapters that follow will chart the cultural significance of such texts in their particular intellectual contexts.

The reassessment of politics, aesthetics, and early modernism that results from these detailed studies offers a significant revision to current accounts of literary history. The productive, communal ideal of art associated with socialism was an important counterweight to the contemporary developments of decadent aestheticism at the fin de siècle and both of these models, I argue, went on to play a part in shaping modernist aesthetics in the decades that followed. Crossing the conventional divide between Victorians and modernists, I show how the socialist debates of the 1880s and early 1890s persisted and were refracted in the works of modernist writers and critics such as Virginia Woolf, Roger Fry, and Alfred Orage in the early twentieth century. The pages of socialist journals reflect an enduring conflict between different beliefs about the nature and aims of art: between decadence and ethical purposiveness in criticism; playful self-reflection and earnest communal idealism in poetry; style and content in the novel. Regenia Gagnier has argued that the 1880s and 1890s were increasingly dominated by an aesthetic of consumption, but socialist writers and activists in the same period disseminated a model of virile production in which the making of goods, rather than the delectation of refined style was championed as the ultimate access to beauty.[9] That some writers, most notably William Morris, but also Dollie Radford, espoused such socialist aesthetics whilst being co-opted as aesthetes by the decadents is just one example of the complex intertwining of political and literary history traced through in this book. A politicized (and gendered) aesthetic permeated the broad spectrum of socialist thought at the turn of the century and, as I shall

---

[8] Yeo, 'New Life', p. 5.
[9] Regenia Gagnier, *The Insatiability of Human Wants: Economics and Aesthetics in Market Society* (Chicago: University of Chicago Press, 2000), pp. 54–9.

argue in the final chapters of this book, seeped out into the wider literary community to form part of the dialectic from which modernist aesthetics emerged.

That the development of the modern British socialist movement in the early 1880s was marked by a particular preoccupation with aesthetics as well as politics has been as evident to recent scholars as it was to Oscar Wilde. In part this fusion of questions of artistic production, taste, and the nature of beauty with capitalism, class-consciousness, and revolution can be attributed to the cultural origins of British socialism. Whilst some eminent socialists such as George Bernard Shaw and Beatrice Webb moved from the radical Liberal inheritance of the Utilitarian tradition to Fabian municipal socialism—from calculating the 'greatest happiness for the greatest number' to planning what William Morris dismissed as 'gas and water socialism'—many others traced a path from a very different, but equally indigenous, tradition of social criticism. The works of both William Morris and Edward Carpenter, for example, reveal a profound debt to John Ruskin and Thomas Carlyle: critics whose jeremiads against the age of machinery were grounded in the discourse of aesthetics and put this ideal to work in the realm of ethics and economics. Stanley Pierson argues that the form of Marxism disseminated in Britain from the early 1880s was thus shaped to fit such pre-existing romantic idealist critiques of capitalism.[10] We shall see shortly how Ruskin and Carlyle's projection of 'their intense . . . aesthetic feelings into vivid pictures of transformed social relations', as Pierson puts it, informed the move towards socialism on the part of numerous later nineteenth-century writers and activists.[11] For Pierson this attempt to fuse aesthetics and politics, Ruskin and Marx, most notable in the work of William Morris, resulted in the stunted growth of British Marxism and social democracy.[12] It is, however, this very co-articulation of the political and the aesthetic—of necessity and desire— that E. P. Thompson commemorates as William Morris's legacy to the British socialist movement. According to Thompson, Morris 'grafted Ruskin to the stem of Marx', allowing the sap of historical materialism to give new life to Ruskin's aesthetic concerns.[13]

The debate between Pierson and Thompson is an instructive reminder here that, from a twentieth-century critical perspective, politics and aesthetics

---

[10] Stanley Pierson, *Marxism and the Origins of British Socialism: The Struggle for a New Consciousness* (Ithaca, NY: Cornell University Press, 1973), pp. 22–38, 75–80.
[11] Ibid. 22.
[12] Ibid. 80.
[13] E. P. Thompson, *William Morris: Romantic to Revolutionary* (London: Lawrence & Wishart, 1955), p. 733.

always started out as either/or, rather than both/and.[14] Even Thompson's metaphor of hybridization implies a need for artificial selection: socialism and aesthetics develop as inorganic growth, nature's bastards. But no such profound sense of disarticulation is visible in the writings of the ethical socialists and romantic revolutionaries whose works are studied in this book. The last two decades of the nineteenth century witnessed a remarkable disregard, in this respect, of boundaries that over a century later seem impassable divides. That desire among radical critics of late nineteenth-century capitalism to find a new life led to an eclectic collation of belief systems: spiritualism, theosophy, Emersonian transcendentalism, Nietzschean notions of the will, Ruskinian medievalism, alongside the more material influences of Marx and Engels.

Scanning the minute books and lecture programmes of early metropolitan socialist organizations reveals that, as both speakers and audience members, individuals who are now affixed to one particular group by the lens of carefully focused historical monographs in fact glided over the capital, surfacing wherever suitably radical fare was on offer. The desire for synthesis outweighed the inevitable scoring of lines in the sand between fracturing socialist groupings such as H. M Hyndman's Marxist Social Democratic Federation and Morris's anarchistic-tending Socialist League. As Terry Eagleton has observed, fin-de-siècle intellectuals 'blend belief systems with staggering nonchalance, blithely confident of some invisible omega point at which . . . Emerson lies down with Engels'.[15] The pleasures of the archive offer up an object that correlates Eagleton's summary in the shape of the first minute book of the Fabian Society executive. On the inner front cover is written bold, 'Society for Psychical Research: Haunted Houses Committee Notebook', by the future Fabian secretary Edward Pease, followed by the stubs of several excised pages of notes, before the book starts a new life recording meetings with socialists, rather than apparitions.[16] Far from a firm boundary existing between the spiritual and the material, the utopian and the reformist, the seeming opposites are literally bound together in this past.

The careful work of social historians has done much to uncover the integration of aesthetic culture within socialists' theory and practice from the

[14] This useful distinction is found in Ruth Robbins, 'The Genders of Socialism: Eleanor Marx and Oscar Wilde', in John stokes (ed.), *Eleanor Marx: Life, Work, Contacts* (Aldershot: Ashgate, 2000), pp. 99–113.

[15] Terry Eagleton, 'The Flight to the Real', in Sally Ledger and Scott McCracken (eds.), *Cultural Politics at the Fin de Siècle* (Cambridge: Cambridge University Press, 1995), pp. 11–22 (p. 12). On the particular debt of British Socialism to Emerson see Mark Bevir, 'British Socialism and American Romanticism', *English Historical Review*, 110 (1995), 878–901.

[16] BLPES archives, LSE, Fabian Collection C1.

1880s into the early twentieth century. Chris Waters and Carolyn Steedman, for example, have both concluded that a belief in the capacity of natural beauty and art to reform the individual underlay socialist activities at the turn of the century as diverse as the choirs and cultural tours of the Clarion movement and Margaret McMillan's open-air kindergarten experiments.[17] Although the self-styled scientific and gradualist socialists of the Fabian Society were notable for their explicit attempts to distance themselves from this aesthetic dimension of socialism from the late 1880s onwards, Ian Britain's work also reveals the continued interest in the arts on the part of many prominent activists.[18] As we shall see in later chapters, however, the best-known Fabian writer, George Bernard Shaw, remained sceptical about the practical use of the arts in advancing real improvement in the lives of the working classes. Sitting through an ecstatic idealist address from Edward Carpenter in 1886 forced Shaw into voicing his doubts in the margins of the meeting's minute book. Carpenter's lecture praised the ethical value of returning to the 'simple life' of subsistence farming to a collection of middle-class ladies and gentlemen in a Bloomsbury drawing-room and Shaw found a release for his sense of the futility of such projects by scribbling down a description of the fidgety audience:

> Awfully dull meeting. [Charlotte] Wilson yawning like anything—no wonder. Infernal draught from the window. Coffin fidgeting—putting coals on the fire, distributing ipecacuanha lozenges and so on. Miss Coffin sitting on the land-ing, evidently bored . . . Somebody making a frightful noise like the winding of a rusty clock. Mrs Bland [E. Nesbit] suspected of doing it with the handle of her fan. Wish she wouldn't.

Shaw concluded that 'two or more meetings like this should finish off any society' and went on to play a central part in redirecting the work of the Fabian Society away from the numinous idealism of Carpenter's return to the land towards political lobbying and urban social investigation.[19] Britain's work, however, presents a very different analysis of the relationship between Fabianism and culture from Shaw's simple dismissal of Carpenter's aesthetic idealism. Not only were a large number of artists and writers members of the Fabian Society during the late nineteenth and early twentieth centuries, but also the *New Age*, a journal central to the dissemination of

---

[17] Chris Waters, *British Socialism and the Politics of Popular Culture, 1884–1914* (Manchester: Manchester University Press, 1990); Carolyn Steedman, *Childhood, Culture and Class in Britain: Margaret McMillan, 1860–1931* (London: Virago, 1990), pp. 87–97.
[18] Ian Britain, *Fabianism and Culture: A Study in British Socialism and the Arts* (Cambridge: Cambridge University Press, 1982).
[19] BLPES, Fabian Collection C36.

early modernist literature, was established by members of the Fabian Arts Group in 1907. Articles on guild socialism as a source for the rebirth of the arts and on art and revolution appear in the *New Age* as late as 1914 and rub up against the early works of Ezra Pound and F. T. Marinetti's Futurist Manifesto. The distinctive pluralism of 1880s socialism and its promise of the both/and of aesthetics and politics thus left a legacy within the socialist movement well into the twentieth century.

In this inclusive context of emergent socialism during the 1880s, the aesthetic aspect of socialist debate provided a space in which the deep-seated idealism that underlay earlier radical traditions of political critique could be brought together with historical materialism. The ethical socialists who founded the Fellowship of the New Life in the early 1880s, for example, and who later, as Pierson suggests, exerted a profound influence over the identity of the ILP, argued that the goal of socialism was nothing less than the perfection of human character.[20] Hubert Bland, Percival Chubb, Isabella Ford, James Ramsay MacDonald, and many other members of the Fellowship went on to join socialist organizations with more materialist manifestos such as the Fabian Society and the ILP. But these ethical socialists retained a belief in the necessity of revolution both within the individual subject and in the organization of the means of production. Whilst they expressed the necessity of change within the individual in terms of ethics, or the 'religion of socialism', it was, I want to argue, the category of the aesthetic that provided the vector between an idealist revolution in the ethics of the subject and a material revolution in the organization of the means of production.

In 1894 Katherine St John Conway co-authored a pamphlet, titled *The Religion of Socialism: Two Aspects*, for the socialist Clarion organization with her husband John Bruce Glasier. Conway's section of the text was a secular parable, in prose that echoes the cadences of the King James Bible, recounting a rich young man's encounter with (and subsequent conversion by) the deity of the religion of socialism. The young man's guide tells of his desire for the socialist future, envisioned as:

> A race of men and women who work together for the need of each, and who strive in every way that the powers of every man, woman and child, may be called forth to the uttermost, that real wealth may abound and that never a beautiful picture, a glorious song, or a triumph over nature may be lost to the human race.[21]

---

[20] See Pierson, *Marxism*, and *British Socialists*, pp. 45–80.

[21] Katherine St John Conway, 'The Religion of Socialism', in Katherine St John Conway and J. Bruce Glasier, *The Religion of Socialism: Two Aspects* (Manchester: Manchester Labour Press, 1894), p. 5.

Conway's text is a good example of the double work of aesthetic discourse—work of both form and of content—within the late nineteenth-century socialist movement. The register of the prose marks it as something outside political polemic and closely reasoned argument (the register favoured by Bruce Glasier in his contribution). The use of the form of parable demands a reader who grants a special status to the ethical value of stories—who endows the art of narrative with the autonomy and authority to comment on the world. The form thus constructs a space of alterity and possibility; a space Morris identifies in his socialist utopian visions as that of hope and which Olive Schreiner also draws upon in her dreams and allegories. Like Schreiner and Morris, Conway not only uses a self-consciously aesthetic form, but the content melds together aesthetics and economics in its vision of socialism. The 'real wealth' that will be called forth under socialism will be aesthetic value rather than that determined by use or exchange: 'beautiful pictures, glorious songs'. The revolution in economic organization will liberate the individual subject into labour for the commune and thus the human 'race' will become a thing of beauty. The prospect of a new life of beauty in the socialist hereafter thus fuelled the latent idealism of many seeking a new belief system: the aesthetic and the political were inseparable in enthusiasm for the 'religion of socialism'.

The category of the aesthetic provided late nineteenth-century socialists like Conway with a means of imagining a world without the capitalist system of commodification, whilst the use of aesthetic form ensured that readers themselves engaged with this process of imagining. As Andrew Bowie has argued, with the rise of industrial modernity from the beginning of the nineteenth century, the 'aesthetic becomes a utopian symbol of the realization of freedom: in it we can see or hear an image of what the world could be like if freedom were realised'.[22] The idealist tendency within the socialist movement meant that this alternate world of the aesthetic served not just as a utopian vision of the new life of socialism but also as a means of bringing the new life into being. The encounter with beauty stimulated hope and desire within the individual subject and these transitive qualities formed a bridge between the aesthetic ideal and the material world: wanting socialism was one means of making it so. Looking back to the early years of the socialist movement, Olive Schreiner noted how her friend Edward Carpenter's long poem, *Towards Democracy*, evoked that intense idealism of the 1880s: 'Of course Ed. Carpenter's book touches us in a way it can't others, just because it brings us back to that time—"All we have

---

[22] Andrew Bowie, *Aesthetics and Subjectivity from Kant to Nietzsche* (Manchester: Manchester University Press, 1990), p. 47.

dreamed or hoped or willed of good shall exist"'.[23] Katherine St John Conway also reflected that, after hearing Edward Carpenter lecture during the 1880s, 'the earth reborn to beauty and joy' seemed just around the corner, wanting only the popular spread of desire for this new life to make it real.[24] Although the degree of power granted to such individual acts of desire in hastening the revolution varies between the socialist writers studied in this work, there is a general agreement between these writers that if any sphere can retain some autonomy from the material determinations of capitalism, it is that of the aesthetic. Carpenter's belief that capitalism could be ended by individuals desiring and evolving themselves closer to the Neoplatonic idea of the beautiful is evidently somewhat distant from Morris's assertion that revolution must be a result of hope for the beautiful as well as the necessity of a proletarian uprising. Both, however, saw the aesthetic as the means by which individual subjects could gain critical consciousness of the material conditions of their existence and work towards social change.

Despite the differences between them, both William Morris and Edward Carpenter formulated a socialist aesthetic in which subjects were joined in communal fellowship through their response to beauty. Carpenter certainly would not have disagreed with Morris's assertion that the 'Socialist ideal of art is that it should be common to the whole people' and that art itself must pervade all life as a result of the 'harmonious co-operation of neighbours'.[25] Art under socialism would be the product of communal workshops in which tradition would guide the latent sensuous intuition of beauty within the labourer, and the product that resulted would evoke pleasure in all who encountered it. Such beliefs were founded on an understanding of aesthetic democracy: an expectation of audiences of intense subjectivity, possessed of an innate intuition of aesthetic value and truth. If the comments of one reader of the *Clarion* newspaper are anything to go by, socialist writers certainly did not over-estimate the aesthetic susceptibilities of their readers. An anonymous subscriber commented in promotional copy for the paper that 'Clarion men do not preach to their readers, they sing to them'. Such a remark takes for granted a shared understanding of the distinction between preaching and singing and their effects on the listener. Whilst the former maintains the gap between preacher and laity, subject and object, in the process of ethical instruction, the latter requires a sensuous intuition of aes-

---

[23] Olive Schreiner to S. C. Cronwright-Schreiner, 8 May 1908, in *Letters of Olive Schreiner*, pp. 278–9.
[24] Conway cit. Yeo, 'New Life', p. 12.
[25] William Morris, 'The Socialist Ideal: Art' (1891), in *The Collected Works of William Morris*, ed. May Morris, 24 vols. (London: Longmans, 1912–15), xxiii. 260.

thetic value. Such responsiveness to beauty suggested that the self was not wholly subject to material determinism and it was this willingness to grant relative autonomy to the category of the aesthetic that enabled ethical idealism and historical materialism to rub along together in the last decades of the nineteenth century. That the same issue of aesthetic autonomy forced idealism and materialism apart within the socialist movement in the early years of the twentieth century is part of the history of an increasingly individuated notion of aesthetic response that I relate in the final chapters of this book.

Wilde, for one, certainly seems to have been aware of the tension between the communal, productive aesthetic embodied in Carpenter's *Chants of Labour* and his own individuated, avant-garde theories of art and he expresses his consequent dissent in terms of sex. After carefully cataloguing the various professions of the contributors to Carpenter's collection—from bootmakers and printers to clergymen and soldiers— Wilde inverts the logic of this volume designed to be used as a secular hymnal in draughty socialist meeting halls. The commune of diverse producers labouring manfully to initiate the new life through this 'songbook of the people' is transformed by a turn of phrase and socialism becomes, in effect, a salon hostess: 'She [Socialism] welcomes many and multiform natures. She rejects none and has room for all.'[26] Wilde's playful feminization of socialism brings into sharp relief the inherent masculinity of the communal, productivist aesthetic popular within the late nineteenth-century labour movement. The transposition of the subject of socialism from masculine to feminine, from labouring producers to a singular, delightful consumer with a 'wonderful personality', is a move freighted with political significance. For Wilde's vision of aesthetic socialism as a singular, feminized salon maven brings the works of Carpenter and others back within the bounds of late nineteenth-century aestheticism.

The gender inversion performed by Wilde is so highly charged in this context because Morris and many of his followers were, as I argue in the following chapter, reacting against the effeminacy associated with the individuated consumption of the decadent aesthetes.[27] In resisting this decadent aesthetic, Morris formulated a theory of the arts grounded in the pleasurable somatic sensations of physical, 'manly' labour. For many middleclass men of letters, then, socialism became a site for the reclamation of

---

[26] Wilde, 'Poetical Socialists', p. 3.
[27] Richard Dellamora, *Masculine Desire: The Sexual Politics of Victorian Aestheticism* (Chapel Hill, NC: University of North Carolina Press, 1990) revisits central works of aestheticism to reveal more complex paths of male–male desire than this association with effeminacy.

manhood lost within capitalist modernity: a place in which even a poet could conceive of himself as a labourer. If late nineteenth-century socialism had a sex, it was male. This is not to say, of course, that the early years of the British socialist movement were a normative masculine affair. Edward Carpenter's *Towards Democracy* (1883) and later writings on what he termed 'the intermediate sex' celebrate the transformational power of love between men in the quest for social change.[28] For Carpenter such radical sexual dissidence was an act of will and social engagement at odds with sensuous consumption and effeminacy.[29] Just as effeminacy cannot be equated with a putative homosexual identity in this period, so too the manly vigour celebrated by many socialist writers at the time served, for a while, as an inclusive principle to which sexually dissident men, and women, could subscribe.[30]

Carolyn Steedman and June Hannam's biographies of the ILP activists Margaret McMillan and Isabella Ford, for instance, demonstrate the contributions both women made to the early twentieth-century labour movement, and Karen Hunt's study of the Social Democratic Federation (SDF) ensures that women's participation in that Marxist organization cannot be overlooked.[31] It is the very wealth of such research—the solid assurance that women too, played a major part in the socialist movement—that enables this study to examine how such women (and men) negotiated an aesthetic model that rested on masculinized production. And negotiate it they did: Olive Schreiner, Clementina Black, and Dollie Radford all found a means of making this manly aesthetic their own in an age in which conventional literary history gives a very different account of the woman writer.

The model of communal, artistic production associated with the late nineteenth-century socialist movement offered a means for the rehabilitation of female artistry in an era in which successive literary movements parodied and denigrated the feminine as the antithesis of the aesthetic. As David Weir (drawing on the work of Andreas Huyssen) notes, the late

---

[28] Sheila Rowbotham and Jeffrey Weeks, *Socialism and the New Life: The Personal and Sexual Politics of Edward Carpenter and Havelock Ellis* (London: Pluto, 1977) played a vital part in the rereading the sexual politics of late 19th-century socialism to which this work is indebted.
[29] My thanks to Michael Hatt for an illuminating discussion of this distinction.
[30] See Alan Sinfield, *The Wilde Century: Effeminacy, Oscar Wilde and the Queer Moment* (New York: Columbia University Press, 1994); Thais Morgan, 'Victorian Effeminacies', in Richard Dellamora (ed.), *Victorian Sexual Dissidence* (Chicago: University of Chicago Press, 1999), pp. 109–27.
[31] Steedman, *Childhood, Culture and Class*; June Hannam, *Isabella Ford* (Oxford: Blackwell, 1989); Karen Hunt, *Equivocal Feminists: The Social Democratic Federation and the Woman Question, 1884–1911* (Cambridge: Cambridge University Press, 1996).

nineteenth-century decadent movement was shaped by a double negation of gender. First, the separation of art and literature from the nineteenth-century masculine marketplace served to render the man of letters effeminate, leading several decadent writers to self-idealize themselves as women. It is this habit that Wilde throws over Carpenter's edition, idealizing its 'delightful' femininity, despite the latter's attempt to frame the work as a manly, communal endeavour.[32] Second, this tendency to (self-)idealize the feminine was 'coupled with the negative fantasy of woman as the embodiment of all that is natural and therefore antithetical to the art he practices'.[33] As Rita Felski argues concerning the dandiacal decadent aestheticism of the 1890s, 'the female body comes to function as a primary symbolic site for confronting and controlling the threat of an unruly nature':

> If the dandy-aesthete embodies an aspiration to the ideal, then woman, according to the dualisms of nineteenth-century thought, represents materiality and corporeality, or the 'triumph of matter over mind'.[34]

As we shall see in the next chapter, despite Morris's own early association with aestheticism, his later socialist aesthetic theory of the 1880s was in many ways a reaction against this final flowering of the movement into the figure of the individuated, anti-naturalist aesthete. Morris and other socialist writers attempted to resist the effeminate aesthetic of consumption associated with the aesthetes and reintegrate the material and corporeal into a productive aesthetic ideal. One consequence of this move was that the material body—both male and female—found a place on an aesthetic continuum rather than being exiled as the antithesis of art. In framing the pleasure of the body in the act of creation as the source of the aesthetic, the materiality of womanhood is brought in from the cold in the works of socialist aestheticians. In fact, as we shall see, both Olive Schreiner and Grace Black extrapolate the productive, somatic aesthetic to the point at which women's biological reproduction becomes the creation of a work of art.

---

[32] On the relation between the dandy-aesthete and parody more widely see Dennis Denisoff, *Aestheticism and Sexual Parody, 1840–1940* (Cambridge: Cambridge University Press, 2001), pp. 3–9.

[33] David Weir, *Decadence and the Making of Modernism* (Amherst, Mass.: University of Massachusetts Press, 1995), p. 19. See also Andrew Huyssen, *After the Great Divide: Modernism, Mass Culture, Postmodernism* (Bloomington, Ind.: Indiana University Press, 1986), p. 45; Elaine Showalter, *Sexual Anarchy: Gender and Culture at the Fin de Siècle* (London: Virago, 1990), pp. 169–87.

[34] Rita Felski, *The Gender of Modernity* (Cambridge MA: Harvard University Press, 1995), p. 109.

Despite the evident disdain for the 'natural' body of woman in decadent aestheticism, the work of Talia Schaffer and other recent scholars has done much to interpolate women writers into accounts of the movement. Far from being exiled from the world of the aesthetes and the doctrine of 'art for art's sake', Schaffer has demonstrated the significant role of women writers in disseminating aestheticism. Like many recent revisionist accounts of the place of women writers in established narratives of literary history, Schaffer's invaluable work involves redefining what, exactly, it is we mean by 'aesthete' and 'aestheticism'. It is significant, for example, that the majority of the writers she identifies as 'forgotten female aesthetes' responded to the cultural programme of the aesthetic movement—the vogue for blue china, peacock feathers, archaic picturesque dress, and the house beautiful—rather than the aesthetic manifesto and prose stylistics associated with Walter Pater and his followers.[35] In this sense, Schaffer's work is a counterpart to Ann Ardis's recent reconsideration of the class and gender conflicts that remained unspoken in previous accounts of the rise of literary modernism at the turn of the century.[36] It is important however, that we retain some sense of the core definitions of such literary-historical terms as aestheticism and modernism, even whilst accepting their instability and porousness. The writers examined in this work were writing from and against an epoch in which 'high' art developed an interest in aesthetic style over ethical content and encouraged the cultivation of a sharply individuated aesthetic response that insisted upon the absolute autonomy of art. It is this conventional understanding of aestheticism as a proto-modernist doctrine of the individuating and perfectly autonomous aesthetic that proved so problematic to the socialist writers, particularly the women socialist writers, studied here.

The next chapter traces this complex history of aestheticism, socialist aesthetics, and early modernism through a study of the development of William Morris's works in the later nineteenth century. Placing Morris's aesthetic (and political) development in the context of the writings of John Ruskin and Walter Pater enables me to explore Morris's resistance to (and complicity with) an emerging aesthetic that emphasized individual taste and

---

[35] Talia Schaffer, *The Forgotten Female Aesthetes: Literary Culture in Late Victorian England* (Charlottesville, Va.: University of Virginia Press, 2000), pp. 86–102. Weir dissociates Pater's literary aestheticism from the later aesthetic movement in fashion and taste in *Decadence and the Making of Modernism*, p. 65. See also Kathy Alexis Psomiades, *Beauty's Body: Femininity and Representation in British Aestheticism* (Stanford, Calif.: Stanford University Press, 1997) throughout for an instructive discussion of the gendered politics of what she terms feminized 'lifestyle aestheticism'.

[36] Anne Ardis, *Modernism and Cultural Conflict, 1880–1922* (Cambridge: Cambridge University Press, 2002), pp. 1–14.

consumption, rather than communal production. In his socialist essays, *Signs of Change* (1888) Morris developed an aesthetic continuum that enabled him to collapse the distinction between art and bodily labour and imagine a future of communal artistic production after the revolution. Both the radical nature of Morris's aesthetic and its preoccupation with productive masculinity are emphasized by contrasting his work to Wilde's essay 'The Soul of Man under Socialism' (1891).

Morris's concern with the rebirth of 'manly' art should not be seen as an exclusionary tactic that prohibited women socialist activists and writers from working with his politics and aesthetics. Chapter 2 examines the lives and writings of three sisters, each of whom responded to Morris's works with enthusiasm: Grace, Constance (Garnett), and Clementina Black. The chapter explores the rhetoric of 'fellowship' that permeated the mixed-sex discussion groups and early socialist organizations frequented by the Blacks and all the writers whose works are subsequently studied in the book. During the course of the 1880s, however, this ideal of working in fellowship regardless of class or gender came under increasing strain as middle-class women struggled to find roles within the active socialist movement. I examine the Black sisters' idiosyncratic political beliefs and their various attempts to advance the socialist cause through labour organization. The chapter also explores the extent to which the Blacks' work and writing for the socialist movement forced them to address the 'Woman Question' as a concern in its own right by the late 1880s. The chapter closes with an analysis of Clementina Black's historical romances published in the late 1890s and suggests that these texts can be read as a negotiation of the gendered politics of 'history', 'revolution', and 'romance' evident in Morris's aesthetic.

On her arrival in London in the early 1880s, Olive Schreiner became a regular visitor to many socialist clubs and debates and developed her interest in the movement hand in hand with her pursuit of the 'Woman Question'. Chapter 3 explores Schreiner's feminist works, 'The Woman Question' (1899) and *Woman and Labour* (1911), in the context of her exchanges with the eugenicist socialist Karl Pearson and her good friend Eleanor Marx. In the latter work, Schreiner adopts and revises the rhetoric of manly artistry familiar from Morris's works: a revision that defines women as virile labourers rather than 'sex parasites'. It is, however, in her creative collection of allegories and fragments, *Dreams* (1890), which Schreiner composed during her time in Europe, that she insists upon the autonomy of the aesthetic as an ideal that transcends gender divisions and holds out hope for a future radically different from the capitalist present. For Schreiner, at least, voracious feminized consumption lies at the heart of the hell of capitalism and imperialism and needs to be reformed through a vision of collective beauty.

Schreiner's good friend Edward Carpenter was her chief source of news about the socialist movement during her self-imposed exiles on the continent throughout the later 1880s. If Schreiner tested the limits of female desire, then Carpenter sought to reshape masculinity and civilization through sexual desire itself. In Chapter 4 I examine how the 'fads' of vegetarianism, Jaegerism, and sandal wearing came to be associated with socialism in the last decades of the nineteenth century. I argue that for Carpenter and George Bernard Shaw these ascetic regimes provided a means of investigating and reforming conventional ideals of masculinity. Both writers represent such 'fads' as bodily labour and discipline, thus overcoming the opposition between the man of letters and the manly labourer. Whilst Carpenter's theory of Lamarckian biological idealism concluded that such practices would result in species change and a socialist utopia of liberated sexual bodies, Shaw's regime aimed to supplement the necessary redistribution of capital. Finally, Shaw's emphasis on the 'superman'—prophet, saint, and genius—as an individuated harbinger of the socialist future is contrasted to Morris's utopia of communal labouring artistry.

Chapter 5 uses the case of the poet, Socialist League member, and Fabian, Dollie Radford, to examine the relationship between socialism and fin-de-siècle aestheticism. After outlining Radford's conversion to socialism in the context discussed in Chapter 2, I go on to examine her (unsuccessful) attempts to publish her work in the socialist journal *Today*. Radford's work from the 1880s forms a marked contrast with that of her widely published fellow Fabian E. Nesbit and the contrast highlights the oft-remarked 'feminine' lyricism of Radford's poetry. This 'femininity' was underlined in the exquisite, aesthetic production of her first volume of verse. Nevertheless, I argue that, like Schreiner's *Dreams*, Radford's 'A Ballad of Victory', published in the *Yellow Book*, uses allegory to render political questions in an aesthetic register. The chapter concludes by comparing Radford's work from the 1890s with that of her fellow in the League, William Morris. I suggest that Radford's experiments with a communal lyric subjectivity reflect her engagement with his ideals of aesthetic production outside individualism whilst insisting on the place of feminized affect in a political poetics.

The next chapter moves outwards to analyse the dissemination of socialist aesthetics in the press up until 1914. During the 1890s the rise of the ILP shifted the locus of such debates from London to northern manufacturing towns, as is evident from the contributions of Isabella Ford, Margaret McMillan, Robert Blatchford, and Alfred Orage to the *Clarion*, *Labour Leader*, and the Leeds Arts Club. The chapter focuses on the development of Orage's politics and aesthetics from his early work with Isabella Ford and Edward Carpenter in Leeds to the peak of his influence as editor of the *New*

Age in 1914. Orage came to reject both the 'sentimental' aesthetics of the ILP and the compromises of the Parliamentary Labour Party in the early twentieth century, turning instead to the model of guild socialism. Whilst this model constantly alluded to the inheritance of Morris, it was matched with increasing misogyny, homophobia, and arguments aimed at removing women from the field of labour. I argue that there is a dialectic between guild socialism and intense artistic individualism in the pages of the *New Age* and conclude that this dialectic is important for our understanding of the emergence of a 'virile' literary modernism in the years before the war.

The final chapter examines the afterlife of 1880s socialism in the early modernist generation. It focuses upon Virginia Woolf and Roger Fry and examines their negotiations with (and negations of) the productive, engaged aesthetics of those Bloomsbury socialists before the Bloomsbury Group examined in Chapter 2. Both Woolf and Fry had significant relations with writers examined in earlier chapters of this work. Woolf encountered Constance Garnett and the group of London socialists who had left the capital for the Surrey village of Limpsfield in the 1890s through her friendship with Rupert Brooke and his fellow young Fabian 'Neo-Pagans' in the early twentieth century. Woolf's writings concerning the Women's Co-operative Guild reflect her rejection of the socially engaged and productive aesthetics of that generation in favour of a radical statement of aesthetic autonomy and the individualism of the artist. Thanks to his friendship with Edward Carpenter, Roger Fry's aesthetics strained between a belief in a democracy of aesthetic responsiveness and a conscious attempt to rewrite the aesthetic legacy of Ruskin and Morris. In the debacle that surrounded Wyndham Lewis's secession from Fry's collective Omega Workshops, however, Lewis himself sexed Fry's aesthetics as effeminate traces of the fin de siècle. The Bloomsbury Group, according to Lewis, were nothing more that a party of 'strayed Dissenting Aesthetes', unable to 'rise above the level of a pleasant tea-party', and hence outside the bounds of virile modernism, whatever their debts might have been to Morris's 'manly' socialism.[37]

---

[37] Wyndham Lewis, cit. Francis Spalding, *Roger Fry: Art and Life* (London: Granada, 1980), pp. 186–7.

1

William Morris and the Aesthetics of Manly Labour

In April 1914, the architect and journalist Arthur J. Penty devoted his column in the journal the *New Age* to the subject of 'Aestheticism and History'.[1] Despite breaking free of its origin as an adjunct of the Fabian Society and championing the aesthetic avant-garde in the pre-war years, the *New Age* had retained a considerable readership on the radical left. Even so (or, perhaps, as a result), Penty's reflections on the nineteenth century sparked off a heated correspondence in the letters page over the next month.[2] Penty's article sought to defend what he saw as the embattled ethical and aesthetic origin of the British socialist movement. He argued that in the contemporary modernist 'state of flux' and relativity, it was time once more to look towards the fixed point of John Ruskin's certain 'aesthetic truth that the artist and the craftsman must be one':

> I have no hesitation in saying that the discovery that the artist and the craftsman should be one was the greatest discovery of the nineteenth century. Once grasp that fact and everything follows from it. The social fabric may be reconstructed from that one fragment of truth.[3]

Pushing aside both Marx and Darwin, developments in both public health and technology, Penty (a self-confessed medievalist) framed Ruskin and William Morris as the greatest discoverers of the industrial age. Thanks to their aesthetic interests, both medieval history and contemporary capitalism had become objects of critical inquiry and thus 'aesthetics have led to history, as they have led to economics, and will one day to social reform'.[4]

Here, at the limit point of the capacious 'long' nineteenth century, on the eve of the First World War and in the pages of a journal that has been identified as one of the engines of literary modernism, Penty immerses his

---

[1] Arthur J. Penty, 'Aestheticism and History', *New Age* (2 April 1914), 683–4.
[2] Penty's correspondents included G. D. H. Cole, a prominent Fabian, and later one of the foremost proponents of the Guild Socialist model outlined by Penty in the early 20th cent.
[3] Penty, 'Aestheticism and History', p. 683.
[4] Ibid. 684.

readers in what seems to be a thoroughly nineteenth-century understanding of the relationship between art and society.[5] Art, in Penty's argument, should be a force for social good, lived through the physical and mental labour of all workers and not limited to an elite, autonomous sphere to be glossed by aesthetes and connoisseurs. The way forward for politics and aesthetics was, Penty asserted, the restitution of the medieval guild (or, in his archaism, 'gild') system: industrial devolution to a state of localized politics and handicraft production. Well after 1910, the year Virginia Woolf playfully identified as the watershed of modernism in Britain, the legacy of nineteenth-century aesthetic socialism thus claimed its space in cultural discourse.[6] The significance of this particular debate on guild socialism and its relationship to modernism is examined in due course in the penultimate chapter of this book. At this point, however, Penty's work helps to illuminate the peculiarly aesthetic genealogy of British socialism: a genealogy in which, to borrow Ruth Robbins's useful phrase, politics and aesthetics were never an either/or but always a both/and.[7] It also illustrates the longevity of desire on the part of political radicals to (re)claim that most unstable of categories, aestheticism, as the natural adjunct of social engagement, rather than aesthetic autonomy.

Both the aesthetic genealogy of nineteenth-century socialism and the attempt to formulate a theory of socially productive aesthetics converge in the life and works of the subject of this chapter, William Morris. But Morris is more than just a historical exemplum and convenient starting point for this discussion of socialism and aesthetics in the late nineteenth and early twentieth centuries. Morris's works feature throughout this study as a counterweight to some well-established narratives of literary history in the

---

[5] In the preface to his socialist manifesto *The Restoration of the Gild System* (London: Swan Sonnenschein, 1906), p. viii, Penty frames his work as a practical application of Ruskin's co-operative ideal in conjunction with Edward Carpenter's 'theory put forward ... in "Civilization: Its Cause and Cure"'. On the *New Age* and early modernism see Wallace Martin, *The New Age under Orage: Chapters in English Cultural History* (Manchester: Manchester University Press, 1967), pp. 108–92.

[6] Virginia Woolf, *Mr Bennett and Mrs Brown* (London: Hogarth Press, 1924), p. 5. See also Peter Stansky, *On or About December 1910: Early Bloomsbury and its Intimate World* (Cambridge, Mass.: Harvard University Press, 1996).

[7] Ruth Robbins, 'The Genders of Socialism: Eleanor Marx and Oscar Wilde' in John Stokes (ed.), *Eleanor Marx: Life, Work, Contacts* (Aldershot: Ashgate, 2000), pp. 99–113. Penty's rejection of Soviet communist collectivism in favour of Mussolini's corporate state fascism will be studied in the last two chapters as one of the uneasy destinations of this both/and of political aesthetics in the 20th cent.: 'Fascism is the social subconscious reasserting itself against that ugly and menacing thing, Bolshevism, and that poisonous and corroding thing which springs from the same root, Modernism', Penty argued in 1937; unlike communism, fascism appreciated the 'strong sense of reality' imbued in 'traditional things'. A. J. Penty, *Tradition and Modernism in Politics* (London: Sheed & Ward, 1937), p. 58.

period 1880–1914. That aesthetic and chronological boundary between the
Victorian aesthetic movement and literary modernism—questioned,
revised, and blurred as it has been by scholarship in the past decade—is
one which Morris (in typically 'ungovernable' fashion) refuses to settle on
either side. His problematic place in accounts of the politics of aestheticism
and early modernism is thus a consideration in this chapter: a consideration
that requires some attention to the development of the nineteenth-century
aesthetic movement. For just as Morris's socialist theory of the arts was
rooted in his early involvement with the aesthetic movement and the works
of Ruskin and Walter Pater, then so too it grew out of a reaction against the
later stages of that movement in the 1880s and 1890s as it edged towards the
aesthetic preoccupations of literary modernism.

Morris has long proven troublesome to those seeking to place him in the
history of the aesthetic movement and the rise of modernism. Nikolaus
Pevsner, for example, had to split Morris in half in order to slot him into a
narrative of how the 'pioneers of the modern movement' had got to the
Bauhaus.[8] The half of Morris's doctrine that made 'a chair, a wallpaper, or
a vase a worthy object of the artist's imagination' made him a 'true prophet
of the twentieth century'. But, Pevsner argued, the remainder of Morris's
beliefs, his medievalism and abhorrence of 'the pride in artistic genius [as]
some special form of inspiration' relegated him to the dowdy realms of
'nineteenth century style[,] . . . prejudices' and 'historicism'.[9] In typically
high modernist fashion (the work was first published in 1936), Pevsner
thus erases the continuity between late nineteenth-century aesthetic
interests and his own modernist moment.

Recently this conception of modernism as sleek impersonality, perfect
aesthetic autonomy, propelled by individuated artistic genius through the
heavy atmosphere of tradition, has started to recede before us. Although
the idea of a 'great divide' somewhere on or around 1910 remains a useful
one for understanding modernist writers' self-definition as an iconoclastic
avant-garde, close attention to aesthetic theory either side of that divide
has revealed—inevitably—a subtle weaving of continuities.[10] Such revisionist accounts of the coming of the modernist moment have stemmed
largely from a renewed interest in that very movement from which Pevsner

---

[8] Nikolaus Pevsner, *Pioneers of Modern Design: From William Morris to Walter Gropius*
(London: Faber & Faber, 1936).
[9] Ibid. 22–3.
[10] See for example Ann Ardis, *Modernism and Cultural Conflict, 1880–1922* (Cambridge:
Cambridge University Press, 2002); Morag Shiach, *Modernism, Labour and Selfhood in
British Literature and Culture, 1890–1930* (Cambridge: Cambridge University Press, 2004).

and his fellow modernists sought to distance themselves: the aesthetic movement. Both Linda Dowling and Jonathan Freedman, for example, have argued persuasively that the influence of late nineteenth-century aestheticism in the emergence of literary modernism lies precisely in those traits of style and historicism that Pevsner relegates to the white elephant stall.[11] Freedman suggests that 'the concern with the purification of language and style; the simultaneous desire to evade or annul history and an intense, even obsessive historicism . . . are the permanent gifts of aestheticism to the . . . modernists'.[12] In such an estimate (primarily derived from the works of Walter Pater) Morris himself seems to fit neatly into the aesthetic movement as it fed into modernism.

Morris, however, remains intractable due to his particularly complex relationship with Paterian aestheticism and the aesthetic movement itself. Morris's theories of the beautiful grew out of a mode of mid-nineteenth-century criticism that drew upon a (relatively) autonomous aesthetic sphere to comment unfavourably on the qualities of the contemporary industrial world in comparison to an idealized past. The works of John Ruskin in particular, as we shall see, helped to disseminate the German idealist philosophic tradition—most notably that of Immanuel Kant—in which the free play of aesthetic judgement was a symbol for morality. The exercise of taste and the feeling for the beautiful was, in such an understanding, the realm in which both the common sensations shared by mankind and the individual's autonomy from material determinism were most evident. It is this idea of aesthetic autonomy and the consequent interplay between individual judgement and collective feeling that proved so attractive to socialist aestheticians at the end of the nineteenth century.

The theories of beauty associated with the socialist movement were, however, only one set of responses to the aesthetic moment of mid-nineteenth-century Britain. As the labels 'aesthetic movement', 'aestheticism', and 'aesthete' came into increasingly common use in the latter half of the century, the terms accreted a number of conflicting meanings quite at odds with Ruskin's own ethical aesthetic. It was Morris's fate to be caught up in the midst of this conflict and to see his own works co-opted in the emergence of an aestheticism that negated the purposiveness of mid-nineteenth-century aesthetic criticism. In common with other recent scholarship in the field I have found it useful for the sake of clarity to thus differentiate between two

---

[11] Linda Dowling, *Language and Decadence in the Victorian Fin de Siècle* (Princeton: Princeton University Press, 1986), p. 238.
[12] Jonathan Freedman, *Professions of Taste: Henry James, British Aestheticism and Commodity Culture* (Stanford, Calif.: Stanford University Press, 1990), p. 128.

sorts of developments that emerged from aesthetic criticism in the 1850s.[13] The first—which I term aestheticism—is that critical pursuit of 'art for art's sake' associated with the work of Walter Pater. The second is the commodification of such aesthetic concepts into desirable consumer goods (blue and white china, craft furniture) which I collect under the more general category of the aesthetic movement. What has been termed the Paterian 'stylism' of late nineteenth-century poetry and prose here then stands in a complicit, but slightly quizzical attitude towards the marketing of an aesthetic lifestyle. Morris himself could display little such detachment in the 1880s, inescapably implicated as he was in the marketing of the aesthetic movement by his work for his firm, Morris & Co. The 'aesthetic drawing room', he declaimed, was part of the 'miserable wreckage' of capitalist society.[14] His socialist aesthetic theory of this period thus emerged in part as a passionate reaction against his complicity in the commodification of the aesthetic movement.

I

In 1894, Morris reflected back on his conversion to socialism in an article for *Justice*, the journal of the avowedly Marxist Social Democratic Federation. Disarmingly (but pointedly, given the context) Morris confessed to a total ignorance of economics prior to his political education. Even after his conversion to socialism, Morris admitted that the economic sections of Marx's *Capital* gave him 'agonies of confusion of the brain' in comparison to his thorough enjoyment of the historical part of the work.[15] Yet Morris suggested that the framework of his political critique had been established, prior to his encounter with Marxism, through reading earlier critics of the blithe optimism of nineteenth-century capitalist narratives of improvement. Carlyle and Ruskin, Morris argued, were the only two in 'open rebellion' against the 'Whiggery' of industrial 'progress' in the mid-nineteenth century, and the latter, 'before my days of practical Socialism, was my master

---

[13] Dowling, *Language and Decadence*, pp. 3–4, also differentiates between what she calls the aestheticism or decadence of the 'cultural surface', typified by Gilbert and Sullivan's *Patience* and Oscar Wilde's green carnations, and the deeper literary decadence of style.

[14] William Morris, 'The Aims of Art', in *The Collected Works of William Morris*, ed. May Morris, 25 vols. (London: Longmans, 1912–15, hereafter *CW*), xxiii. 91.

[15] William Morris, 'How I Became a Socialist' (1894), *CW*, xxiii. 278.

towards the ideal'.[16] He concluded 'I cannot help saying, by the way, how deadly dull the world would have been twenty years ago but for Ruskin'.[17]

Although tossed away as a characteristically brusque aside, Morris's choice of the adjective 'dull' to characterize a world without Ruskin is one that clarifies the texture of the latter's contribution to the fabric of late nineteenth-century socialism. A dull world here is not simply one that is boring, but one that lacks discriminating vision and the keen edge of desire for the good and the beautiful. The world that Ruskin's *Modern Painters III* (1856) and *The Stones of Venice* (1853) offered William Morris in his Pre-Raphaelite Brotherhood days at Oxford—and which filtered through to a younger generation of socialists in reading groups across the country—was a world which was improved ethically by whetting the aesthetic appetite.[18] To learn to see the moral and historical truth in a work of art, to desire to realize the self in the labour of the hand, these were the means by which a dull world of material progress was found wanting by the sharp focus of Ruskinian romantic idealism. If it seems extraordinary that, for example, a volume about the architecture of medieval Venice should act as a catalyst for the development of the British socialist movement, then, to paraphrase Ruskin, we must attend more closely. We must attend to the mental tendencies legibly expressed in Ruskin's *The Stones of Venice* as well as to its material form.[19] It becomes clear then that, in addition to the explicit rejection of the division between the artist and craftsman championed by Penty, Ruskin's mode of criticism made the relationship between aesthetics and politics inescapably reciprocal.

In the following passage from 'The Nature of Gothic' Ruskin pauses to consider the 'general uses of variety in the economy of the [nineteenth-century] world'. After seamlessly shifting his point of focus in the preceding paragraphs from the capacity for perpetual novelty inherent in gothic architecture and hence to the legible freedom of medieval craftsmen, Ruskin comes to dwell on the nature of constancy and change:

> a strong intellect will have pleasure in the solemnities of storm and twilight, and in the broken and mysterious lights that gleam among them, rather than

---

[16] Ibid. 279. Dowling argues that Morris's rebellion against Whiggism was rooted in the 'Whig aesthetic tradition itself'; Linda Dowling, *The Vulgarization of Art: The Victorians and Aesthetic Democracy* (Charlottesville, Va.: University of Virginia Press, 1996), p. 61.

[17] Morris, 'How I Became a Socialist', p. 279.

[18] For the effect of Ruskin's *Stones of Venice* on Morris and his circle in Oxford in the 1850s see E. P. Thompson, *William Morris: Romantic to Revolutionary* (rev. edn. New York: Pantheon, 1976), pp. 33–8, and Fiona MacCarthy, *William Morris: A Life for our Times* (London: Faber & Faber, 1994), pp. 69–70.

[19] John Ruskin, *The Stones of Venice*, II. vi. 4 in *The Complete Works of John Ruskin*, ed. E. T. Cook and Alexander Wedderburn, 39 vols. (London: George Allen, 1903–12), x. 183.

in mere brilliancy and glare, while a frivolous mind will dread the shadow and the storm; and as a great man will be ready to endure much darkness of fortune in order to reach greater eminence of power or felicity, whilst an inferior man will not pay the price; exactly in like manner a great mind will accept, or even delight in, monotony which would be wearisome to an inferior intellect . . . But in all cases it is not that the noble nature loves monotony . . . But it can bear with it . . . while those who will not submit to the temporary sameness, but rush from one change to another, gradually dull the edge of change itself, and bring a shadow and weariness over the whole world from which there is no more escape.[20]

Ruskin's general economy is structured here by an apprehension of the experience of time and history as sensuous texture. Progress and change, whether actual alterations in light and dark, sunshine and rain, or that metaphorical storm cloud that was, in Ruskin's later formulation, the nineteenth century itself, are felt as lived experience, rather than intellectually apprehended. Even great minds and noble natures are trapped in the 'weariness' of a world dulled by a mass of inferior men seeking the transitory stimulus of variety: nothing, at first, seems to exist outside the inescapable shadow of history. Everything is subject to the organization of labour in a given historical moment, to the 'great cry that rises from our manufacturing cities . . . that we manufacture everything except men'.[21] Everything, that is, apart from the capacity of those noble minds to aestheticize the very experience of their moment of history. The discriminating eye that accompanies the great mind and noble nature is still free to feel pleasure and delight in the sharp contrasts of the age; or, at least, look up to the clouds and endure in the knowledge that as the beauty of nature requires some variety, so too man-made storm clouds cannot last for ever. It is this aestheticized vision that enables 'noble natures' to develop criticism of their historical moment through their access to the super-sensible ideal of beauty, past and to come.

Ruskin's imperative, then, is that his readers look.[22] This primacy of the eye is of course a mode that Ruskin shares with Pater and the wider host of aestheticist writers. Think, for example, of Dante Gabriel Rossetti's dramatic monologue 'Jenny' in which the artistic young male speaker tries (and, most interestingly, fails) to assert the primacy of his vision of his 'fallen' companion, read from her sleeping form. Whilst Rossetti's speaker

---

[20] John Ruskin, *The Stones of Venice*, II. vi. 37 (p. 211).
[21] Ibid. II. vi. 16 (p. 196).
[22] On Ruskin and the eye see Robert Hewison, *John Ruskin: The Argument of the Eye* (London: Thames & Hudson, 1976); Alexandra Wettlaufer, *In the Mind's Eye: The Visual Imperative in Diderot, Baudelaire and Ruskin* (Amsterdam: Rodopi, 2003); Susan P. Casteras (ed.), *John Ruskin and the Victorian Eye* (New York: Harry Abrams/Phoenix Art Museum, 1993).

ends up implicating himself in his vision of Jenny's morally denuded life, Ruskin's visual imperative penetrates through the material object in view, to the historical moment of its creation, and past that to the ideal it thus embodies:

> First, See if it looks as if it had been built by strong men; if it has the sort of roughness and largeness, and nonchalance, mixed in places with the exquisite tenderness which seems always to be the sign-manual of the broad vision, and massy power of men who can see past the work they are doing, and betray here and there something like a disdain for it. If the building has this character, it is much already in its favour; it will go hard but it prove a noble one.[23]

Material and ideal vision, the object and the subject, slip and slide into one another throughout this passage. The building is a legible sign of the noble masculine character of its makers, rough, large, nonchalant, tender: we are told to look at a work of art, but find ourselves instead looking at the artists; and yet again we see them not as artists but as ideals of masculinity. Indeed, the very nobility of the work stems from the (paradox) that we can see from its material surface that its makers disdained such material surface in favour of realizing their own ideals. Ruskin thus plucks at the tension between the social visionary and aesthetic vision: one must see an ethical ideal whilst looking at art's surface.

For Morris, Ruskin's *Stones of Venice* pointed out 'a new road on which the world should travel' at its moment of publication.[24] Yet in retrospect, Morris reflected, neither Ruskin nor his devotees understood at the time 'what the equipment for that journey must be, and how many things must be changed before we are equipped'.[25] Certainly, even in 1855 Morris had internalized Ruskin's dictum of the necessity of finding pleasure in labour to the point at which it formed a core of resistance to his mother's desire that he should take holy orders. In proposing his alternative career as an architect he added 'you know too that in any work that one delights in, even the merest drudgery connected with it is delightful too—I shall be master too of a useful trade'.[26] In this earnest attempt to prove his mature commitment to a new profession (Morris was 21), there are hints already of that sense of missing the right equipment to set out along Ruskin's road. The

---

[23] Ruskin, *Stones of Venice,* II. vi 111 (p. 264).
[24] William Morris, 'Preface' to *The Nature of Gothic: A Chapter of the Stones of Venice by John Ruskin* (Kelmscott Press, 1892), p. i.
[25] Ibid., p. i.
[26] William Morris to Emma Shelton Morris, Nov. 1855 in *The Collected Letters of William Morris*, ed. Norman Kelvin, 4 vols. (Princeton: Princeton University Press, 1984–96, hereafter *CL*), i. 25.

delightful prospect of a career devoted to some sort of artistic creativity has
to be hastily counterbalanced by the rugged language of masculine mastery
and utility in the nineteenth-century marketplace: the pleasure of labour
strains against the requirements of capitalism.

In Morris's meditations on his choice of profession, his ever-present
sense of lack intertwines the pressures of the marketplace and the dominant
nineteenth-century definition of 'manliness'. Morris initially selected architecture, Jan Marsh argues, because it seemed the most 'manly' of the arts.[27]
Even this, however, did not prevent him deriding himself as 'a lazy, aimless,
useless dreaming body', 'the adjectival antithesis', as Marsh puts it, of
nineteenth-century manliness.[28] That Ruskin's work could lead to such anxieties of masculinity seems unlikely at first: it was Ruskin, after all, who in
his lecture 'Of Kings' Treasuries' encapsulated the material of nineteenth-
century middle-class manliness, battered into shape by robust encounters
with the world. Yet Ruskin's early emphasis on the pleasures of the eye, that
instruction to find an ethical ideal in the art of the past and thus stand apart
from the cloud of history, ran counter to the model of masculinity that
insisted upon material productivity and the rational subjugation of sensuousness. Ruskin's aesthetic theory attempted to hold together both the
celebration of manual labour and the imperative that the most effective,
engaged activity for his readership was to look: both these activities fell
outside of mainstream middle-class manliness on the grounds of class and
gender respectively.

Morris's letters from the 1850s are thus filled by what can be typified as
a late romantic anxiety concerning the masculinity of the artist and poet in
the age of industry. Writing to Cormell Price in 1856, Morris seemed almost
relieved that his new hero, Dante Gabriel Rossetti, had decreed that Morris
should be a painter rather than an architect or poet. He had little hope of
his own abilities in any direction without a master to guide him:

> I can't enter into politico-social subjects with any interest, for on the whole I
> see that things are in a muddle, and I have no power of putting them right in
> ever so little a degree. My work is the embodiment of dreams in one form or
> another . . . I am glad that I am compelled to try [painting] anyhow; I was
> slipping off into a kind of small (very small) Palace of Art.[29]

The reference to Tennyson's 'The Palace of Art' (1832) emphasizes that this
abiding sense of impotence and solipsism is intimately connected to

---

[27] Jan Marsh, 'William Morris and Victorian Manliness', in Peter Faulkner and Peter Preston
(eds.), *William Morris: Centenary Essays* (Exeter: University of Exeter Press, 1999),
pp. 185–200 (p. 179).
[28] Ibid. 191.
[29] William Morris to Cormell Price, July 1856, Morris, *CL,* i. 28.

Morris's identity as a poet. The reference to Tennyson also serves to remind us that Morris was one among many late or post-romantic poets who explored the anxiety of the latecomer, writing in an age in which the aesthetic seemed disarticulated from social and political necessity.

Morris, of course, returned to writing poetry after his experiment in painting, and for the critic Walter Pater the volumes that Morris produced over the next two decades remained the archetype of contemporary wanderings in the Palace of Art. Reviewing Morris's works, *The Defence of Guenevere and Other Poems* (1858), *The Life and Death of Jason* (1867), and *The Earthly Paradise* (1868) in 1868, Pater luxuriated in the 'secret of enjoyment' of the works, which was:

> that inversion of home-sickness known to some, that incurable thirst for the sense of escape, which no actual form of life satisfies, no poetry even, if it be merely simple and spontaneous. It is this which in these poems defines the temperament or personality of the workman.[30]

This characteristic inverted home-sickness of what Pater was later to dub 'aesthetic poetry' sublimated the ideal world of ordinary poetry to create one beyond it 'still fainter and more spectral, which is literally an artificial or "earthly paradise"'.[31] The male Victorian poet, unable to reconcile his vocation with the contemporary equation of masculinity, material production, and a rationalized public sphere, embodies the crisis of art in industrial modernity. He explores the ideal realm of aesthetics which has somehow now become unhitched from history: he is an exile from the processes of modernization and at the same time, emblematic of the self-estranged, dislocated subjectivity of modernity. Pater's use of the term 'workman' to describe the creator of such evanescent visions is a good example of his subversion of Ruskin's writings in order to deny the communal nature of the aesthetic. Rather than the 'broad vision' and 'massy power' of Ruskin's manual labourer giving form to an ethical ideal in traditional material, the individual 'temperament or personality' of Pater's 'workman', Morris, can only give shape to an ideal that has no communal material correlative, no collective ethical response.

It was this negation of the aesthetic as a site of the *sensus communis* that formed the most radical thrust of the latter part of Pater's review of Morris's poetry. Pater reprinted this material as the conclusion to *Studies in*

---

[30] [Walter Pater], 'Poems by William Morris', *Westminster Review*, 34 n.s. (1868), 300–12 (pp. 300–1).
[31] Ibid. 300. Pater republished the first half of his essay as 'Aesthetic Poetry', in *Appreciations* (London: Macmillan, 1889).

the History of the Renaissance in 1873, which can justly claim to be a manifesto of aestheticism.[32] Pater's distinctive contribution to aestheticism in
this text lies not so much in his suggestion that 'success in life' lies in gathering 'the fruit of a quickened, multiplied consciousness' from 'the love of
art for art's sake' as in the radical individualism that is its premise.[33] Pater's
rehearsal of German Idealism and its concurrent aesthetic autonomy
would, for example, be relatively familiar to readers of Ruskin. Yet whereas
Ruskin's ethical aesthetic idealism tends away from solipsism to the collective experience of the aesthetic, Pater's aestheticism (and, indeed, Pater's
Morris) does precisely the opposite.

> And if we continue to dwell on this world, not of objects in the solidity with
> which language invests them, but of impressions unstable, flickering, incon-
> sistent, which burn and are extinguished with our consciousness of them, it
> contracts still further; the whole scope of observation is dwarfed to the nar-
> row chamber of the individual mind. Experience, already reduced to a swarm
> of impressions, is ringed round for each one of us by that thick wall of per-
> sonality through which no real voice has ever pierced on its way to us from us
> to that which we can only conjecture to be without. Every one of those
> impressions is the impression of the individual in his isolation, each mind
> keeping as a solitary prisoner its own dream of a world.[34]

Whereas Morris feared slipping into solipsism in his small poetic Palace of
Art, Pater takes Morris's poetry to insist that aesthetic experience must
necessarily build up the palace walls ever thicker, until the aesthete is confined to a single cell of the self. Pater pursues an inversion of Matthew
Arnold's critical imperative: an inversion slipped in by sleight of hand in his
preface to *The Renaissance*.[35] Rather than us all agreeing to see the object
'as in itself it really is', Pater insists that there is nothing beyond radical subjectivism. One can only see an object by realizing one's impression of it distinctly. All aesthetic experience is thus individualizing and solipsistic. To
encounter beauty, in the Paterian formula, is not to achieve transcendence
with some communal spirit more deeply interfused through the aesthetic
object, but to add yet more substance to the 'thick wall of personality' that
is the critic. The aesthetic critic's skill, after all, consists in him or her

---

[32] [Pater], 'William Morris'.
[33] Walter Pater, *Studies in the History of the Renaissance* (London: Macmillan, 1873), p. 213.
[34] Ibid. 209.
[35] Rather than flatly contradicting Arnold's dictum from 'The Function of Criticism at the
Present Time' Pater attaches a rider to the original quotation that completely inverts its meaning: '"To see the object as in itself it really is," has been justly said to be the aim of all true
criticism whatever; and in aesthetic criticism the first step towards seeing one's object as it
really is, is to know one's impression as it really is, to discriminate it, to realise it distinctly.'
Pater, *Renaissance*, p. viii.

filtering out a particular impression of an object and returning that impression to the world as a sign of his or her uniquely sensitive temperament. Paterian aestheticism is so deeply anti-materialist that language itself is the thing nearest to being granted 'solid' status: all else exists in the impressionistic flux of the idea. Only the structure of language provides that substance which prevents experience existing as a mere unstable flicker and transforms it into a 'hard gem-like flame'.[36]

Pater extrapolates from Morris's poetry an aestheticism that requires the refined taste of individual experts and a historicism that exists only to provide pleasure in the transient moment of the present. Whereas Ruskin's historicism provided Morris with a model of heroic artistic labour and hope that the art of collective social engagement might once more be a possibility, Pater glosses Morris's historicism as the delicate flower of decadent solipsism. Mourning for an idealized past, struck with the modern disease of nostalgia, and estranged from the cultural connotations of his own gender identity, the poet takes hold of a feminized 'wild, convulsed sensuousness' as a trope to escape the limitations of the present through the possibilities of the past.[37] This is historicism as nostalgia, the affect of a mournful masculinity that desires the aesthetic to remain at a remove from the historical conflict that is the world. Important as Ruskinian historicism was for Morris's works, without a Marxist analysis of history, such ventures into the past risked being mere flickers in the mind of a dreamer: Paterian aestheticism encouraged Morris to make his history material.

II

In later years, when Morris had absorbed a very different model of history from Marx, he was able to understand his prolonged youthful anxieties about his poetic (and gender) identity as a product of the historical conditions of his existence. Writing to James Henderson, a young socialist in Norwich who had gingerly sent some of his poetry for scrutiny, Morris tempered some bad news regarding Henderson's talents by contrasting the experience of his generation with the current opportunities for manly heroism available to the young:

> we were born into a dull time oppressed with bourgeoisdom and philistinism so sorely that we were forced to turn back on ourselves, and only in ourselves and the world of art and literature was there any hope. You on the contrary

---

[36] Ibid. 210.
[37] [Pater], 'William Morris', 303.

have found yourself confronted by the rising hope of the people, and have
been able to declare yourself a soldier of the Cause: that is a serious and
solemn step to take: it may lead you into tribulation of various kinds, but it
will certainly provide you with aspirations, which will after all make your life
a pleasure to you, and an honour also: believe me this is better than *mere*
poetry-writing.[38]

By the time Morris wrote this letter he had spent over two years taking part
in the socialist propaganda campaigns coordinated by the Social
Democratic Federation. He had found his own 'rising hope' in the people: a
hope that promised an end to solipsism and the beginning of pleasure in
communal life. Biographers and scholars have provided a variety of expla-
nations for Morris's new-found political beliefs and activism in the 1880s,
from his encounter with Iceland and its heroic sagas and his involvement in
the practical politics of the Eastern Question Association during the 1870s,
to his ongoing and troubled marital situation.[39] It is clear, however, that one
major channel for Morris's exit from his 'own dream of a world' was his
practical interest in the craft techniques involved in the making of goods for
the Firm, Morris & Co. Morris's meticulously researched lectures on the
'lesser arts' or crafts delivered during the later 1870s constantly draw attention to the relationship between the organization of means of production,
the definition of wealth and value, and the state of the arts in his own time
in a manner highly reminiscent of Ruskin's own ethical aesthetic criticism.
Certainly, Morris had established the Firm in the 1860s with high hopes that
he, along with his 'brotherhood' of fellow artists and craftsmen, could revolutionize the world of and by art. By the early 1880s, however, the effects
of the Firm looked rather different, as the aesthetic interiors of Morris
& Co. became the mark of tasteful consumption on the part of wealthy
individuals.

   Linda Dowling suggests that Morris's work for the Firm thus
thwarted his aim of achieving aesthetic democracy. Driven 'by his own
high and implacable standard of craftsmanship, which would not allow
tawdry approximations produced by machine manufacture', she argues,
'Morris watched helplessly as the democratic ideal of a luxury of taste
was wholly absorbed and recontained within a crassly plutocratic luxury

---

[38] William Morris to James Frederick Henderson, Oct. 1885. Morris, *CL,* iib. 472. Emphasis
in orginal.
[39] For the influence of Morris's encounter with Iceland and Icelandic saga upon his ideas of
manly heroism and social action prior to the early 1880s see Ruth Kinna, *William Morris and
the Art of Socialism* (Cardiff: University of Wales Press, 2000), pp. 79–87. See also Linda
Dowling, *The Vulgarization of Art: The Victorians and Aesthetic Democracy* (Charlottesville,
Va.: University of Virginia Press, 1996), pp. 60–2; Thompson, *William Morris*, pp. 192–243.

of costliness.'[40] Dowling's analysis of nineteenth-century aesthetic democ-racy is instructive in many respects, but here she seems to underestimate the extent to which Morris's aesthetic theories published during the 1880s emerged as a reaction against both the 'luxury of taste' and the 'luxury of costliness'. For both of these categories are forms of individuating aes-thetic consumption: the individual subject either receives the fleeting impression of the object and signifies his or her exceptional sensuous dis-crimination in selecting it as a good worthy of display or simply pur-chases an object that signifies the distinction of wealth. Morris's writings on the arts from the late 1870s onwards, however, attempt to construct a theory of aesthetic response that stems from production rather than consumption.

The numerous recollections of Morris emerging from his workshop up to the elbows in home-made dye, or sitting at his handloom weaving before breakfast suggests the extent to which this interest in the aesthetic of pro-duction resulted from his own practice. This free play as a craftsman had, for Morris, become the ethical symbol of the possibilities of pleasurable labour in a different model of society. Rather than Pater's workman of aes-theticism, making nothing but an escape from the material world styled by temperament, Morris could be a labourer back in tradition and history. During the last two decades of the nineteenth century aestheticism and the aesthetic movement edged ever more into the marketplace with the profes-sionalized taste of the aesthete performing against the mass culture of modernity and the increasing commodification of aesthetic goods.[41] If the seemingly irresistible forces of capitalism assimilated the beautiful goods of the Firm and put these works of revolutionary intent on the marketplaces as markers of plutocratic distinction, then something had to be found to con-quer capitalism and do away with that marketplace altogether. Morris com-mented to an American correspondent that he had struggled to 'understand thoroughly the manner of work under which the art of the Middle Ages was done, and that that is the only manner of work which can turn out popular art'. This manner of work and hence truly popular art, Morris concluded, however, 'is impossible in this profit-grinding society':

---

[40] Dowling, *Vulgarization*, p. 59. See also Freedman, *Professions of Taste*, pp. 59–64.
[41] As will be seen in Ch. 4, however, the resources of capitalism did not let late 19th-cent. socialism escape without also commodifying some of its most marketable fads, although Edward Carpenter's sandal manufacture never quite reached the global scale of cheap knock-offs of Morris & Co.'s Sussex chairs.

So on all sides I am driven towards revolution as the only hope, and am growing clearer and clearer on the speedy advent of it in a very obvious form,
though of course I cannot give a date for it.[42]

The new earthly paradise of collective heroism and beauty was seemingly
just around the corner during the 1880s and this belief gave Morris the
chance to sustain his alternative model of productive aesthetics in the face
of the late flowering of individuated aestheticism.

In July 1883, Morris wrote a letter to the Christian Socialist, C. E.
Maurice, that made clear how far he had travelled during the early 1880s
from Ruskin's (and Maurice's own) beliefs concerning the need to 'moral-
ize' capitalism. After an account of the transition from feudalism to capitalism that evidently reflected his recent reading of Marx, Morris concluded
that art was handcuffed by the present system of capital and labour and
would die out if that system lasted. It was the resultant decadence of the
aesthetic when detached from labour that, for Morris, carried with it 'the
condemnation of the whole system' of capitalism. Above all, however,
Morris admitted that it had been his fears for the arts which had 'drawn my
attention to the subject in general'.

> Now it seems to me that, feeling this, I am bound to act for the destruction of
> the system which seems to me mere oppression and obstruction; such a sys-
> tem can only be destroyed, it seems to me, by the united discontent of num-
> bers; isolated acts of a few persons of the middle and upper classes seeming
> to me . . . quite powerless against it: in other words the antagonism of the
> classes, which the system has bred, is the natural and necessary instrument of
> its destruction.[43]

If we look closely here, we can see Morris inscribing the distance between
his new historical materialism and Ruskinian historicism: the dangerously
effete and 'powerless' acts of 'isolated' persons of the upper classes against
the communal, martial, material actions of the class struggle. Ruskin,
Morris confided to a fellow socialist, was quite sound in some respects, 'but
he does not understand this matter of classes' and that the 'class struggle is
really the only lever for bringing about change'.[44] The collective mechanism
of class struggle overcame that fearful solipsism and individualism that
threatened to keep the Ruskinian artist looking hard at the storm cloud of
the nineteenth century, but doing little other than dreaming of the hopes of
the past.

[42] Morris to unknown American woman, March 1885, Morris, *CL*, iib. 395.
[43] Morris to C. E. Maurice, July 1883, Morris, *CL*, iia. 202.
[44] Morris to Fred Pickles, Oct. 1885, Morris, *CL*, iib. 462.

Morris's socialist lectures of the 1880s led his listeners along this, his own aesthetic route to socialism. It was a route shaped by what Morris perceived as the cracks and flaws in late nineteenth-century aesthetic practice, pinched in the grip of capitalism. The socialist aesthetic that Morris disseminated in his collection of lectures, *Signs of Change* (1888), challenged the form of aestheticism that fed into early modernism at the end of the nineteenth century on the grounds of its individualism, its autonomy, and its decadence. Morris thus forms a case in point of what Freedman identifies as a common paradox within the development of British aestheticism: the paradox of the proponents of aestheticism reacting against the legacy of their work and becoming its most stern critics.[45] In Morris's case this was perhaps all the more keenly felt because that recurrent fin-de-siècle representation of the artistic soul as consumer, collector, and exhibitor of enlightened taste in the arrangement of interiors and the experience of surfaces owed so much to the work of the Arts and Crafts Exhibitions Society with which Morris continued to be involved during this period.[46]

As the exercise of elite, educated taste—what Regenia Gagnier has termed an aesthetics of consumption—came to dominate art and criticism at the fin-de-siècle, Morris constantly reaffirmed the democratic, productivist nature of 'true' art.[47] Despite Morris's implication in the development of aestheticism and the aesthetic movement, it is that emblem of early modernism—the aesthete exercising ahistorical, individuated taste in the collection of sensuous surfaces—that we see Morris working against in his account of his conversion to socialism. The 'study of history and the love of the practice of art', Morris writes,

> forced me into a hatred of the civilization which, if things were to stop as they are, would turn history into inconsequent nonsense, and make art a collection of curiosities of the past, which would have no serious relation to the life of the present.[48]

History and aesthetic production are threatened by a capitalist modernity that rewrites the former as fragmentary stories lacking an originary, causal logic, and the latter as arbitrary consumption, necessarily detached from

---

[45] Freedman, *Professions of Taste*, p. xxi.

[46] For Wilde too, Morris was a central figure in his promotion of the aesthetic movement. Wilde's 1882 lecture tour of the USA consisted largely of his performance of Morris's aesthetic theories as published in *Hopes and Fears for Art* (1882). See Richard Ellmann, *Oscar Wilde* (London: Hamish Hamilton, 1987), pp. 165–200. See Peter Stansky, *Redesigning the World: William Morris, the 1880s and the Arts and Crafts* (Princeton: Princeton University Press, 1985), pp. 171–262, for the Arts and Crafts Exhibitions Society.

[47] Regenia Gagnier, *The Insatiability of Human Wants: Economics and Aesthetics in Market Society* (Chicago: University of Chicago Press, 2000), pp. 123, 167.

[48] Morris, 'How I Became a Socialist', CW, xxiii. 280.

the everyday. The negative attributes of civilization here can be equated with the decadent aesthete himself: think of those collectors, Dorian Gray and Des Essientes, gathering up the art and narratives of the past with no inherent logic but individual desire, personal, jaded tastes. 'Soon there will be nothing left', Morris argues, 'except the lying dreams of history, the miserable wreckage of our museums and picture galleries, and the carefully guarded interiors of our aesthetic drawing rooms, unreal and foolish, fitting witness of the life of corruption that goes on there'.[49]

The historical materialism that Morris gleaned from reading Marx in the early 1880s provided him with a means of explaining the aesthete, placing him back into history whilst also figuring the hope of change. The decadence and detachment of the aesthetes was but the result of high capitalism and the necessary alienation of the worker from his task. There could be no true, manly art under such a system, just the 'sham art' that resulted from the simulation of aesthetics by 'dilettanti fine gentlemen and ladies without any help from below'.[50] Looking forward through his hopes of the past, Morris envisioned the rebirth of aesthetics after the overthrow of capitalism. The inevitable processes of history would sweep away the possibility of art as self-interested consumption, and it would be Nature (whose gender I will return to), Morris argues, that will be 'recovering her ancient beauty, and . . . teaching men the old story of art'.[51]

Art is indeed an 'old story' for Morris, but it is a story that exists outside civilization and history in terms of its origins. The pure wellsprings of the aesthetic lie in man's primal contest with Nature, when he learnt to mimic 'her' in her adornment of her work. For Morris art therefore originates in the somatic inheritance of tradition rather than the momentary inspiration of individual genius. Through copying the productions of Nature, man would learn again to adorn his work after the revolution and hence stamp 'all labour with the impress of pleasure'.[52] Quite at odds with the tenets of Paterian aestheticism—though of course owing much to the early inspiration of Ruskin—Morris locates aesthetics in the realm of the body via the pleasures of labour. With the sweeping away of the capitalist system, he argues:

> our working hours would rather be merry parties of men and maids, young men and old enjoying themselves over their work, than the grumpy weariness it mostly is now. Then would come the time for the new birth of art, so much talked of, so long deferred; people could not help showing their mirth and

[49] Morris, 'Aims of Art', *CW*, xxiii. 91.
[50] Ibid. 93.
[51] Ibid. 95.
[52] Morris, 'Useful Work versus Useless Toil', *CW*, xxiii. 114.

pleasure in their work, and would be always wishing to express it in a tangible and more or less enduring form, and the workshop would once more be a school of art, whose influence no one could escape from.[53]

The 'definite sensuous pleasure' of the labour of the hand contains the seeds of a new art ready to blossom forth, once historical developments sweep away the burden and slavery of work under capitalism.[54] The embodied tradition of aesthetic pleasure is, as Morris indicates in *News from Nowhere* (1891), something that outlasts the end of history. Even though the inhabitants of Nowhere have little notion or need of history in that utopian 'epoch of rest' after historical materialism, their pleasure in nature and the architectural repositories of tradition feed a new communal artistry.

Morris's somatic aesthetic theory was in tension with two major currents of nineteenth-century thought regarding the relationship between art and the people, aesthetics and politics. First his insistence on communal tradition as a school of art was at odds, as we have seen, with aestheticism and the Paterian doctrine of individuating taste during the 1880s.[55] True artistic individuality for Morris could, paradoxically, only develop through working within authentic popular tradition. Oscar Wilde responded to Morris's socialist aesthetics—as we shall see shortly—by trying to fold socialism back into the mainstream of aestheticism. Socialism, Wilde argued, would liberate the artist from a concern with popular tradition into states of intense creative individualism. Art under socialism, in Wilde's formulation, is not only an autonomous but also a self-reflexive process: 'Its beauty comes from the fact that the author is what he is'; from self outwith, rather than within, tradition.[56] At the same time as Morris rejected such ideas of the autonomy of artistic creativity, his somatic aesthetic of tradition also diverged from the dominant forms of cultural philanthropy in the late nineteenth century. By concentrating on the 'lesser arts' in his writing, Morris refused the possibility that the ethical affect of the aesthetic—Arnold's 'sweetness and light'—was a perquisite of the bourgeoisie. For Morris the tradition of the productive hand, rather than the culture of the consuming,

---

[53] Morris, 'How we Live and How we Might Live' (1888), CW, xxiii. 21.

[54] Morris, 'Aims of Art', p. 84.

[55] Josephine Guy, *The British Avant Garde: The Theory and Politics of Tradition* (Hemel Hempstead: Harvester Wheatsheaf, 1991), p. 135, suggests that, despite his divergence from the aesthetes concerning the nature and function of the arts, Morris was connected to writers such as Pater by means of a shared strategy of using tradition to undermine 'contemporary orthodoxies'. Despite Guy's subtle reading of Morris's place among the British avant-garde, I would argue that the 'tradition(s)' invoked by Morris and Pater (medieval craftsmanship and Hellenist elitism) were so radically opposed to each other in political effects that the differences between them remain irreducible.

[56] Oscar Wilde, *The Soul of Man under Socialism* (London: Journeyman, 1988), p. 29.

tasteful mind was the source of aesthetic transformation: a transformation
that could therefore be led by popular revolution and not by doses of culture
de haute en bas. Hope was to be found in seeking not the 'dead exterior' of
art itself, but the aims of art, in the production of human subjects not the
consumption of aesthetic objects.

III

In returning the aesthetic to a logic of production as opposed to consumption, Morris attempted to reinscribe the 'manliness' of art. No longer lost
in his small palace of art, or walled up in his solitary Paterian cell of impres-
sions, the poet could once more be a 'makere', the socially engaged labourer
whose work spoke from the people and returned their pleasures to them.
Even in a hastily drafted poetic address for a gathering of the Socialist
League in 1885 it is possible to see Morris's aversion to the troubling privilege of the modern, self-centred 'luxurious mood', the inwardness and
individualism of bourgeois lyric subjectivity.[57] Morris urges his socialist
audience to let their politics interpenetrate their play and let 'the cause
cling':

> About the book we read, the song we sing,
> Cleave to our cup and hover o'er our plate,
> And by our bed at morn and even wait.

Morris contains the troubling solipsism of the lyric by referring to the ballad form: that affirmation of poetry as engaged collective experience, signified, as Anne Janowitz indicates, in both the rhythmic structure and the
titles of the 'songs' and 'chants' that Morris produced after his conversion
to socialism in the early 1880s.[58]

Art is the offspring of labour in a non-alienated, pre- or post-capitalist
world, and the desire for labour for Morris is an inherent trait of mankind:
the urge 'for due work to do' is, he argues, most important of demands in
constituting happiness. Even rough or nasty work possesses aesthetic potential. 'I should not think much of the manhood of a stout and healthy man',
Morris sniffed, 'who did not feel a pleasure in doing rough work.'[59] The aim
of art, he writes, is to give men 'hope and bodily pleasure' in their work so

---

[57] William Morris, *Socialists at Play: An Address to the Entertainment of the Socialist League*
(London: Socialist League, 1885).
[58] Anne Janowitz, *Lyric and Labour in the English Romantic Tradition* (Cambridge:
Cambridge University Press, 1998), p. 199.
[59] Morris, 'How we Live', p. 21.

that even swinging a pickaxe and road mending, as Morris suggests in *News from Nowhere*, finds its place on an aesthetic continuum.[60] *News from Nowhere* is thus that paradox of an aesthetic utopia in which there are no more works of art as such. It is, as Patrick Brantlinger argues, an anti-novel, in which the specific aesthetic forms which flourished under the system of capitalist individualism (in this case, the realist novel) simply make no sense any more.[61] Instead its muscular inhabitants participate in the aesthetic democracy every time pleasure is felt along the body, every time the body moves in labour.[62] The aesthetic quality of the manly road-mender was of course nothing new to the nineteenth-century reading public. Ford Madox Brown's *Work* and Ruskin's philanthropic road-building scheme using Oxford undergraduates had both associated aesthetic muscular masculinity with so-called Christian Socialism during the 1870s. In Morris's somatic aesthetic such manual labour was not the mere healthy, corporeal counter-balance to elite, intellectual art, but the source of the aesthetic itself. It was this placement of the natural body at the centre of the aesthetic that proved crucial to women socialist artists trying to negotiate their way within the aesthetic of production.

It is highly probable that Wilde had read the serialization of *News from Nowhere* in *Commonweal* during 1890 and that this work was one among the many that Wilde drew on in writing 'The Soul of Man under Socialism' that winter.[63] Although Wilde's article barely caused a ripple in the socialist press at the time—and should, as Josephine Guy suggests, be seen as topical entertainment in response to current journalism, rather than as considered political analysis—'The Soul of Man under Socialism' wittily debunks Morris's somatic aesthetics.[64] The figure of labouring masculinity straddled the divide between aesthetics and politics for Morris because Morris believed that man was created as man the maker, man the labourer. Far from labour being the punitive consequence of a fall into civilization and history, for Morris joyful labour is there from the outset. The aesthetic is therefore

[60] Morris, 'Aims of Art', p. 85; William Morris, *News from Nowhere* (1891; repr. London: Routledge, 1992), p. 39.

[61] Patrick Brantlinger, '*News from Nowhere*: Morris's Socialist Anti-Novel', *Victorian Studies*, 19 (1975), 35–49.

[62] Dowling, *Vulgarization*, pp. 70–2, contains a sophisticated discussion of how the consequent transformation of the moral-aesthetic into the *sensus communis* of Nowhere creates aesthetic democracy at the price of denuding the aesthetic of that critical autonomy that made it a source of resistance in the Whig tradition.

[63] Lawrence Danson, *Wilde's Intentions: The Artist in his Criticism* (Oxford: Clarendon, 1997), p. 163; Josephine Guy, '"The Soul of Man Under Socialism": A (Con)Textual History' in Joseph Bristow (ed.), *Wilde Writings: Contextual Conditions* (Toronto: University of Toronto Press, 2003), pp. 61–83 (p. 64).

[64] Guy, 'Soul of Man', p. 67.

not spawned in a pre-lapsarian primal relationship, cradled in the bosom of Nature, but in the effortful labour needed to mimic her pleasures whilst mastering her resources. Pleasure, labour, and manliness need to be inter-linked categories within this political aesthetic: categories that have been strained apart by the corruption of art, production, and the subject under capitalism, but that will return to Edenic identity after the revolution, out-side history once again. Wilde, however, neatly dissects these three and rein-scribes the boundaries between them by insisting that the nature of pleasure, labour, and pain are essentially unaffected by socialism and eco-nomic revolution: art will still be the source of pleasure and labour (often) that of pain.

Although Wilde concedes, in a phrase reminiscent of Morris, that 'Pleasure is Nature's test, her sign of approval' of the value of any activity, he denies that such pleasure is necessarily linked to labour.[65] Nonchalantly launching an attack on Morris's aesthetic socialism, informed perhaps by his own experience in Ruskin's road gang, Wilde adds, 'I cannot help saying that a great deal of nonsense is being written and talked nowadays about the dignity of manual labour . . . many forms of labour are quite pleasureless activities and should be regarded as such.'[66] And homing in on one end of Morris's aesthetic continuum in *New from Nowhere*, Wilde concludes that '[t]o sweep a slushy crossing for eight hours a day when the east wind is blowing is a disgusting occupation'.[67] So, under the Wildean socialist scheme, machines would fulfil tasks currently allotted to manual labourers and humanity would be free for its chief, true, aim in life: 'enjoying culti-vated leisure'.[68] This is more than just a generalized joke against contem-porary ideals of masculine earnestness, divisible, as Robbins suggests, from the article's critique of socialism.[69] It is rather a careful attempt to decon-struct the figure of effortful labouring manhood, a pointed attack on the politicized aesthetic of 1880s socialism that foreshadows (in a typically Wildean manner) the increasingly rigid demarcation between art and labour in the twentieth century.

Wilde's insistence upon the boundary between, on the one hand, art and leisure, and on the other, politics and labour is the fruit of what Gagnier has identified as the dominant late nineteenth-century aesthetic of consump-tion. Freed by the machinery of state socialism and automated crossing sweepers from the burden of altruism and the tradition of manual labour,

---

[65] Wilde, 'Soul of Man', p. 64.
[66] Ibid. 26.
[67] Ibid.
[68] Ibid. 27.
[69] Robbins, 'Genders of Socialism', p. 107.

the Wildean aesthete is able to construct himself through acts of taste, states of 'admiration and delight'. And so that democratization of art under socialism through the communal experience of labour and the inheritance of tradition imagined by Morris is simply an impossibility for Wilde. Man is not made for the corporeal processes of labour for Wilde, but for the exercise of pleasurable taste; art is not the expression of communal tradition, but rather of individual personality. Such art may in turn have a revolutionary effect in reconstructing its audience, as Gagnier suggests, however, this would be the paradox of a socialist state crafted by 'the most intense mode of individualism that the world has known'; that is, by Wildean art.[70] Wilde's individualism in 'The Soul of Man' is, as Jonathan Freedman argues, nothing less than his translation of Pater's idiom of aestheticist solipsism 'into the language of ethics'.[71]

In 'The Soul of Man under Socialism' Wilde develops that latitudinarian fantasia of socialism as a feminized consumer with a 'wonderful personality' which he outlined in his review of Edward Carpenter's *Chants of Labour* in 1889.[72] For Wilde, socialism is to be a salon hostess drawing out the individuated artistic elite into even more dazzling performances of their own personality. For Morris, however, the future of socialist hope took the shape of 'some noble communal hall' that bespoke the manly labour of the many by whom it would be built.[73] As the salon is to the communal hall, so too is Wilde's 'personality' to Morris's 'manliness': the former alluding to the erotic aesthetics of delectable individualism against the mass, the latter to the impulse of self-forgetful labour that paradoxically forges subjects in the process of making objects. 'A man at work', Morris declaimed, 'making something which he feels will exist because he is working at it and wills it, is exercising the energies of his mind and soul as well as of his body'. And with a final biblical cadence he concluded 'if we work thus, we shall be men, and our days happy and eventful'.[74] Morris's manly subjects are making (them)selves through tradition, out of the historical conditions of their existence into a future of socialist hope.[75]

---

[70] Regenia Gagnier, *Idylls of the Marketplace: Oscar Wilde and the Victorian Public* (Stanford, Calif.: Stanford University Press, 1986), p. 29; Wilde, 'Soul of Man', p. 29.

[71] Freedman, *Professions of Taste*, p. 36.

[72] [Oscar Wilde], 'Poetical Socialists', *Pall Mall Gazette* (13 Feb. 1889), 3.

[73] Morris, 'How we Live', p. 23.

[74] Morris, 'Useful Work', *CW*, xxiii. 100.

[75] Jeffrey Spear, *Dreams of an English Eden: Ruskin and his Tradition in Social Criticism* (New York: Columbia University Press, 1984), pp. 223–34, argues that this phase of Morris's work should be understood as 'realized romance'. This analysis receives more attention in the following chapter.

It is this move from the consumption of 'high' art to the production of social goods, from aesthetic autonomy to social engagement, which for many years led to the exclusion of Morris from our account of modernism (and modernity). On the one hand, his belief that the super-sensible effects of the aesthetic retained relative autonomy from historical materialism resulted in his dismissal from much twentieth-century Marxist thought as a mere utopian. On the other, Morris's refusal to disaggregate the ends of art from art itself required early historians of modernism, such as Nikolaus Pevsner, to relegate him to a role in social science rather than aesthetic innovation. For both he is simply too medieval to be modern. It is rather to the aestheticism of Pater and Wilde that we look for the avant-garde of literary modernism. But Morris's resistance to aestheticism in the late nineteenth century foregrounds the gendered politics of style at the turn of the last century and reminds us that modernism itself emerged from the dialectic of effeminate consumption and virile aesthetic production at the fin de siècle.

IV

By the time of his death in 1896 Morris had endured more than a decade of splits and fractions within the various socialist organizations that claimed to be heir to the true Marxist heritage. Morris joined the Democratic Federation of the former Tory Radical, H. M. Hyndman, in January 1883, at a point so early in British socialist propagandism that even Hyndman had not yet added 'Social' to his organization's title to reflect his new-found economic analysis. Less than two years later, Morris was at the forefront of a breakaway group that included Karl Marx's daughter Eleanor and her partner Edward Aveling, who, guided by the advice of Friedrich Engels, formed the Socialist League. Morris and his fellow dissidents argued that Hyndman's leadership of the SDF was overly autocratic, uninterested in the need to educate the workers and the aim of 'making socialists'.[76] Hyndman himself, it was hinted (unfairly, as it turned out), was a mere political opportunist who hoped that his agitation would lead to a seat in Parliament.

Over the years that followed, Morris doggedly completed his education in the Marxist interpretation of classical Ricardian economics through drafting his series of articles, 'Socialism from the Root up', with Ernest Belfort Bax, published in *Commonweal*, the journal of the Socialist League in 1886 and 1887. Such intellectual effort was accompanied by an endless

---

[76] For a detailed (if partisan) account of the split and its aftermath see Thompson, *William Morris*, pp. 331–65.

round of speaking engagements and practical propaganda that extended far beyond the hub of the Socialist League, the meeting room Morris constructed from his former coach house in Hammersmith. Eschewing electoral politics, the League was committed to 'realising the change towards social order' and steering the people through the 'irresistible movement' of the coming revolution.[77] Although a certain indefiniteness about the means of advancing the revolution and the shape of the society to come enabled a broad spectrum of anarchists and socialists to join the League, such lack of clarity put pressure on the 'frankness and fraternal trust in each other, and single-hearted devotion to the religion of socialism' that Morris inserted as the conclusion to the manifesto.[78] By 1888, the Bloomsbury Socialist Society, a branch of the League that named Eleanor Marx and Edward Aveling as its most prominent members, had already developed an autonomous programme that included the possibility of achieving socialism through parliamentary means. Upon the subsequent suspension of the Bloomsbury branch, Morris found himself isolated within an increasingly anarchist-leaning League, which refused to contemplate anything other than an immediate total overthrow of the existing social and political order. In 1891 Morris broke his links with the League and concentrated his efforts on his own Hammersmith Socialist Society. In the mean time Morris was reconciled with Hyndman and the SDF and by 1894 he candidly admitted in an interview in *Justice* that some sort of parliamentary palliative to the sufferings of capitalism might be a desirable stop-gap.[79]

In the context of this troubled history, Morris's explicit reference to Ruskin in his 1894 article, 'How I Became a Socialist' acts as a gesture of reunification. It was a means of emphasizing the native romantic idealism of Morris's own beliefs in the context of an institution (and an individual) that had been increasingly associated with continental 'scientific' socialism and socialists over the last decade.[80] As will become clear in the following chapters, whilst the Fabian Society and the Independent Labour Party emerged from domestic traditions of radical Utilitarianism and the ethical idealism of the secularist movement, both the SDF and the SL were content to claim the ground of scientific socialism in the mode of Marx and Engels. Morris's onetime collaborator, Ernest Belfort Bax, for instance, set out stringent criteria in his article 'Unscientific Socialism' which purged true socialism of the 'nominally socialistic' movements of Christian,

---

[77] *Manifesto of the Socialist League* (1885), ibid., appendix I, p. 737.

[78] Ibid. 737.

[79] *Justice* (27 Jan. 1894); Thompson, *William Morris*, p. 617.

[80] That is, 'native' only insofar as filtered by a couple of generations of modification and transmission by British writers. Both Marx and Carlyle, of course, shared an intellectual origin in German Idealism.

'Sentimental', and utopian socialism alongside anarchism.[81] With a scarce-concealed jab at the actual Fellowship of the New Life, Bax scoffed at the vagueness of societies with names 'such as the "Brother[hood] of the Higher Life", or . . . the "Communion of Noble Aspirations"'.[82] Such organizations were nothing other than manifestations of the 'morbid self-consciousness of our Christian and middle-class civilisation run to seed': a solipsistic indulgence of young men and women who required a 'stimulus' of some sort.[83] This stimulus, Bax concluded, 'may be aesthetic, philanthropic or social. It may consist in languishing and vapouring on art, on improved dwellings, on social reconstruction. Just now it wears the latter aspect.'[84] However it cloaked itself, this youthful twitch of idealism was unrelated to Bax's thorough-going Marxist socialism.

Bax's diatribe is a fairly neat summary of youthful fads in the 1880s, but it also dissects the various tendencies that emerged from the aesthetic critical mode of the 1850s. By the later 1880s, the figure of the aesthete 'languishing and vapouring on art' had become common currency in the commodified aesthetic movement as the figure of the dandy played with his audience. Earlier in the decade philanthropic ventures into the East End of London had been fuelled (and, in the case of the housing management schemes of Octavia Hill, funded) by Ruskin's later explicit interventions in the social sphere. But it was the ethical socialist movement, which gained increasing force nationally during the 1890s, that claimed Ruskin as a native source of inspiration for political action. In 1894, Morris thus attempted to recuperate Ruskin's aesthetic and historical interests specifically for a united future for the British socialist movement. The voices of 'our friends' who question the relevance of such matters and argue that they want 'by means of Social-Democracy to win a decent livelihood, we want in some sort to live, and that at once', needed Ruskin's legacy more than anyone else, Morris argued.[85] They simply did not want enough for themselves:

> It is the province of art to set the true ideal of a full and reasonable life before [the worker], a life to which the perception and the creation of beauty, the enjoyment of real pleasure that is, shall be felt to be as necessary to man

---

[81] Ernest Belfort Bax, *The Religion of Socialism: Essays in Modern Socialist Criticism* (London: Swan Sonnenschein, 1887), p. 92. The title of Bax's work is rather a Trojan horse, since the 'religion of socialism' was most often associated with the very form of socialism Bax here dismisses as 'Sentimental'. This particular section was first published as 'Unscientific Socialism', *Today*, 1/3 (March 1884), 192–304.

[82] Bax, *Religion of Socialism*, p. 100.

[83] Ibid.

[84] Ibid.

[85] Morris, 'How I Became a Socialist', p. 281.

as his daily bread, and that no man, and no set of men, can be deprived of this except by mere opposition, which should be resisted to the utmost.[86]

The ethical aesthetics here could not be further from the decadent aestheticism of the 1880s and 1890s. The aesthetic ideal must be available to all, Morris argues, in order to stimulate material change. Only the aesthetic has the capacity to stand outside the shadow of history: it is the only place left for idealism in Morris's socialist theory; the only means by which will and desire can have relative autonomy from the material determinations of capitalism. In a turn of phrase, here towards the end of his life, oddly reminiscent of Wilde, Morris suggests that in the present state of society 'happiness is only possible to artists and thieves'.[87] Only these two groups are free from commercialism's success in denuding production of pleasure. However, unlike Ruskin or Wilde, Morris insists upon the necessity of historical materialism as the engine of revolution: desire for the beautiful alone is never enough.

[86] Ibid.
[87] Morris, 'The Socialist Ideal: Art', CW, xxxiii. 256.

2

Politics, Fellowship, and Romance: Clementina Black and the Culture of Socialism in 1880s London

From 1885 to 1889 the socialist journal *Today* carried one of the longest running and least sensationalist serials in literary history: James Broadhouse's translation of Karl Marx's *Capital* in forty-four instalments. These monthly bit parts ran under vociferous debates in the pages of *Today* and beyond concerning the nature and destiny of British socialism throughout the 1880s. It was the space of these few years, for example, that saw the distinct development of the Fabian Society as a middle-class and explicitly non-Marxist socialist society which aimed to permeate existing political parties.[1] At the same time as the Fabians, George Bernard Shaw and Sidney Webb dismissed *Capital* on the basis of Marx's reliance upon the outdated wage fund theory of classical economics, H. M. Hyndman's Marxist Social Democratic Federation sought to educate and agitate among the working class in hope of an imminent revolution.[2] Sydney Olivier, a prominent Fabian socialist, insisted that Marxism alone would do nothing to overcome the real enemy, 'Individualism, Personalism or Egoism', and that socialists should be attentive to personal ethics, but the SDF activist Henry Hyde Champion dismissed such thinking as 'socialism of the armchair'.[3] Such 'wordy sympathy', Champion argued, demonstrated that the Fabians and most of the middle class 'could not grasp what the life of the many really

---

[1] See Norman and Jeanne MacKenzie, *First Fabians* (London: Weidenfeld & Nicolson, 1977); Patricia Pugh, *Educate, Agitate, Organize: 100 Years of Fabian Socialism* (London: Methuen, 1984).

[2] George Bernard Shaw, 'The Jevonian Criticism of Marx', *Today*, 3/12 (Jan. 1885); Phillip Wicksteed, 'The Jevonian Criticism of Marx (a Rejoinder)', *Today*, 3/15 (April 1885), 173–6. On the history of the SDF see Stanley Pierson, *Marxism and the Origins of British Socialism: The Struggle for Consciousness* (Ithaca, NY: Cornell University Press, 1973), pp. 59–89, 174–98; Karen Hunt, *Equivocal Feminists: The Social Democratic Federation and the Woman Question, 1884–1911* (Cambridge: Cambridge University Press, 1996).

[3] Sydney Olivier, 'Perverse Socialism II', *Today*, 6/34 (Aug. 1886), 114; Sydney Olivier, 'Perverse Socialism I', *Today*, 6/32 (Aug. 1886), 51.

is', for 'they could not sit still in their armchairs if the sights of our great cities haunted them as they haunt men who have got to understand what needless misery there is in the world'.[4]

This impassioned concern with taking the right route to the socialist future reflected the widespread view among socialists of all persuasions in the 1880s that the revolution, or at least an opportunity for profound political transformation, was imminent. Writing to Fred Pickles in October 1885, William Morris was pleased to note that 'things are going on very fast, and … my hopes of the great change coming speedily are much higher than they were a year ago'.[5] The repression of the socialist demonstrators on 'Bloody Sunday' in November 1887 and the increasing fractions from and within the SDF sobered such optimism somewhat a few years later. But the rise of labour activism around the great dock strike of 1889 seemed to promise a way forward for socialism in the new union movement at the end of the decade. This shared sense amongst socialists of standing at the brink—or, *On the Threshold*, as the socialist activist Isabella Ford titled her novel set in this time, this place—of a new life naturally lent a sense of urgency to debates on the shape of the socialist future. They were at the heart of a struggle that promised millenarian redemption and, for many socialists, the events of the 1880s seemed to represent what Jeffrey Spear has termed in a different context as a 'realised romance'.[6] Marxist dialectic melded into pre-existent understandings of the form of epic romance and created a sense among socialists that they were participating in a mythic cycle of change and renewal. Working together in fellowship, men and women activists moved from that ethical aesthetic origin examined in the previous chapter to practical efforts to organize and agitate in London during the 1880s.

The Fellowship of the New Life, founded in October 1883, formed one such common ethical aesthetic meeting ground for many socialists who later rejected its nebulous mission in favour of political action.[7] The Fellowship's stated aims were to cultivate 'perfect character in each & all' by founding a 'communistic society' in which 'material things would be subordinated to spiritual things' and manual labour pursued 'in conjunction with

---

[4] H. H. Champion, 'Socialists of the Arm Chair', *Today*, 6/35 (Oct. 1886), 151.

[5] William Morris to Fred Pickles, Oct. 1885, *CL*, iib. 462.

[6] Jeffrey Spear, 'Political Questing: Ruskin, Morris and Romance', in Robert Hewison (ed.), *New Approaches to Ruskin* (London: Routledge, 1981), pp. 174–93; Jeffrey Spear, *Dreams of an English Eden: Ruskin and his Tradition in Social Criticism* (New York: Columbia University Press, 1984), pp. 223–34.

[7] For a recent reassessment of the influence of the FNL see K. Manton, 'The Fellowship of the New Life: English Ethical Socialism Reconsidered', *History of Political Thought,* 24 (2003), 282–304.

intellectual pursuits'.[8] Its founder, the ethical socialist Percival Chubb, actively encouraged both men and women to join the Fellowship in pursuit of this new life and such an agenda drew together a wide range of interested parties. Indeed, Chubb's improbably inclusive reading list suggests just how broadly the Fellowship interpreted socialism. Marx and his fellow economists were, Chubb suggested, the 'enlighteners, but not [the] inspirers and instigators' of the Socialist movement:[9]

> These latter we find in such names as Wordsworth, Shelley, Byron, Carlyle, Emerson, Dickens, Ruskin, George Eliot, Thoreau, Whitman and the younger Swinburne, who have quickened and nourished in us a deeper sense of human dignity, a more exacting demand for freedom, a keener susceptibility to beauty and recoil from ugliness, a wider sympathy, and more uniting spirit of comradeship.[10]

As a result of such inclusiveness a meeting in 1883, for example, brought together the Social Democrats Henry Hyde Champion and James Leigh Joynes and the Hintonian sexual radicals, Caroline Haddon and her sister, Mrs James Hinton. Havelock Ellis found a common interest for all in his suggestion that Robert Owen's daughter should be invited along to a meeting explain her father's utopian socialist experiment, New Harmony.[11] The editors of *Today*, Hubert Bland and his wife Edith Nesbit, were present at these early discussions, but soon became exasperated with the planned commune that never quite materialized and seceded with Frank Podmore and others in 1884 to form the Fabian Society, dedicated to research into the question of the 'working-man'.[12]

The future labour activist Isabella Ford and her sister Bessie had also been at the founding meeting of the Fellowship of the New Life in 1883, inspired by the charismatic ethicist, Thomas Davidson.[13] Over a decade later, as an active union organizer and member of the Independent Labour Party, Ford wrote *On the Threshold* (1895), a novel set in London when 'we

---

[8] BLPES archives, LSE, Fabian Collection C36, Fabian Society Meetings Minutes 1883–1888; 24 Oct. 1883.

[9] See Mark Bevir, 'British Socialism and American Romanticism', *English Historical Review*, 110 (1995), 878–901 (pp. 878–92). On the aesthetic interests of the founders and inspirers of the FNL see Ian Britain, *Fabianism and Culture: A Study in British Socialism and the Arts, 1884–1918* (Cambridge: Cambridge University Press, 1982), pp. 25–52.

[10] Percival Chubb, 'The Two Alternatives', *Today*, 8/46 (Sept. 1887), 72–7 (p. 76).

[11] BLPES Fabian Collection C36, 24 Oct. 1883.

[12] BLPES Fabian Collection C36, 4 Jan. 1884. Despite this split Sydney Olivier, among others, retained a membership of both organizations throughout 1880s.

[13] One of the founders of the FNL was the Fords' cousin Edward Pease, who later acted as Secretary of the Fabian Society for 30 years. See Bevir, 'British Socialism', pp. 882–5, on Thomas Davidson.

were all socialists more or less' which gently satirized the idealism and millenarian optimism of the movement in the previous decade.[14] Her student
heroines of the 1880s, recreated with terrible, tender nostalgia, just *know*
that they are in a realized romance: an epic quest narrative in a cityscape
charged with good and evil. Ugly lodging houses are transformed into 'a
fairy-land of freedom' as the two heroines, Kitty and Lucretia, swear
solemnly over cocoa 'that we will set about changing all this': poverty, prostitution, policemen, all will be removed by the imminent social revolution.[15]
As Carolyn Steedman has pointed out, we hardly need the meticulous exca-
vations of the intellectual origins of the socialist movement carried out by
scholars such as Stanley Pierson when Ford encapsulates that aesthetic journey of the 1880s so perfectly with a brief mention of her heroines' changing
literary tastes.[16] Ruskin's later works replace those of John Stuart Mill and
Whitman's poetry Emerson's essays as Kitty and Lucretia confront the city
and move through the varied ethical idealist and socialist meetings on offer
there.

Ford's novel picks apart the tensions between men and women within
such idealist socialist organizations during the 1880s, as it becomes clear
that the leaders of the thinly disguised socialist debating society expect their
women members to do the housework and not much else in their future
commune.[17] But the form of the novel itself poses a question about the
ethics of seeing socialist activism as romance: a question that the women
activists examined here all had to face by the end of the 1880s. Could the
ethical ideal of fellowship and the hope for a new life of beauty under
socialism really make a difference to the lives of working-class women? For
the cluster of women writers and artists studied in this chapter, the mid-
1880s offered a moment in which the socialist aesthetic ideals of fellowship
and comradely labour shared by men and women alike could be lived in the
city in pursuit of the cause. The narrative genre of epic romance, to paraphrase Frederic Jameson, offered these socialists the possibility of sensing
and living through another historical rhythm, the spectre of a future
utopian transformation.[18] And yet those characteristics of romance which

[14] Isabella Ford, *On the Threshold* (London: Arnold, 1895), p. 29.
[15] Ford, *Threshold*, pp. 10, 52.
[16] Carolyn Steedman, 'Fictions of Engagement: Eleanor Marx, Biographical Space', in John
Stokes (ed.), *Eleanor Marx: Life, Work, Contacts* (London: Ashgate, 2000), pp. 23–39.
Steedman provides an extensive discussion of the significance of the novel's retrospective
setting and its fond nostalgia.
[17] The leading proponent of the new commune in Ford's novel is called Perchet—only two
letters from Chubb's fellow freshwater fish.
[18] Frederic Jameson, *The Political Unconscious: Narrative as Socially Symbolic Act*, 2nd edn.
(London: Routledge, 1996), p. 104.

made it so amenable to the energy of the socialist utopian impulse played no small part in forcing these women to readdress their own part in the labour movement by the early 1890s.

I

Ford's novel opens, like another, and rather better known text, with Beatrice. Glimpsed on the threshold of Ford's novel, this Beatrice—Beatrice Ratcliffe—is none other than the maid of all work at Kitty and Lucretia's lodging house, whose name, the narrator suggests archly, 'was not in the least descriptive' (9). Thomas Davidson had urged the more strictly Dantean title of the *Vita Nuova* upon the founders of the Fellowship of the New Life in order to connect their quest for a new life back into an aesthetic tradition of ethical enquiry. Ford's reference to Beatrice thus makes for a purposefully improbable allusion to the object of Dante's spiritual and romantic quest. This Beatrice's role is to lead the heroines out of their world of armchair socialism into the material determinism of poverty in the East End: she is not the ideal love of the *Vita Nuova*, but their guide in a divine comedy that never reaches Paradise. 'We were quite sure', the narrator Lucretia reflects on her youthful beliefs, 'that the oppressed in this world were the good, and the oppressors, the bad' (11):

> However, after we had known Beatrice a few days, Kitty suddenly announced that our creed had changed . . . and that henceforward we must understand, first, that people who are oppressed are often more wicked than their oppressors, and, second that wicked people require more love and help than good ones. (12)

The impulse to follow Beatrice starts in the realm of romance, but ends up somewhere else altogether. A few chapters into the novel, Ford's heroines, fired up by the founding meeting of their new drawing-room socialist society aimed at doing away with class distinctions, industrialism, and top hats in favour of a new life in communes, discover that Beatrice has been turned away from her employment. Whilst they have been planning the perfect ideal of human relations in a middle-class utopia, this resolutely material Beatrice has been erased from their lives as so much expendable physical labour.

As they search for Beatrice in the streets of 'darkest London', Kitty and Lucretia come to realize that the aestheticized ideal of fellowship—the sort of collective romance that sustained the 'religion of socialism' in groups like the Fellowship of the New Life—simply cannot incorporate the labour and desires of a Beatrice from the Ratcliffe Highway rather than a Rossetti painting or translation. Once she is discovered in a common lodging house in the company of a prostitute, Beatrice refuses to be recuperated either by the heroines' idealization of the virtue of the oppressed or more conventional philanthropy.

> 'I cannot go back to that house. I've no pleasure there; I've nothing but hard words and hard work. I've never had nothing else all my life! And now [Beatrice's lover] Jim's turned agin me, I've no one left nor nothing. You've been kind to me, kinder nor any one; but you'll be going home soon, and I shall never see you again, The likes of you, miss, can't understand what it is.' (49–50)

Beatrice's pleasures in the popular culture of the lively slum streets are ones that can simply never be met by a pair of art student ladies with aesthetic ideals for the socialist future. As the novel progresses, naïve excitement at this world on the threshold of transformation is gradually worn away as the heroines' male socialist acquaintances are seen to condone the prostitution of working-class women, whilst sheltering their lady friends from such realities. Shortly before her death after a pub brawl with her lover, Beatrice underscores the limitations of socialism as a spiritual quest narrative to Lucretia: 'You're a lady, miss, that's what it is' (155). Nothing, it seems, can transcend this implacable barrier between women of different classes, but Lucretia (and Ford) pose a plangent question which remains unanswered in the bounds of the text: 'Then must I always be outside your life, always something different from you? Can I never reach you, Beatrice?' (155).

The encounter with Beatrice forces Kitty and Lucretia into an awareness of the material and psychological rifts underlying the ideal of revolutionary labour in fellowship regardless of sex or class. She takes them out of socialism-as-romance to the threshold of a new political realism in which sexual difference must be addressed and where middle-class women must recognize the connection between themselves and 'that great tramp and beating of feet . . . sounding from all over this mysterious wonderful city' (189). Ford's novel thus reflects on the very specific dynamic of this period of the 'religion of socialism' when all it was seemingly going to take to achieve the revolution was to travel to the East End, spread the word and share the vision of a beautiful world around the corner. It was a moment in which many young men and women writers and artists set aside their aesthetic activities in pursuit of fellowship and a new life in which it seemed that differences of sex and class could be resolved. It was also a moment that, as Ford's novel makes clear, could be the subject only of nostalgia ten years later.

In the early 1880s Ford's contemporary, Clementina Black, who was, like Ford, to become a labour organizer, had already established herself as a writer of popular historical romances. Black's journey into the labour movement began as she circulated in the various radical and literary clubs open to men and women alike that sprang up in the capital during this period.[19] After moving from the family home in Brighton, where she had been responsible for running her solicitor father's household following the death of her mother in 1875, Black was soon a regular visitor at the home of the Marx family thanks to her friendship with their daughter Eleanor, or 'Tussy'. In April 1881 Karl Marx looked on benevolently as Tussy, Miss Black, and the poet Dollie Maitland paid fearful court to a 'new Wunderkind' called Ernest Radford, whom they had met at the British Museum and invited to their Dogberry dramatic society.[20] Radford in turn invited all three women along to a men and women's social discussion group, known simply as 'the Club', which he had joined the previous year, with among others, Isabella Ford's sister, the artist Emily Ford.[21] Clementina Black scraped by on her earnings from writing for the next few years, occupying her spare time by acting with Dollie Radford (who married Ernest in 1883) as President and then Secretary of the club. Black proceeded to invite her sisters to join her in the club: Emma, a successful artist; Constance, who was studying at Newnham College with the poet Amy Levy from 1879; and Grace, who shuttled between the family home in Brighton and studying art in London.[22]

During the early 1880s the Black sisters and their circle lived out a form of female autonomy in the metropolis that was at odds with much of the later outpouring of print that constituted the 'literary product' of the New Woman of the 1890s.[23] As they moved from days working in the British

---

[19] The most extensive study of Black's life and works remains Liselotte Glage, *Clementina Black: A Study in Social History and Literature* (Heidelberg: Carl Winter Universitatlag, 1981). Glage concludes that Black's political education came via her sister Constance's membership of the Fabian Society and her friendship with Eleanor Marx and that, rather than identifying her as a socialist, 'it is probably safest to say that [Clementina Black] was bourgeois and pro-Labour' (p. 36). Glage's chronology and account of Black's socialism is contested here.

[20] Karl Marx to Jenny Longuet, 11 April 1881, in *Karl Marx and Friedrich Engels Correspondence, 1846–1895* (London: Martin Lawrence, 1934), pp. 389–90.

[21] The records of this original club are found among those of its successor, Karl Pearson's Men and Women's Club: University College London Archives, Pearson Collection 10/2. On the transition between the two clubs see pp. 78–81.

[22] Emma Keriman Mahomed (née Black) exhibited portraits of Grace Black (entitled 'Sweet and Twenty' with verses by Ernest Radford) and Dollie Radford (see Figure 6) at the Royal Academy in 1883 and 1884. The Blacks' maternal grandfather was the fashionable mid-19th-cent. portraitist, George Patten.

[23] Talia Schaffer, '"Nothing but Foolscap and Ink": Inventing the New Woman', in Angelique Richardson and Chris Willis (eds.), *The New Woman in Fiction and Fact* (Basingstoke: Palgrave, 2001), pp. 39–51 (p. 43); see also Sally Ledger, *The New Woman: Fiction and*

Museum reading room to evenings at literary societies and political clubs, these women actively downplayed sexual difference and individualism in favour of an idea of heterosocial friendship and fellowship.[24] In the 1880s Clementina Black argued that 'original differences [between the sexes] are often extremely minute' and that the remaining tensions could be resolved by offering men and women more opportunities to know each other as friends and comrades before even considering marriage.[25] For Black the city of modern capitalism 'compelled' women of her class and situation to be free and treated 'with the same respect and consideration' as men in a manner never before experienced.[26] Such necessary freedom resulted from the simple fact that her work had been assigned a monetary value: her labour was, as Black put it, a commodity in the marketplace. As it was thus accepted that some middle-class women like herself 'have to work, have to live alone, and go about alone at all hours', it was now 'possible for all women to do so'.[27] Labour offered Black material freedom from sexual difference and sustained her sense of participating in an ideal of fellowship.

This novel self-definition of middle-class women as workers seems to have been widespread amongst what Deborah Nord has termed the 'urban female community' of radical London during the 1880s. Nord concludes that her subjects—Amy Levy, Black's socialist acquaintance Margaret Harkness, and the latter's cousin, Beatrice Webb—'vacillated between an identification with masculine forms and postures and a need to adopt or reinterpret feminine modes and traditions'.[28] For the women of Black's club, this coupling of a new identification as an independent worker with older notions of woman's mission as writer, poet, or philanthropist played a significant part in their interest in the socialist movement. In the space of a few

---

Feminism at the Fin de Siècle (Manchester: Manchester University Press, 1997), pp. 1–3, on the 'New Woman' as a 'discursive response' to the actual work of the woman's movement.

[24] Angelique Richardson, *Love and Eugenics in the Late Nineteenth Century: Rational Reproduction and the New Woman* (Oxford: Oxford University Press, 2003), pp. 186–9, proves the slipperiness of the New Woman debates by contrasting Mona Caird's liberal individualism with the eugenic anti-individualism of Sarah Grand. Nevertheless, Grand's writings emphasize women's individual self-determination in eugenic sexual selection, rather than fellowship and community.

[25] Clementina Black, 'On Marriage: A Criticism', *Fortnightly Review*, 47 (1890), 586–94 (p. 593).

[26] Clementina Black, 'The Organisation of Working-Women', *Fortnightly Review*, 46 (1889), 695–704 (p. 696).

[27] Ibid.

[28] Deborah Nord, *Walking the Victorian Streets: Women, Representation and the City* (Ithaca, NY: Cornell University Press, 1995), p. 205. See also Liz Stanley, *Feminism and Friendship: Two Essays on Olive Schreiner*, Studies in Sexual Politics, 8 (Manchester: Department of Sociology, University of Manchester, 1985).

short years, the poets, artists, journalists, and would-be actresses of the club had moved from distanced debate on 'Some Recent Socialistic [sic] Tendencies in Our Legislation' to active affiliation with the movement.[29] The turning point for Dollie Radford came after attending William Morris's lecture 'How we Live and How we Might Live' in Hammersmith in November 1884. Radford left the meeting with Constance Black, 'more than ever convinced of the seriousness and beauty of the Socialistic [sic] movement', a feeling she had not gained from listening to either the leader of the Social Democratic Federation, H. M. Hyndman, or her friend Eleanor Marx's partner, Edward Aveling.[30] Constance Black seems to have shared Radford's political and aesthetic response to socialism, joining her at further lectures, and evolving her own interest in the literary dimension of Russian radicalism thanks to her friendship with the political exile, Sergius Stepniak.[31]

Morris's preoccupation with fellowship, labour, and art in his socialist lectures provided a particularly important means of authorizing these women's involvement in the movement. At first glance, this enthusiastic response to Morris's socialist aesthetics on the part of women activists seems surprising. Morris's aesthetic theory was, as the previous chapter suggested, constructed on the basis of a manly and productive future for the arts after the social revolution and most of these women were themselves aspiring to be artists of some sort in the early 1880s. But the masculinization of the artist within Morris's socialist aesthetic should not be seen as an exclusionary tactic that prohibited the possibility of women drawing upon it for their own ends. A close reading of Morris's invocations of the manliness of the artist—for example that biblical cadence, 'If we work thus, we shall be men and our days will be happy and eventful'—suggests that manhood is not primarily contrasted with a maligned femininity. In fact the key opposition here, hinted at by the Old Testament rhetoric of a chosen people, is between the possibilities of free, independent manhood and the

---

[29] UCL Pearson 10/1. The meeting to discuss these 'socialistic tendencies' was held on 20 Dec. 1881. Both Clementina Black and Dollie Radford were present.

[30] UCLA Clarke Library, MS R126 M3, Dollie Radford Diaries, entry dated 30 Nov. 1884. Dollie and Ernest Radford joined the Hammersmith branch of the Socialist League in early 1886. The Radfords were also members of the Fabian Society from 1888 until their deaths. Constance Garnett (née Black) joined the Fabian Society in 1893 and was later elected to the executive, only to resign in 1897. See Minutes and Papers of the Hammersmith Socialist Society, British Library Add. Mss. 45891; BLPES Archives, Fabian M (Members Cards Index). There is no record of Clementina Black ever being a member of the Fabian Society and Black criticizes a fictional version of the Fabians for knowing nothing of the labour question and the working class in her novel *An Agitator* (1894). A review of that novel in *The Times* (26 Dec. 1894), 9, identifies the author as a member of the Independent Labour Party.

[31] See Richard Garnett, *Constance Garnett: A Heroic Life* (London: Sinclair Stevenson, 1991).

emasculation of labour under capitalism. For Morris continues, 'all other work' but that which has hope in it 'is slave's work'.[32] Morris's emphasis on the pleasure of free labour must have resonated with this generation of women seeking to define themselves through paid work and thus experience a freedom never before possible for them.

As Clementina Black, her sisters, and friends became increasingly involved in the labour and socialist movements over the next two decades, their divergent political affiliations created new tensions between them. But despite Eleanor Marx's role within the schisms of the SDF, Dollie Radford's membership of the Socialist League, Grace and Constance's interest in the Fabian Society, and Clementina Black's work organizing women's labour in the East End, Morris's works offered the possibility of consensus. As June Hannam suggests with regard to Isabella Ford, the 'broad ethical' and, it should be added, aesthetic, 'appeal of Morris's vision of a socialist future based on fellowship . . . provided a common point of contact for socialists who were otherwise divided along tactical and theoretical lines'.[33]

Like many socialists of their generation, Clementina and Constance Black's abstract political discussions in socialist drawing-room meetings were given painful urgency by their encounter with the poverty of the East End of London in the mid-1880s. Constance Black was employed as a tutor for the oldest children of Charles Booth during the period in which he embarked on his major investigation of poverty, *Life and Labour of the People of London* (1889).[34] Booth recommended Constance for the post of librarian at the new People's Palace in the Mile End Road and by 1888 she was living in worker's dwellings in Royal Mint Square in the East End surrounded by a colony of fellow philanthropists, including her future husband Edward Garnett.[35] Clementina Black seems to have involved herself in the community of philanthropists around Toynbee Hall prior to her sister's employment in the area.[36] In early 1886 she was present when her friend the rent-collector Ella Pycroft faced down a protest by the tenants of Katherine Buildings, adjacent to Royal Mint Square and populated by

---

[32] William Morris, 'Useful Work versus Useless Toil', CW, xxiii. 100.

[33] June Hannam, *Isabella Ford* (Oxford: Basil Blackwell, 1989), p. 28.

[34] Garnett, *Constance Garnett*, p. 53.

[35] Richard Garnett claims that his grandmother was the author of 'Life in Model Dwellings' by 'A Lady Resident' in the second volume of Booth's survey, but I have been unable to verify this.

[36] For the politics of Toynbee Hall see Standish Meachum, *Toynbee Hall and Social Reform, 1880–1914: The Search for Community* (New Haven, Conn.: Yale University Press, 1987); Seth Koven, *Slumming: Sexual and Social Politics in Victorian London* (Princeton: Princeton University Press, 2004), pp. 228–78.

what Beatrice Webb termed the 'aboriginals of the East End'.[37] Within the
year, Black had taken up a paid post that was to take her beyond such
philanthropic endeavours to a new engagement with the labour movement.

In early 1887 Black was appointed as Secretary of the Women's
Protective and Provident League. The WPPL had been founded by Emma
Paterson in 1874 with the aims of organizing unions of women workers in
various trades and encouraging habits of thrift by collecting savings against
illness and unemployment.[38] Black's appointment came at a time when the
organization seemed to be moving away from such philanthropic roots to
more direct political engagement. At the annual meeting in 1886, Adolphe
Smith 'feared the League was in bad repute among working-men [and some
of the women] who spoke of it as a "goody-goody" society and declined to
help its work because of the air of patronage which the names and sub-
scriptions of rich people gave it'. [39] Stuart Headlam, a long-term supporter
of the WPPL, proposed that the WPPL renew its emphasis on the protective
element of the work—that is, the formation of unions to secure a living
wage—rather than the promotion of thrift and rational recreation. Despite
the fears voiced that such a move would alienate some wealthy, anti-trade
union, supporters of the League, Headlam's motion was carried, along with
the rider that a full-time secretary be appointed to develop new women's
unions, at the salary of £100 per annum.

By the time that Black took up this post, the sudden death of Emma
Paterson had led to the election of a new president of the League, the liberal radical and art critic, Emilia Dilke.[40] Sir Charles Dilke, Emilia's second

[37] BLPES, Passfield Papers 2/1/2/7, Ella Pycroft to Beatrice Webb, 9 Feb. 1886. The identification of 'Miss Black' as Clementina comes from Rosemary O'Day, 'How Families Lived Then:
Katherine Buildings, East Smithfield, 1885–1890', in Ruth Finnegan and Michael Drake (eds.),
Studying Family and Community History (Cambridge: Cambridge University Press, 1994),
pp. 129–65. See also Ruth Livesey, 'Women Rent Collectors and the Rewriting of Space, Class
and Gender in East London, 1870–1900', in Lesley Whitworth and Elizabeth Darling (eds.),
Women and the Making of the Built Environment in Britain, 1870–1950 (Aldershot: Ashgate,
2007).

[38] On this aspect of Black's work see Rosemary Feurer, 'The Meaning of Sisterhood: The
British Women's Movement and Protective Labour Legislation, 1870–1914', *Victorian Studies*,
31 (1988), 233–60; Philippa Levine, *Feminist Lives in Victorian England: Private Roles and
Public Commitment* (Oxford: Blackwell, 1990), pp. 157–75. On the history of the WTUL see
Ellen Mappen, *Helping Women at Work: The Women's Industrial Council, 1889–1914*
(London: Hutchinson, 1985). Emma Paterson also supported Isabella Ford's work with the
Leeds tailoresses in 1885.

[39] *The Women's Union Journal: The Organ of the Women's Protective and Provident League*,
11 (July 1886), 70.

[40] According to Amy Levy, Black was appointed over 72 other applicants: see Amy Levy to
Vernon Lee, Feb. 1887 in Linda Hunt Beckman, *Amy Levy: Her Life and Letters* (Athens,
Ohio: Ohio University Press, 2000), p. 257. For an account of Emilia (Francis Strong Pattison)

husband, had a well-established record of supporting the legalization of unions and protective labour legislation during his career in Parliament, which had an abrupt hiatus during the League's years of political influence from 1886 to 1892.[41] For the next two years, Clementina Black researched the conditions of female labour and attempted to unionize women workers in various London trades in affiliation with the League. She experienced a profound 'thrill of horror' at the realization that the present capitalist system had driven poor women to 'slavery . . . worse than any of which record exists in the world' at the very same time as it had compelled 'educated' women like herself into economic freedom.[42] Black attempted to convey this message to a drawing-room meeting of the Fabian Society in June 1888 by delivering a lecture on the conditions of women's labour at the Bryant and May match factory. Despite the Society's usual distance from labour agitation, one member, Annie Besant, initiated a publicity campaign on the basis of this 'capital' lecture which led to a successful strike by the workers the following month and marked one of the most memorable triumphs of the new union movement.[43]

Amidst the increasing momentum of strike activity in the late 1880s, Black became frustrated at the reticence of the League's leadership in engaging with the wider labour movement.[44] The renaming of the organization as the Women's Trade Union League in September 1888 seems to have only paid lip-service to such collaboration for Black and she resigned from her post in May 1889. A few months later Black and the labour activist John Burns founded a new organization to foster the unionization of women workers, the Women's Trade Union Association. The WTUA was far less hesitant in coordinating strike action and enabled Black to adopt a more public political stance in her journalism. Black's energies were soon directed into supporting the strike of women confectionery workers in the capital; an enterprise that 'meant 16 to 18 hours work daily for the "agitators" who have been managing it'.[45]

Dilke's diverse lives see Kali Israel, *Names and Stories: Emilia Dilke and Victorian Culture* (New York: Oxford University Press, 1999).

[41] The hiatus was a result of Dilke's citation as a corespondent in an infamous divorce case. See Israel, *Names and Stories*, pp. 198–240.

[42] Clementina Black, 'Organisation of Working-Women', pp. 698, 695.

[43] *Bernard Shaw: The Diaries, 1885–1897*, ed. Stanley Weintraub, 2 vols. (London: Pennsylvania State University), i. 385. Entry dated 15 June 1888. Annie Besant cit. Yvonne Kapp, *Eleanor Marx: The Crowded Years 1884–1898* (London: Virago, 1976), p. 268.

[44] See Henry Pelling, *A History of British Trade Unionism* (London: Macmillan, 1963); Yvonne Kapp, *The Air of Freedom: The Birth of New Unionism* (London: Lawrence & Wishart, 1989).

[45] Clementina Black, 'The Chocolate Makers' Strike', *Fortnightly Review*, 48 (1890), 305–14 (p. 311).

For Clementina Black and her fellow women socialists, 1889 was a heady year in which the organization of women workers seemed to promise a new life in which the exploitation of women could be resolved through the fellowship of labour. Whilst Black worked with the chocolate makers, Eleanor Marx organized the labourers of the Silvertown gasworks in London's Isle of Dogs, Isabella Ford led out the Leeds' Tailoresses and Machinists Union on strike, and Margaret Harkness did what she could to support the action of the London dockers.[46] 'Every day', Black recalled, 'there were boxes to open',

> to screw up, to label, and to distribute to the collectors; every day there were some £7 worth of copper to be counted and packed in rolls of 5s, and only those who have counted East End coppers on a wet day know the unpleasantness of the task. [47]

Black was thoroughly absorbed by her new identity, not as a lady taking a philanthropic interest in women workers, but as a labour 'agitator' in her own right, working for a cause that seemed to transcend gender. Letters concerning the confectionery makers' strike came 'addressed to Messrs. [John] Burns and Black, a style and title which', Clementina commented, 'made us feel as if ... we were running a factory on our own account'.[48] Despite Black's own role as a woman in an organization dedicated to women workers, her account of the strike elides gender difference in favour of the fellowship of labour. She is just one of the 'agitators', as much a part of the struggle as her co-organizer John Burns and happy to revel in the misapprehension that she is part of that partnership of masculine labour activism, 'Messrs. Burns and Black'.

II

During the 1880s Clementina Black set her career as a novelist to one side as she took part in the struggle to bring on that seemingly imminent great change. But for some other women socialists, like her sister Grace and, as we shall see in a later chapter, her friend Dollie Radford, the mass unionization and demonstrations in London towards the end of the decade only served to underline their own incapacity to contribute to the cause. In contrast to her sisters, Grace Black spent the best part of her time from 1887 to 1889 caring for her invalid father in Brighton. She did her best with the

[46] See Kapp, *Eleanor Marx*, pp. 261–420; Hannam, *Isabella Ford*, pp. 33–42.
[47] Black, 'Chocolate Makers' Strike', p. 311.
[48] Ibid. 312.

inhabitants of the seaside resort, founding a proto-socialist society there in 1888. Grace Black was forced to confess to Karl Pearson, however, that its 'composition is not very hopeful for conversion to socialism, being mostly grown-up and married people', only there because 'socialism was the fashion a little while ago & Brighton people have just waked [sic] up to it'.[49]

Grace Black shared her frustration at her enforced inaction with George Bernard Shaw, whom she had met at Fabian meetings whilst staying with her sisters in London. 'You know I am a Socialist', Black wrote in 1887, 'but I can't look to myself to helping on Socialism much, it would be folly', settled as she was in Brighton, and lacking the organizational skills of her eldest sister. It was not folly, though, Black asserted with percipience, to expect Shaw to do 'a great deal' because of his 'greater power of seeing truth than most'.[50] What Grace Black feared, however, was that Shaw's socialism would tend away from her own ethical beliefs towards something much more mechanistic. Black berated Shaw for his own lack of hope and enthusiasm 'for the good that lies in people' and the inattention to 'the building up part of Socialism' within the movement as a whole. 'Socialism', she argued, 'cannot be the outcome only of a desire for freedom: it must come from the desire for solidarity.'[51]

> What I fear is that you do not care for nor believe in people sufficiently, and you won't be able to understand them unless you do, and your socialism must be warped if you don't understand human nature . . . If you think [this letter] needs an excuse (wh[ich] I don't) say that it is because I care for socialism.[52]

Shaw dismissed the letter as evidence that she was in love with him. 'So I am', she replied gamely, 'but that has nothing to do with my letter and it is a pity if that thought has clouded my meaning.'[53]

This exchange between Shaw and Black reflects some of the strains within the ideal of socialist fellowship in the later 1880s. On the one hand the research-driven programme of the middle-class Fabian Society promised an increasingly bureaucratic route to the socialist future in which the collective was the state, rather than any more aesthetic notion of communalism. On the other, the ideal of fellowship between men and women

[49] UCL Pearson 636/8, Grace Black to Karl Pearson, 18 Oct. 1888.
[50] BL Add. Mss. 50511 ff. 321, Grace Black to George Bernard Shaw, 24 May 1887.
[51] BL Add. Mss. 50511 ff. 321; 50512 ff. 112, Grace Black to George Bernard Shaw, 24 May 1887, 8 April 1889.
[52] BL Add. Mss. 50511 ff. 321, Grace Black to George Bernard Shaw, 24 May 1887.
[53] BL Add. Mss. 50511 ff. 323, Grace Black to George Bernard Shaw, 25 May 1887. In old age Shaw seems to have confused Constance with Grace Black, confiding to Constance's son, David Garnett, that he would have married his mother during the 1880s if only he had been better established in his career.

socialists in the more radical organizations was under pressure as numerous activists turned their attention to the 'Woman Question' in relation to socialism and women's role within the movement itself. As we will see in the next chapter, Eleanor Marx, Olive Schreiner, Karl Pearson, and many others all insisted on the intimate interdependence of female emancipation and socialism in the mid-1880s. The social democrat Ernest Belfort Bax, however, was having none of this. For him, women members of the socialist movement could never truly participate in its fellowship thanks to the absolute identification of women's sex with their personality as a whole:

> Discourse in any drawing room with the 'ladies' assembled there and you have an irresistible but uneasy sense that, however well-feigned may be the interest in the subject of your conversation, the real interest of the woman centres round the fact that she is female and you are male.[54]

Middle-class women, Bax suggested, could simply never break away from the sexed individualism of the drawing-room, where socialism was but the latest consumer good to be absorbed and retailed to the next likely conquest.[55] Annie Besant's response was that most women socialists, like her, would simply not be found in such drawing-rooms. They were instead at work in the East End with 'working women' for whom 'sex is a much less prominent matter . . . than . . . women of [Bax's] social grade'.[56]

By the end of the 1880s, however, Clementina Black was only too aware that friendships between men and woman working for the cause in the East End could also be (mis)read as a commonplace affair, rather than communal fellowship. In early 1889, rumours began to circulate concerning the novelist and activist, Margaret Harkness, and her friendship with H. H. Champion. Champion was from a wealthy military family but had thrown himself into the socialist cause from the early 1880s and had married a working-class woman who developed alcoholism.[57] Harkness had worked with Champion and John Burns during the 1889 dock strike and had doubtless acquainted herself with Champion's difficult marital situation, as her *roman à clef* set during the strike, *George Eastmont: Wanderer* (1905) makes

---

[54] Ernest Belfort Bax, 'Some Heterodox Notes on the Woman Question', *Today*, 8/44 (July 1887), 25–6. The clinching evidence for Bax's argument concerning the evident mental inferiority of women was that one had recently survived falling off the Clifton Suspension Bridge—a piece of logic which Annie Besant had considerable fun with in her witty response to Bax the following month.

[55] See Hunt, *Equivocal Feminists*, pp. 57–63, for an account of Bax's misogyny and its effects within the SDF.

[56] Annie Besant, 'Misogyny in Excelsis', *Today*, 8/45 (1887), 54.

[57] *Dictionary of Labour Biography*, ed. Joyce Bellamy and John Saville, 11 vols. (London: Macmillan, 1972–), viii.

clear.[58] It was Shaw, once again, who instigated a romantic interpretation in the case of Harkness and Champion. He met Clementina Black at William Archer's house in February 1889 and talked 'mostly about Champion & Maggie Harkness'.[59] Black did her utmost to resist such speculation concerning fellow comrades, the former of whom was a good friend and regular correspondent of hers. In 1894, both Harkness and Champion happened to be in Australia at the same time, a fact that John Burns had mentioned to Black in the course of their correspondence. Black admitted that 'a hint of the same kind' had been made to her before, but 'though the news of a happy marriage would seem about the best news that could be heard of Mr Champion I sh[oul]d be sorry—and I think you and Mrs Burns would agree with me—if this particular marriage were to be contemplated'.[60]

Black proceeded to deflect the rumours with a light touch that protected her friends and the ideal of male and female comradeship for the cause:

> I hope, however, that the idea merely arises out of that sort of talk which some people always begin when any man and woman are thrown [?] together by any circumstances. I myself have at various times been reported engaged to various different people without the slightest foundation in fact—indeed I am not sure whether two of my brothers-in-law haven't jilted me in favour of younger and prettier sisters.[61]

Such prurience and speculation among fellow workers did little to aid middle-class women, whose socialist commitments were trivialized and dismissed often enough without being fitted up for a wedding every time they left drawing-room meetings behind in favour of more active propaganda.[62] By the early 1890s misogyny within the socialist movement and a newly invigorated women's movement had led many women socialists to address the question of sexual difference and separatism in a positive manner. The proposal for women-only shortlists in the Fabian Society in 1892 is but the most tangible evidence that the ideal of socialism as fellowship without sex

[58] John Law [Margaret Harkness], *George Eastmont: Wanderer* (London: Burns & Oates, 1905). The eponymous hero is a labour activist from a wealthy military family, married to an alcoholic woman from a lower social class, who craves the company of a middle-class woman socialist writer in her peaceful ladies' chambers.

[59] *Shaw: Diaries*, p. 469, 15 Feb. 1889.

[60] BL Add. Mss. 46294 ff. 226, Clementina Black to John Burns, 1 Nov. 1894. Black and Champion ceased to correspond after he left London, though not, Black assured Burns, through any quarrel. By 1907 Black was able to thank her 'old friend' Champion for supplying information concerning sweated labour in Australia in *Sweated Industry and the Minimum Wage* (London: Duckworth, 1907), p. vi.

[61] Ibid.

[62] In 1893, for instance, Shaw yet again dismissed Constance Garnett's candidacy for the Fabian Society executive, suggesting that she only wanted to join because it was fashionable.

had passed, taking with it the belief that the romance of the movement would resolve the question of sexual equality.[63] In *On the Threshold* Kitty Manners insists that '*My* socialism regards men and women as equals, as co-workers, as each other's helpers and friends'.[64] Although the testaments of women socialist activists record many such moments of collaboration, the persistent argument that the women's movement was an individualist, middle-class affair hampered the work of many who sought to combine the struggle to secure sexual equality in the present with a belief in an imminent socialist future. As we shall see in the final chapters, these tensions were to re-emerge in the early twentieth century and, as prominent members of the National Union of Women's Suffrage Societies, Clementina Black and Isabella Ford were both to play their part in determining the future of feminism and socialism.

III

In the late 1880s, however, the most visible conflicts within the movement were not about sex, but about defining socialism and determining its future. Never one to gloss over political differences, George Bernard Shaw proposed in June 1887 that the various socialist factions in London—gradualist, parliamentarian socialists, revolutionists, and those of an anarchist tendency—should meet and have a proper 'Shindy' courtesy of the Fabian Society. William Morris, that 'walking Etna in debate', was sure to provide an entertaining spectacle of volcanic explosion as parliamentarian socialists tried his temper by pointing out that his Socialist League was slipping into the hands of anarchists.[65] The Black sisters, being as their old friend Amy Levy asserted, 'quiet & completely domestic, unless when they are attending Socialist or Anarchist meetings', were bound to attend.[66]

However quiet and domestic the Blacks were, they attempted to make an ethical connection between their personal lives and the wider cause which had captured their interest and this commitment led to them entertaining a visitor on the evening of the meeting. Amy Levy had described the Blacks' novel shared living arrangements in London's Fitzroy Street, where they did

---

[63] *Fabian News* (3 May 1892). The prominent Fabian Emma Brooke opposed such measures arguing that 'the prominent introduction into the Fabian Society of the Woman Question in any of its departments is unnecessary; further, that it is desirable the selection of candidates for the Executive should have sole regard to the ability of the nominees and their fitness for the position'.

[64] Ford, *Threshold*, p. 31.

[65] George Bernard Shaw, 'A Word for War', *Today*, 8/46 (Sept. 1887).

[66] Hunt Beckman, *Amy Levy*, p. 255, letter dated 26 Nov. [1886].

all 'their own housework' to the aesthetic critic and novelist, Vernon Lee (Violet Paget). Although Levy admitted that her own 'Philistine, middle-class notions w[ould]d not be met by their ménage' this did not prevent her from inviting Lee to sample this experiment in living on her annual visit from Italy in June 1887.[67] Lee could not resist the prospect of cataloguing these oddities in her collection of literary lions of the salon. She found the Blacks' 'anti-servitoress lodging . . . extremely picturesque': 'In a large kitchen, looking like that of an old farm, I found a charming young creature with superb eyes & a complexion like a peach, a sort of delightful dairy maid Duchess of Devonshire. This was Miss Grace Black.'[68] The Blacks (who were, Lee reassured her mother, 'perfect ladies . . . in *their* way') capped off Lee's evening by inviting her along to the 'stormy conference between the moderate Socialists & the Immoderate Ones' so that she could witness the larger cause that shaped their domestic arrangements.[69]

'We all went on the bus to St James Hall', Lee reported to her mother, 'where a socialist conference "for the Rich Classes" was going on in a small room'.[70] Lee took her place with the Blacks in the 'well dressed audience' mainly made up of women 'with a sprinkling of aesthetic looking men'.[71] The Fabians, Lee decided, 'seem mostly gentlemen' and 'extremely courteous', but only Annie Besant spoke well enough for them to be striking. The members of 'more revolutionary' clubs (Lee failed to retain even the names of the SDF and Socialist League), on the other hand, appear in Lee's account as a set of music-hall turns who have misconceived themselves as epic heroes. Black's friend John Burns stars as 'a sort of comic get up between a workman & a comic opera sailor', whose speeches are rendered by Lee in stage cockney. William Morris himself features as 'a fine, grey, excitable, good-natured, rather theatrical creature', sounding more like a pantomime horse than a political activist.[72]

Lee's rendition of the Black sisters and the metropolitan socialist scene is, of course, a triumph of aestheticist wit and style in which surface

---

[67] Ibid.

[68] *Vernon Lee's Letters*, ed. Irene Cooper Willis (privately printed, 1937), letter dated 13 June [1887]. Lee had visited her friend Emily Ford at the Fords' family home, Adel Grange outside Leeds the previous summer, during which time she recorded visits to Isabella Ford's clubs for the women mill workers.

[69] Ibid., 19 June [1887].

[70] Ibid., 13 June [1887].

[71] Ibid.

[72] Ibid., 19 June [1887].

performance becomes substance.[73] But Lee's brief tour in the regions of socialism also demonstrates how vulnerable the sort of ethical socialist lifestyle adopted by the Blacks was to being denuded of political content. In Lee's letters, the Blacks are translated into a purely autonomous aesthetic realm, in which despite her 'curious & very determined ideas', Grace Black becomes an object of delight, and, despite the odd lack of servants, the Blacks' kitchen becomes a source of aesthetic pleasure.[74] By rendering Grace Black as a painting of a lady pretending to be a rustic ('a sort of delightful dairy maid Duchess of Devonshire') the stern-sounding 'anti-servitoress lodging' can be inserted into an aesthetic tradition of the pictur-esque. The servantless kitchen thus seems to have as little to say about conditions of female labour as the backdrop of rustic cottages would in any eighteenth-century portrait of an aristocrat posing as shepherdess.

At the same time that Lee made Grace Black the object of delightful aes-thetic consumption, the latter was moving closer towards the idealism of Edward Carpenter's evolutionary socialism.[75] Black took issue with Shaw's increasing (and idiosyncratic) individualism and political pragmatism and tried to explain to him her own sense of the relationship between 'the *Ideal & Real*'.[76] After awkwardly blurting out the fact of her engagement to the engineer, Edwin Human (who was, she underscored, 'a socialist'), Black went on to explain that, for her, works of art, like a child, were socially engaged, inter-subjective works, even at the moment of their conception.[77] Socialism itself, she argued, as the hope of the future, must turn away from individual 'self-realization' and replicate that original moment of commu-nal solidarity.[78] The very super-sensible quality of such aesthetic socialism that made it so appealing to metropolitan writers and artists like the Blacks during the early 1880s, however, made it susceptible to being consumed as just another lifestyle preference of the aesthetic movement. Experiments in living such as the Blacks' servantless lodgings or Edward Carpenter's self-sufficient smallholding, could be read merely, in Vernon Lee's phrase, as

---

[73] For an analysis of Lee's interest in competing aesthetic theories see Diana Maltz, 'Engaging Delicate Brains: Vernon Lee and Kit Anstruther-Thompson's Psychological Aesthetics', in Talia Schaffer and Kathy Alexis Psomiades (eds.), *Women and British Aestheticism* (Charlottesville, Va.: University of Virginia Press, 1999), pp. 211–29.

[74] *Vernon Lee's Letters*, 19 June [1887].

[75] The epigraph to Grace Black's collection of short stories, published by her brother-in-law, comes from Carpenter's *Towards Democracy*: 'Turn from these words and look again at the world around you, the work you have to do'. Grace Black, *A Beggar and Other Fantasies* (Henhurst Cross, Holmwood, Surrey: Edward Garnett, 1889).

[76] BL Add. Mss. 50512 ff. 117, Grace Black to George Bernard Shaw, 31 March 1889.

[77] Ibid.

[78] BL Add. Mss. 50512 ff. 122, Grace Black to George Bernard Shaw, 8 April 1889.

'extremely picturesque' arrangements, that obscured the labour involved in their own production.

As her engagement with the labour movement developed, Clementina Black, in contrast to her sisters, became increasingly aware of this divide opening up between ideal identification with labour on the part of middle-class women (and men) and the material determinates that circumscribed the lives of the working class. In her work as a union organizer, Black's aim was to raise the value of working-class women's labour as a commodity in the marketplace, refusing to let it stay in the invisible realm of supplementary 'pin money' and insisting that it was needed to support whole families. The servant question and domestic work was, for instance, no less a part of the politics of labour for taking place in the home. The 'domestic servant', she wrote, 'still lives under a system of total personal subservience' and 'a feeling has gradually grown up that personal subservience is intolerable and degrading'.[79] The very private nature of going into service made such women workers all the more vulnerable to exploitation by their employers. If she was a mother of girls 'who had to choose between factory work and service', Black concluded, 'I should give my voice unhesitatingly for the factory'.[80]

Black's attempts to bring domestic labour to the foreground as labour were all the more significant, given the tendency of those earliest movements towards communal living to overlook women's work altogether. In Ford's *On the Threshold* the would-be leader of a new commune, Perchet, argues that 'Woman is a spiritual being, and ought to be treated as such . . . Women must be the inspired of the world; and men the workers.' In his co-operative household,

> 'the men . . . must do all the really hard work . . . must go out into the world and earn money, and the women must—er—must—'
> 'Do the cooking and scrubbing, and washing and mending?' interposed Kitty, as he hesitated.
> 'Won't you?' he asked gently.
> 'In that case, will you black the boots, and carry up the coals, and, as you express it, do the really hard work?'[81]

As Ann Heilmann points out, Perchet cannot even attach the word 'work' to women's domestic labour; it is Kitty Manners who must emphasize the

---

[79] Clementina Black, 'The Dislike to Domestic Service', *Nineteenth Century*, 33 (1893), 454–57 (p. 455).
[80] Ibid. 455.
[81] Ford, *Threshold*, p. 30.

arduous manual work involved in servicing a nineteenth-century house-hold.[82] 'Gradually a sense is growing up', Clementina Black observed in an echo of Morris, 'of the distinction between vital labour—the labour that does and makes, and deadening labour—the labour that merely repeats for ever without producing anything.'[83] Late in her life, Black was still arguing that domestic service fell into this latter category and thus should be replaced by communal kitchens and cleaning services. By the early 1890s, however, Clementina Black was (like Isabella Ford) aware that the gesture of identification with labour offered by middle-class women doing their own housework (or middle-class men running smallholdings) was a far remove from constructing a joyful common cause with women workers in the East End.

At the Royal Commission on Labour in 1891, Clementina Black was asked to testify concerning the desirability of appointing special 'lady assistant subcommissioners' to investigate the conditions of women's labour in factories across the nation.[84] True to her role in labour politics, Black insisted that where unions existed, their delegates should represent working conditions to the Commissioners, but that the Commission should consider appointing working-class women to investigate unorganized trades. Black and working-class women trade unionists argued that material conditions had shaped a great gulf between 'ladies' like herself and working-class women, one that instinctively bred mistrust and misunderstanding. The factory workers would immediately assume that 'ladies' or 'educated women' investigators would report claims straight back to employers. Symbolic gestures of identification with labour were all very well when imagining socialism as an imminent victory in which beauty would be born from epic struggle. Following the lives of labouring women in the East End over five years had convinced Clementina Black, however, that the change would be no great upheaval, but rather a measured tread of amelioration: 'all people who understand history [know] that . . . gradual evolution is the true course of progress'.[85]

[82] Ann Heilmann, *New Woman Fiction: Women Writing First-Wave Feminism* (Basingstoke: Macmillan, 2000), p. 60.

[83] Clementina Black, *A New Way of Housekeeping* (London: Collins, 1918), p. 38.

[84] For the significance of this debate for feminism in the 1890s see Feurer, 'Meaning of Sisterhood' and Ruth Livesey, 'The Politics of Work: Feminism, Professionalisation and Women Inspectors of Factories and Workshops, 1890–1914', *Women's History Review*, 13 (2004), 233–63.

[85] Clementina Black 'An Appreciation', in *A Modern Humanist: Miscellaneous Papers of Benjamin Kirkman Gray*, ed. Henry Bryan Binns (London: A. C. Fifield, 1910), p. 63.

IV

In the late 1880s that route for women artists and writers towards a knowledge of, and involvement in the struggles of labour, appeared to offer the chance of hastening the great change: Morris's utopia of universal productive aesthetics was just around the corner. Well-publicized victories, such as that of the Bryant and May match girls' strike seemed at first to confirm the coming rebirth of the social order.[86] But this moment of the epic romance of the socialist cause was short lived. In the Annual Report of the WTUA for 1890–1, Clementina Black admitted that 'in completing its second year of work' the organization could not 'make a report that looks upon the surface so encouraging as last year'. Her efforts in organization in 1889 had been carried along on 'a wave of Trade Union feeling after the dock strike': a wave that had long since subsided leaving a good stretch of strand between middle-class women activists and unorganized women's labour in the East End.[87]

By the end of 1889 the door was closing over that threshold moment of hope, when socialist theory seemed to be about to prove itself right and bring in the new birth of art. Writing to Edward Carpenter in September of that year, Olive Schreiner reflected with sadness upon two cases of hopelessness, pain, and exhaustion, in which aesthetic socialism could do nothing to help. One was personal: Schreiner's close friend, the poet Amy Levy, who had dedicated her volume *A London Plane Tree* (1889) to her old friend from Brighton, Clementina Black, had committed suicide earlier that week. Levy was not a socialist, but Schreiner had sent her an extract from Carpenter's epic socialist poem shortly before her death:

> The last thing I sent her was the 'Have Faith' page of Towards Democracy. She wrote me back a little note, 'Thank you, it is very beautiful, but Philosophy cannot help me. I am too much shut in by the personal'.[88]

Unlike the Black sisters and Schreiner herself, Levy had never forged the connection between art and activism, aesthetics and politics.[89] Unlike her closest circle of friends she remained at the end of the decade as she had been at the beginning, identified through her art alone. The millenarian spirit of aesthetic socialism had failed to move even an artist like Levy.

---

[86] See Gareth Stedman Jones, *Outcast London: A Study in the Relationship between the Classes in Victorian Society* (Oxford: Oxford University Press, 1971).

[87] Women's Trade Union Association, Annual Report 1890–91, BLPES, WIC Box B.

[88] Olive Schreiner to Edward Carpenter, Sept. 1889, *Olive Schreiner: Letters, 1871–1899*, ed. Richard Rive (Oxford: Oxford University Press, 1988), p. 157.

[89] For an extended study of this lack see Emma Francis, 'Why Wasn't Amy Levy More of a Socialist? Levy and Clementina Black', in Nadia Valman and Naomi Hetherington (eds.), *Critical Essays on Amy Levy* (Athens, Ohio: Ohio University Press, forthcoming).

Schreiner wearily moved on in her letter to Carpenter to mention a second case where hope seemed not to be forthcoming: 'They say the East End women are getting terribly tired of the strike.'[90] This second case of the failure of hope, that of political organization and labour activism, affected all of the women socialists in this circle very deeply. Although the dock strike marked a new era in the unionization of casual labour and the match girls and confectionery workers secured improved working conditions, by the early 1890s socialist organizers could not but be aware that women's labour organizations were strike-based and contingent.

In the run-up to the 1890 Trades Union Congress this now uneasy conjunction of middle-class women and the labour movement soured the remnants of the old friendship between Clementina Black and Eleanor Marx. Marx wrote to the *People's Press* in August to protest that, despite being the elected delegate of the Gas Workers and General Labourers' Union, her mandate was rejected by the TUC on the grounds 'that I am not a working woman'.[91] Such resistance to women's participation and representation within the union movement is a well-documented part of the contested relationship between women and labour politics well into the twentieth century in relation to issues such as the so-called 'family wage'. But in Marx's case, the snub was made all the worse by the fact that it was directed at her class, rather than gender, identity at the very same time as Clementina Black seemed to be in pride of place. Black and Lady Dilke were only nominated representatives of the WTUA and the WTUL and therefore had no democratic mandate. Moreover, Marx argued, 'I am a working woman—I work a typewriter', whereas 'Miss Black . . . has never done a day's manual labour'.[92] Black assuaged Marx's wrath somewhat by clarifying that she was not a delegate, not holding any position that might entitle her to be one, but had merely been invited to sit at the delegates' table on finding the press table full.[93]

It is no coincidence that, out of all the many means by which Eleanor Marx might have characterized her remunerative work—journalism, translation, labour organization—she chose to represent herself as a machine operative, barely avoiding reducing herself through metonymy to the machine itself: a typewriter.[94] There could be no better way of depicting herself as alienated from the product of her own labour: Marx's machine

---

[90] *Schreiner: Letters*, p. 157.

[91] Eleanor Marx cit. Kapp, *Eleanor Marx*, p. 394.

[92] Ibid.

[93] Kapp, *Eleanor Marx*, p. 395. Marx eventually also took a seat at the press table.

[94] Ibid. 261 identifies Marx's distinct shift in the late 1880s as a move from 'serving a cause' to 'identifying . . . with the men and women that cause was intended to serve'.

consumes her surplus value and obliterates any notion that writing might be a means of self-realization. In order to convince her peers in the socialist movement of her absolute identification with labour, Marx had to evacuate her work of any remaining aesthetic content. Eleanor Marx's increasingly scientific Marxism could not contemplate pleasure in labour or a productive aesthetic prior to the coming revolution.

As a response to the changed climate of the labour movement during the 1890s Clementina Black redirected the WTUA towards research and political lobbying at the Royal Commission on Labour 1891–4, after which the WTUA reformed itself as the purely investigative Women's Industrial Council. From the early 1890s Black's articles and books marked her place as an expert on women's labour and employment legislation.[95] Her works aimed at ending 'sweated labour' in the early twentieth century try to capture the subjectivity of working-class women, and depict them not as mute objects of compassion but as autonomous, independent-minded labourers, deprived of a fair wage for hard work.[96] With the end of the realized romance of socialism came attempts to reframe the relationship between the lady and the woman worker: to campaign for a minimum wage whilst leaving space for the (self-)representation of working-class women.

Black combined these extensive commitments to research and writing with new domestic responsibilities after adopting her brother Arthur's daughter, Speedwell, in 1892.[97] In the midst of such new outlets for her energies during the 1890s, it is easy to overlook the fact that Black also returned at this time to a form of writing she had left behind her in 1884 for her work in the labour movement. In addition to her 'socialist' novel *An Agitator* and numerous periodical articles on women's labour issues, Black published four volumes of historical romances during the 1890s and 1900s and began her involvement with the Duckworth Popular Library of Art series as a translator and contributor. In 1891 Black had confided to John

---

[95] Stephen N. Fox and Clementina Black, *The Truck Acts: What they do and what they ought to do* (London: Women's Trade Union Association, 1894); Clementina Black, *Sweated Industry and the Minimum Wage* (London: Duckworth, 1907); Clementina Black, 'Legislative Proposals', in D. J. Shackleton (ed.), *Woman in Industry from Seven Points of View* (London: Duckworth, 1908), pp. 183–207; Clementina Black and Mrs Carl Meyer, *The Makers of Our Clothes: A Case for Trade Boards* (London: Duckworth, 1909); Clementina Black (ed.), *Married Women's Work* (London: G. Bell, 1915).

[96] For an illuminating account of this aspect of Black's work see Francis, 'Levy and Clementina Black'.

[97] Black cared for Speedwell from 1892 and took over her official guardianship upon the murder/suicide of Arthur, his young son, and wife Jessie, in Jan. 1893. See Garnett, *Constance Garnett*, pp. 90–4.

Burns that there was a real danger of her having to give up her political work as she had not made enough money from it to support herself for the past few years.[98] These returns to romance should not be dismissed, however, as mere frivolous Grub Street productions that subsidized more worthy, explicitly socialist output. As Black came to realize that the practical work of the movement was far from achieving imminent revolution into a new life of beauty, fiction became a crucial aesthetic supplement to her practical work in the labour movement.

This notion of the romances as sites of political resolution can be supported by a brief examination of the one novel of Black's that has received critical attention in the context of her socialism: her strike novel *An Agitator*, published in 1894.[99] At first the novel seems to adhere to those tenets of realism and the portrayal of the typical hero that Friedrich Engels urged upon Margaret Harkness as necessary in a truly socialist novel after reading her work, *A City Girl* (1887).[100] After all, Black's working-class hero, Kit Brand, is depicted in the midst of strike action in Mudford in terms directly lifted from Black's accounts of the confectionery workers' strike: damp coppers counted up and rolled together; conspiracies and committees; the psychological and physiological oppression of working-class women. But as Lynne Hapgood has pointed out, *An Agitator* actually follows one of the most long-standing variants of the romance plot.[101] Thanks to some timely coincidences, it is discovered that Brand is in fact the natural son of a Liberal peer, who recognizes this long-lost heir's abilities and proffers social and political advancement. Brand rejects Sir John Warwick's offer and, after the usual adversity (in this case, imprisonment after being framed for electoral fraud), he emerges to enjoy a new sense of triumph and power as his career as the independent Labour Member of Parliament for Mudford lies before him. No longer an embittered individ-

---

[98] BL Add. 46289 ff 310, Clementina Black to John Burns, 11 March 1891.

[99] Clementina Black, *An Agitator* (London: Bliss, Sands & Foster, 1894).

[100] Harkness's publisher Vizetelly sent Engels a copy of *A City Girl*, based on Harkness's observations during her period of residence in Katherine Buildings in the East End, and the author received the following response: 'If I have anything to criticise it would be that . . . the tale is not quite realistic enough. Realism in my mind, implies, besides the truth in detail, the truthful reproduction of typical characters under typical circumstances . . . In *The City Girl* the working-class figures as a passive mass, unable to help itself and not even making an effort at striving to help itself'. Engels cit. Kapp, *Eleanor Marx*, p. 221. On Harkness's work see Lynne Hapgood, 'Is this Friendship? Eleanor Marx, Margaret Harkness and the Idea of Socialist Community', in Stokes (ed.), *Eleanor Marx*, pp. 129–45.

[101] Lynne Hapgood, 'The Novel and Political Agency: Socialism and the Work of Margaret Harkness, Constance Howell and Clementina Black, 1888–1896', *Literature and History*, 5 (1996), 37–53.

ual standing out from his class, Brand ends by acknowledging his representative part of a greater communal struggle that will eventually abolish class distinctions altogether.

A strike novel that has a happy ending is rare enough in itself to warrant attention, but the romance structure of *An Agitator* also resolves those very difficulties which had confronted the Black sisters during the millenarian years of struggle in the 1880s. Nowhere is this more obvious than in that atypical hero, Kit Brand. It is generally thought that Black based Brand on an amalgamation of John Burns and H. H. Champion, a theory which would account for the class miscegenation he represents. But the very name of the character alludes to Burns and another individual with whom Black paired him as an 'agitator' back in 1889: herself. Although there is no record of Black's being referred to as Kit, it was a common enough contraction of Clementina in the late nineteenth century, adopted by, among others, Vernon Lee's partner Clementina Anstruther Thompson. Whilst the years of imagining the labour movement as a communal epic romance, in which differences of gender and class could be subsumed, were gone for good, romance itself came to provide an aesthetic supplement in which intractable differences could be resolved. When the lost child, Kit Brand, is found in *An Agitator*, the magic of romance suggests not only that a new society without the class system has come to be born, but also that the middle-class woman can be fused into the heart of the labour agitator.

The Princess Désirée, which Black published in 1896, two years after her explicitly socialist novel, *An Agitator*, might seem rather more unlikely material for a political reading. A plot summary might be enough to explain why few socialist feminist historians have been inspired to incorporate Black, the novelist, into existing accounts of Black, the estimable labour organizer and investigator. The novel opens with Ludovic de Saintré, a scion of the French nobility, preparing for a diplomatic mission to the obscure European duchy of Felsenheim. His aim is to secure the marriage of the heiress apparent to the throne, the eponymous heroine Désirée, to the duc de Toulouse. But on arriving in the 'steep and stony and medieval' burg, precisely the right setting for 'a Hugoesque drama' our hero muses, he is caught up in dangerous political intrigues.[102] Naturally, after rescuing the Princess from several fraught situations, the handsome hero and fearless heroine are eventually united in marriage and set upon their rightful thrones in Felsenheim, once the usurping wicked uncle has been disposed of.

[102] Clementina Black, *The Princess Désirée* (London: Longmans, 1896), p. 5.

But that brief aside regarding Hugo provides a clue as to arch uses of historical romance at work in Black's text. With the implied author's tongue firmly in her cheek, the hero of this historical romance denies the present and future possibility of heroism, historicity, and romance:

> 'But alas' [Ludovic] reflected, as he carefully surveyed the set of his cravat before descending to supper with the Marquis, 'the days of romance are over, and our errand here is but the parade of notifying a prosaic royal marriage between two prosaic persons whose fitness for each other resides solely in a balance of rank and fortune'. (5)

The irony of this presumption is not only because the hero is immediately catapulted into a pacey romance, but also to do with its setting. The year is 1847 and Black's novel remembers and reimagines the possibilities of that year on the cusp of revolution, constantly reminding the reader of the power of hope for the future, and the reach of historical change: 'Oh your toy kingdoms! . . . your ninepin princes and princesses! Why, such a tale as this will seem stranger to the men of the twentieth century than any medieval miracle' (9). The kingdom of Felsenheim may be imaginary, but Black takes the historical forces—the truths of what might have been—in 1847 and 1848 and makes a future of possibilities within it: a space of playful, but still political, imaginings. The events of the late 1880s were still too close, perhaps, to be put to work in this fashion and the distance of time and place, the form of romance, allowed Black to exercise the counter-factual privilege and the pleasures of aesthetic production over the effortful struggles of political reform.

Ludovic de Saintré has 'dangerous' republican tendencies, and the Princess Désirée has had an equally dangerous English education. With characteristic resourcefulness, the Princess escapes her uncle's coup disguised as a peasant boy and, once living the honest life of the people, she engages Ludovic in a lengthy discussion of republicanism, whilst hiding up a tree. The Princess convinces Ludovic that it would be wrong to form a republic before 'the people' are 'educated to self-government' (Black's socialism gained a distinctly gradualist bent during the 1890s), whilst he for his part begins 'to enter the idea seldom evolved spontaneously in the mind of man, that a woman may be better able to defend herself than a man is able to defend her' (98, 166). As there is no Sallic law in Felsenheim, the Princess is able to propose a companionate marriage to Ludovic in terms that anticipate Schreiner's *Woman and Labour* and reflect back on the heterosocial fellowship of 1880s socialism: 'I ask you as friend to friend, as comrade to comrade, to stay and help me in the work that falls to my share' (201).

V

In the last decade of the nineteenth century, when the journey from aesthetics to politics no longer held the promise of imminent transformation in both fields, romance ceased to be a means of conceptualizing political activism and became instead its vital aesthetic supplement. As Frederic Jameson has argued, with the reification of realism in late capitalism, romance became 'the place of narrative heterogeneity' and 'freedom from the reality principle'. It offered 'the possibility of sensing other historical rhythms, and of demonic or Utopian transformations of a real now unshakeably set in place'.[103] Romance was the narrative of hope, a means of imagining a history or a future at odds with the realism of high capitalism. Morris himself turned almost exclusively to romance in the last decade of his life, whether in the explicitly socialist forms of *A Dream of John Ball* (1886–7) and *News from Nowhere* (1890) or the five prehistoric tribal fantasies he crafted from *The House of the Wolfings* (1888) onwards.[104] It is only recently that scholars have attempted to counter the argument that the latter late prose romances are evidence of Morris's retreat from socialism in his last years, and have suggested that they rather represent an aesthetic attempt to shake the 'real' of high capitalism.[105] The epic romance complemented his socialist thought in respect of its anti-individualism and liberation from the complications of heterosexual romance. As Carol Silver argues, romance, like socialism, for Morris 'harmonised individual and communal interests' and avoided the 'isolated or escapist point of view'.[106]

What has never been in doubt is that Morris's turn to this form was prompted to a great extent by his frustration with socialist activists and their infighting in late 1888.[107] In June 1889, Morris wrote to his friend Charles Eliot Norton in New England in order to introduce Percival Chubb, who was leaving London and the FNL for a new ethical life in the United States. Morris added,

---

[103] Jameson, *Political Unconscious*, p. 104.

[104] Dates refer to initial periodical publication.

[105] See Amanda Hodgson, *The Romances of William Morris* (Cambridge: Cambridge University Press, 1987); Florence Boos, 'An Aesthetic Ecocommunist: Morris the Red and Morris the Green', in Peter Faulkener and Peter Preston (eds.), *William Morris: Centenary Essays* (Exeter: University of Exeter Press, 1999), 21–49.

[106] Carole Silver, *The Romance of William Morris* (Athens, Ohio: Ohio University Press, 1982), p. xv.

[107] Thompson, *William Morris*, pp. 504, 512–13, explicitly connects the composition of *The House of the Wolfings* with Morris's experiences within the Socialist League in 1888, but sees the prose romances as the resurgence of distracting 'older interests'.

I have been a great customer of the ink-makers of late. I have actually another prose romance in hand whereof I hope to send you a copy before the year is out. I will rather carry out Oscar Wilde's theory of the beauty of lying, as it will have neither time, place, history or theory in it.[108]

Morris's late romances continued a dialogue with that particularly English form of late nineteenth-century socialism, in which the retelling of the past without historical chronology, the dream of a future without a place, and above all, a belief in the connection of the aesthetic to the life of labour were indivisible from the hope of political transformation. As a sense of the deferral of hope crept upon socialist artists from 1889, the need for a supplement to political activism became more pressing. Like Morris's utopias and late romances of the 1890s, we must see Black's fiction in this period as remaining in the both/and of aesthetics and politics. In both cases—those of Morris and Black—history offered the story of a cycle of hope, of possibilities deferred but never lost, which could be rebuilt and strengthened in the long revolution. Desire was to be educated through romance, necessity tackled through the slow process of labour organization. But the illusion of the 1880s, that the former could wait whilst the latter was achieved rapidly, was gone for good.

---

[108] Morris, *CL*, iii. 77.

3

Olive Schreiner and the Dream of Labour

In the winter of 1888, Olive Schreiner wrote to her friend Edward Carpenter from her retreat in Alassio on the Italian Riviera to tell him that she was drafting 'a long dream on socialism'.[1] Carpenter had become Schreiner's chief source of news about the British socialist movement during her extended residences on the continent from January 1887 to her eventual departure for her native South Africa in October 1889. As she drew herself together in the aftermath of her bruising encounter with the eugenicist Karl Pearson and his Men and Women's Club, she assured Carpenter that by contrast '[a]ll socialist news' 'is of intense interest to me & I hear none' when away from London.[2] By early 1889, Schreiner—a writer who was seldom able to complete her work—had the rare satisfaction of chiding Carpenter for his lack of literary output compared to her own. Whilst Schreiner had written another 'little allegory . . . socialistic' in tendency, out soon, she promised (with misplaced optimism), in the *Fortnightly*, Carpenter had ceased publishing new fragments of his evolving socialist prose-poem *Towards Democracy*.[3]

Such facility with brief allegories was however, according to Schreiner some years later, merely a symptom of the difficulties she was having with another, far larger piece of writing. For the previous three years, Schreiner had been struggling to produce what she termed her 'sex book', addressing

---

[1] Olive Schreiner to Edward Carpenter (Dec. 1888). *Olive Schreiner: Letters,* ed. Richard Rive (Oxford: Oxford University Press, 1987), p. 144. Schreiner had become acquainted with Carpenter via Havelock Ellis and the Fellowship of the New Life: see Yaffa Claire Draznin, *My Other Self: The Letters of Olive Schreiner and Havelock Ellis, 1884–1920* (New York: Peter Lang, 1992). The first surviving letters between Carpenter and Schreiner date from June 1886, however Schreiner had read and forwarded the correspondence between Carpenter and Havelock Ellis to Karl Pearson as early as Dec. 1885. See University College London Archives, Pearson Papers, Olive Schreiner Correspondence Mss 840/4/92, Dec. 1885.

[2] Edward Carpenter Collection, Sheffield City Libraries, MSS359/3, 11 April 1887. This important indication of Schreiner's continuing political interests is omitted from the transcription of this letter in *Schreiner: Letters,* ed. Rive.

[3] Olive Schreiner to Edward Carpenter, 10 Jan. 1889, *Schreiner: Letters*, p. 146.

the relation between the sexes in the evolution of the human species, from ancient times to the present and into the future.[4] Schreiner claimed that in the process of drafting and redrafting this 'woman question' work in the late 1880s and early 1890s, a series of allegories, or 'dreams' embodying the 'emotions' were awakened by the 'abstract thoughts in argumentative prose' of the main text.[5] 'It's so easy for a mind like mine', she wrote to Havelock Ellis at the time, 'to produce long logical arguments . . . but when I have done it I feel such a "valch" [loathing] against it: that it is only the material; it has to be combined [with the poetic] and made alive'.[6] Argumentative prose, or at least the positivist method of argument she was trying to use during the mid-1880s under the influence of Pearson, was simply incapable of containing the affect of the question at hand. The material of Schreiner's feminist argument needed an aesthetic ideal to live.

Schreiner's encounters with, and contributions to, social and sexual politics in London during the 1880s have been subjected to extensive study since the late 1970s when the rising disciplines of feminist and post-colonial studies converged on her remarkable body of work.[7] It is only very recently, however, that the mythmaking which accompanies any such process of 'rediscovering' feminist forebears has begun to be addressed in its own right. Over the last three decades, Schreiner has evolved into a 'working-class woman' who went to live in the slums of the East End, or, alternatively a hysterical egotist, whose sexual possessiveness rendered productive friendship with fellow comrades impossible.[8] Liz Stanley's recent reconsideration of Schreiner's life and works lays the latter myth to rest with a trenchant account of how the various legatees of Schreiner's letters edited her correspondence so as to make such a reading inevitable.[9] Carolyn Burdett's study

---

[4] For the history and 'evolution' of *Woman and Labour* and Schreiner's 'sex book', see Carolyn Burdett, *Olive Schreiner and the Progress of Feminism* (Basingstoke: Palgrave, 2001), pp. 47–67. For Schreiner's abstract of the 'sex book' as she saw it in 1886 see Olive Schreiner to Karl Pearson, 10 Sept. 1885, *Schreiner: Letters*, pp. 103–4.

[5] Olive Schreiner, *Woman and Labour* (London: Fisher Unwin, 1911), p. 15.

[6] Olive Schreiner to Havelock Ellis, 2 Nov. 1888. *Schreiner: Letters*, p. 142.

[7] Ruth First and Ann Scott, *Olive Schreiner* (London: Andre Deutsch, 1980), pp. 108–88; Carol Barash, 'Virile Womanhood: Olive Schreiner's Narratives of a Master Race', in Elaine Showalter (ed.), *Speaking of Gender* (New York: Routledge, 1989), pp. 269–81; Anne McClintock, *Imperial Leather: Race Gender and Sexuality in the Colonial Contest* (London: Routledge, 1995), pp. 259–95.

[8] The misreading of Schreiner's class appears in David Waterman, *Disordered Bodies and Disrupted Borders: Representations of Resistance in Modern British Literature* (Lanham, MD: University Press of America, 1999), p. 60; Yvonne Kapp's otherwise incomparable biography, *Eleanor Marx: The Crowded Years, 1884–1898* (London: Virago, 1976), pp. 22–9, contains just such an oddly intemperate arraignment of Schreiner's 'egotism'.

[9] Liz Stanley, *Imperialism, Labour and the New Woman: Olive Schreiner's Social Theory* (Durham: sociologypress, 2002), pp. 108–13.

of Schreiner is also invaluable for its sensitive historicization of Schreiner's evolutionary thought and thus the writer's intellectual relationship with Karl Pearson.[10]

Burdett suggests that Schreiner's works rewrite nineteenth-century narratives of progress to provide alternative visions of modernity and certainly Schreiner's idiosyncratic encounter with late nineteenth-century socialism resulted in her redefining the movement in her own terms.[11] Never consistent and far from programmatic, Schreiner's socialist thought took shape first in the aesthetic collection *Dreams* (1890) and later in the fragments of her much revised, long delayed, 'sex book', publications 'The Woman Question' (1899) and that 'bible' of the suffrage movement, *Woman and Labour* (1911).[12] For Schreiner the allegories in *Dreams* resulted from her ability 'to see our socialist movement much more clearly & as a whole . . . & face many things with regard to it that were not clear to me before' when at a distance from the labour demonstrations in London during the later 1880s.[13] It was in Alassio that Schreiner rewrote the materialist analysis of capital, labour, and the history of men as an idealist dream of consumption, art, and an allegory of woman.

Schreiner was caught up in the division between what she termed 'dream life and real life', between idealism and materialism, individualism and collectivism. Like many of her contemporaries—including Carpenter and George Bernard Shaw, as we shall see in the next chapter—Schreiner took those late nineteenth-century triumphs of materialist thought, Darwinism and Marxism, and tried to forge out of them an idealist correlative. If woman's primary function was, as her antagonist Karl Pearson insisted, race reproduction, then Schreiner's idealism recast embodied reproduction as aesthetic production: 'men's bodies', she argued in 1911, 'are our woman's work of art'.[14] As her friend Eleanor Marx spent the late 1880s in a tireless campaign of organizing and agitating among the workers in London's Isle of Dogs, Schreiner decided that Marx suffered from an excess of uncritical faith. Writing to Gladstone's daughter, Mary Drew in 1888, Schreiner described her friend as 'the only person I know brought up as a freethinker & socialist':

---

[10] Burdett, *Schreiner*, pp. 9, 43.

[11] The most extensive analysis of Schreiner's works in the context of late 19th-cent. ethical socialism is found in Joyce Avrech Berkman, *The Healing Imagination of Olive Schreiner: Beyond South African Colonialism* (Amherst, Mass.: University of Massachusetts Press, 1989), pp. 159–77.

[12] Vera Brittain, *Testament of Youth* (1933; repr. London: Virago 1978), p. 41.

[13] SCL Carpenter MSS359/4, 12 April 1887.

[14] Schreiner, *Woman and Labour*, p. 174. On Pearson's own early interest in idealism however, see Theodore M. Porter, *Karl Pearson: The Scientific Life in a Statistical Age* (Princeton: Princeton University Press, 2004), pp. 65–7.

She is, oddly enough, like nothing so much as a Christian of the old old stamp. She has the same childlike faith which cannot be shaken & all that is great & beautiful for her is bound up in her faith, & for that she lives. She *cannot* understand doubt! She never reasons! She believes & would lay down her life for her faith & sees nothing beyond it. We look before & after; she looks only straight forward.[15]

According to Schreiner, Marx was limited by her reduction of all—even aesthetic responsiveness to the 'great & beautiful'—to a simple faith in materialism. Schreiner's counter to Marx's faith was to write an allegory of capitalist imperialism in the cadences and stock images of Christianity, only to then discard these tropes as empty letters. For Schreiner writing such works was, quite simply, the equivalent of agitating for revolution in Trafalgar Square during the late 1880s. Her use of allegorical form enabled her, as Ann Heilmann has suggested, to speak in a mode and of another category than that of the material world.[16] This aesthetic mode of the allegory nevertheless demanded a reader ready to gloss its applications to the contemporary world even as it spoke of a category that transcended the world's dull material inscriptions of inequality and difference. It was to take her experiences during the South African wars at the turn of the century to fully form Schreiner's understanding of the relationship between capitalism and colonialism; sexual and racial subjugation, as we shall see in the last chapter of this book. But Schreiner's paradoxical espousal of both communalism and the vital force of expressive individualism, of materialism guided by idealism, and of allegory as a mode of political critique during the 1880s and 1890s, was forged out of her resistance to the future of socialism and sex envisioned by Karl Pearson.

I

Schreiner's encounter with the metropolitan socialist movement during the 1880s was marked by the very complexity of her status as a literary celebrity, sprung fully formed, so it seemed, from the South African veldt as a radical commentator upon the destiny of man and woman. Schreiner had travelled to Britain from the Cape in 1881 with the intention of attending medical

[15] Olive Schreiner to Mary Drew, BL Add. Mss. 46344 ff. 149. Undated letter, Alassio cat. 1887, but internal evidence suggests that this unpublished letter should be dated late 1888. Schreiner does not name Marx in the letter but that she is the subject of Schreiner's discussion is almost certain from the description given.
[16] Ann Heilmann, *New Woman Strategies: Sarah Grand, Olive Schreiner, Mona Caird* (Manchester: Manchester University Press, 2004), p. 121.

school in Edinburgh and, whilst persistent ill health forced her to relinquish this ambition, she managed to secure a publisher for a novel she had completed in South Africa. In 1883 Chapman and Hall finally published her novel, *The Story of an African Farm* under the pseudonym Ralph Iron. By September of that year, Schreiner's novel had been adopted by the collection of men and women writers and activists that surrounded the radical secularist journal *Progress*. Edward Aveling, who was deputizing for the journal's editor G. W. Foote whilst the latter was in prison for blasphemy, concluded in an extended review that 'since "Tom Jones" there have been few novels so uncompromising' in their frank address to contemporary life.[17] Rather than the current tendency among writers to dress up their stories in the 'medieval . . . garb' which apparently lent itself 'so much more readily to aesthetic representations than those of today', here was a writer who invested the life of the present times with artistic merit and, in Aveling's reading at least, showed that the 'dear Mistress' and 'true god, Science' was our only refuge.[18] Both the aspiring poet, Ernest Radford, and his good friend Eleanor Marx argued in a pair of articles in the same journal a few months later that 'Ralph Iron's' novel supported their own separate causes of, on the one hand, agnosticism and on the other a determined radical atheism.[19] Steeped as it is in the transcendentalism of Ralph Waldo Emerson and the lingering influence of Herbert Spencer and John Stuart Mill, *The Story of an African Farm* universalized the intellectual journeys of those who frequented radical discussion groups in the early 1880s. Whilst Bolton had its own Walt Whitman fellowship and Sunderland its Emersonian transcendentalist meetings, Schreiner's novel seemed to demonstrate that even an indigent farm labourer and an orphan girl on an isolated farm in Africa were stirring to the same social questions.

Despite later nineteenth- and twentieth-century rereadings of *The Story of an African Farm* by the first- and second-wave feminist movements as a novel primarily concerned with the 'woman question', contemporary receptions of the text were thus preoccupied by its contribution to more general

---

[17] Edward Aveling, 'A Notable Book', *Progress*, 2/3 (1883), 156–65 (p. 162).

[18] Ibid. 157, 165.

[19] Ernest Radford and Eleanor Marx had a spirited exchange in the pages of *Progress* in late 1883 concerning absolute atheism. Radford declared his 'variance with the bellicose atheists in England' and his 'sympathy with the Russian Nihilists in their struggle' for ethical 'truth'. Marx dismissed such temporizing as the characteristic bourgeois trait of putting prudence before valour. Both claimed that Olive Schreiner's *Story of an African Farm* (1883) supported their own views. Neither of the Radfords had any more work published in the journal. See Ernest Radford, 'The Attitude towards Religion', *Progress*, 2/5 (1883), 300–3; Eleanor Marx, 'A Reply to Ernest Radford', *Progress*, 2/6 (1883), 370–2.

ethical and theological debates.[20] Together with Walt Whitman's poetry and the plays of Henrik Ibsen, Schreiner's novel became a node of mutual recognition among young radicals in London, who then co-opted the work for their various causes.[21] The group of around twenty young men and women students and writers who had formed the original men and women's club in 1879 provided one such readership in the early 1880s, numbering, as it did, several of Schreiner's later acquaintances such as Eleanor Marx, Dollie Radford, and the Ford sisters among its members and guests.[22] As we have seen in the previous chapter, the ethic of fellowship ran through the club's social evenings and debates that balanced art and literature with questions of political reform and ethical idealism.[23]

In the spring of 1885 such eclecticism attracted an array of artists and writers, including the poet Amy Levy, Augustine Birrell, and George Bernard Shaw to the last few meetings of the original club at the home of the then president Dollie Radford in Brunswick Square.[24] For the club secretary, Clementina Black, however, the organization had outlived its original purpose. Writing to Karl Pearson, an intermittent member, in December 1884 she acknowledged that the club needed to either gain new members or be dissolved in the near future due to the changing commitments of current members: they were 'not now by any means solitary students and so forth in London'. The club, she concluded, simply no longer held 'so important

---

[20] See, for example, Canon McColl, 'An Agnostic Novel', *Spectator* (13 Aug. 1887). In 1894, at the height of the New Woman debates, W. T. Stead identified Schreiner as the 'founder and high priestess of the school' of novels of the 'modern woman', marking the beginning of the retrospective canonization of *African Farm* as a 'New Woman' novel. See W. T. Stead, 'The Novel of the Modern Woman', *Review of Reviews,* 10 (1894), 64–74 (p. 64).

[21] On the dissemination and reception of Ibsen see Sally Ledger, 'Eleanor Marx and Henrik Ibsen', in John Stokes (ed.), *Eleanor Marx: Life, Works, Contacts* (Aldershot: Ashgate, 2000), pp. 53–67.

[22] Ernest Radford first attended as a guest 13 Jan. 1880 and signed in as a member 23 March 1880. Emily Ford attended the Slade School of Art in the late 1870s and had a successful career as an artist, painting portraits of Josephine Butler and the Russian anarchist Stepniak. Millicent Fawcett presented her painting *Dawn* to Newnham College to celebrate her daughter Philippa's success in the mathematics tripos. Emily was also a close friend of the aesthetic critic and writer Vernon Lee (Violet Paget). See Ch. 6 and June Hannam, *Isabella Ford* (Oxford: Basil Blackwell, 1989), pp. 21, 167.

[23] University College London Archives, Pearson Collection 10/1. The records of 'A Men and Women's Club 1879–1885, precursor of The Men and Women's Club 1885–1889' were preserved by Maria Sharpe Pearson. The first list of members is dated 20 Oct. 1879. William Thompson read a paper on 'The English Stage' on 23 March 1880; Clementina Black led the discussion of Browning on 19 Jan. 1882; Emily Ford opened the debate on government 25 May 1880 and the discussion of socialistic tendencies occurred on 20 Dec. 1881, a meeting attended by both Clementina Black and Dollie Maitland (Radford).

[24] UCL Pearson 10/1, minute of meeting at 27 Brunswick Square, 19 May 1885.

a place as it certainly did to many of its members at the beginning and even at the time when I first belonged' to it.[25]

Pearson, who had recently been appointed Professor of Applied Mathematics at University College London, took the opportunity to try to reconfigure the club's constitution. Whilst neither Clementina Black nor Dollie Radford supported his proposal, by 1885 Pearson had made his point.[26] The original club dissolved and Pearson formed 'The Men and Women's Club', devoted to the formal discussion 'of all matters in any way connected with the mutual position and relation of men and women'.[27] Of the women members of the original club, only Annie Eastty went on to join Pearson's group and the entire executive committee, apart from Radford and Black, seceded with Pearson.[28] Radford and the Black sisters' resistance to Pearson's plans is not surprising given that the mission of the original club was to build upon the shared experiences of young people of both sexes entering upon life in the metropolis. Clementina Black argued that 'original differences [between the sexes] are often extremely minute' and Pearson's decision to make sexual difference the entire object of study in the later Men and Women's Club threatened to fracture the ideal of heterosocial fellowship that had sustained the original organization.[29]

As we have seen in the previous chapter, new political commitments were coming to displace the old diffuse questioning of the original club for the Ford and Black sisters by the mid-1880s, whilst Dollie and Ernest Radford were shortly to join William Morris's Socialist League. But Olive Schreiner responded with enthusiasm when her status as author of *African Farm* led to an invitation to join this newly constituted Men and Women's Club in June 1885 and she signed up to the club's mission statement of open discussion of sexual relations the following month.[30] The personal and political struggles that ensued within the club over the next four years provide a remarkable microcosm of the obstacles faced by middle-class feminists at the turn of the century and proved a lasting influence on Schreiner's own feminist argument.[31] Whilst Pearson encouraged women members to

---

[25] UCL Pearson 10/26, Clementina Black to Karl Pearson 11 December 1884.

[26] Ibid.: 'I don't see that an alternative motion like that you suggest wd. be much use'.

[27] UCL Pearson 10/1, Minute Book of the 'Men and Women's Club' 1885–1889.

[28] Annie Eastty's sister Minnie was married to Clementina's brother, Ernest Black.

[29] Clementina Black, 'On Marriage: A Criticism', *Fortnightly Review,* 47 (1890), 586–94 (p. 593).

[30] For an extensive discussion of Pearson's Men and Women's Club see Lucy Bland, *Banishing the Beast: English Feminism and Sexual Morality, 1885–1914* (1995; repr. London: I. B. Tauris, 2001), pp. 3–47. Judith Walkowitz, *City of Dreadful Delight: Narratives of Sexual Danger in Late Victorian London* (London: Virago, 1992), pp. 135–71.

[31] Bland, *Banishing*, p. 47.

discuss their experiences of sexuality for research purposes, Schreiner found herself caught in a trap in which her very openness was ascribed to her feeling '*sex*-love' for Pearson. 'I do not love you as a soul loves itself', Schreiner asserted to Pearson, but anticipating his habit of validating women's personal testimonies, she added: 'You will say "O.S., you are deceiving yourself, that is sex-love". *I deny it*.'[32]

Like so many of his peers, Pearson found little difficulty in marrying a modish preoccupation with socialism with his other interests (which were unusually diverse ones, even by nineteenth-century standards) and lectured widely on the former subject in the mid-1880s.[33] In a paper delivered to the Men and Women's Club in 1886 at the height of socialist activism in London, Pearson argued that the 'two most important movements of our era . . . [are] the socialistic movement and the movement for the complete emancipation of women'.[34] For Pearson, like Schreiner and her friend Eleanor Marx, the woman question and socialism were 'interwoven in a remarkable and hardly yet fully appreciated manner'.[35] But Pearson insisted in the first paper read to the club in 1885, 'The Woman Question', that 'we have first to settle what is the physical capacity of women, what would be the effect of her emancipation on her function of race reproduction, before we can talk about her "rights"'.[36]

Pearson's socialist state was to be 'an organisation of society turning essentially on capacity for work, on the provision of the best conditions for efficient activity, and on the replacement of individual dependence and personal control by State protection and State regulation'.[37] Socialism was entirely amenable to evolutionary thought, Pearson decided: both were at odds with the individualism of nineteenth-century liberalism and, in the hands of wise statesmen, the socialist state would act as handmaiden to natural selection, ensuring national fitness and progress. In the evolving collective order women would realize that they were bearing children for the future of the state and working-class men that their labour contributed to the economic competitiveness of the nation. Once this had been achieved, Pearson suggested, all individualistic claims for 'rights' would be laid to rest, safe in the knowledge of collective (national and imperial) racial progress. The 'emancipation of women seems to call into question the

---

[32] Olive Schreiner to Karl Pearson, 14 Dec. 1886, in *Schreiner: Letters*, p. 117. Walkowitz, *City*, pp. 137, 145.

[33] See Porter, *Karl Pearson*, pp. 69–81.

[34] Karl Pearson, 'Socialism and Sex', in *The Ethic of Freethought* (London: Fisher Unwin, 1888), p. 430.

[35] Karl Pearson, 'Woman and Labour', *Fortnightly Review*, 329 n.s. (1894), 561–77 (p. 561).

[36] Karl Pearson, 'The Woman Question' (1885), in *The Ethic of Freethought*, p. 371.

[37] Pearson, 'Woman and Labour', p. 574.

economic basis of existing society', Pearson concluded, but a socialist state would resolve this by acknowledging that motherhood was a form of social labour and hence providing financial support for it.[38]

Schreiner pointed out to Pearson that the problem with such an approach to the issue of sexual relations was that it led to an exclusive focus on women—and on women more or less as mothers of the future race. He was wrong, she urged, to take woman alone as his object of study in this field and discuss 'man only in as far as he throws light upon her question'.[39] For Pearson, however, maternalism and the history of womanhood offered a model of that self-renunciation which was the necessary ethical basis of a future socialist state. As Theodore Porter concludes, Pearson believed that it 'was incumbent on woman not only to overcome her own individualism for the sake of socialist morality, but also, through rigorous adherence to an ideal of self-development, to control the individualism of man'.[40] The Fabian socialist Emma Brooke went further than Schreiner and accused Pearson of an 'unsocialistic' attitude towards women, characterized by 'a distinctly dominant tone, an inclination to lay down their duty for them' in his addresses to the Men and Women's Club.[41] By 1894 Pearson argued that the sort of women who resisted his influence in the club—'asexual women' in search of the illusion of 'equality'—were a temporary aberration in the race.

> Such women cannot transmit the asexualism which fits them for competition with men to numerous offspring; they leave the women whose maternal and sexual instincts are strong to be the mothers of the coming generation, and to transmit those instincts to the women of the future.[42]

Pearson's evolutionary account of sex and socialism left no space for the expressive individual self. Despite reformulating the club such that women members were actively encouraged to express their sense of personal sexuality and find a new language for discussing sexual difference, Pearson's interest in the collective state reduced these tremulous selves to a racial function. In the future, women would come to understand that their contribution to national efficiency came in the shape of 'bearing a child to the state—a new citizen to assist the common social growth': in reproduction rather than production.[43]

---

[38] Ibid. 386.
[39] UCL Pearson 840/4, Olive Schreiner to Karl Pearson, July (?) 1885.
[40] Porter, *Karl Pearson*, p. 176.
[41] Emma Brooke, cit. Bland, *Banishing*, 29. On Emma Brooke see Kay Daniels, 'Emma Brooke: Fabian, Feminist and Writer', *Women's History Review*, 12 (2003), 153–68.
[42] Pearson, 'Woman and Labour', p. 568.
[43] Ibid. 564.

For Schreiner, Pearson's demarcation of women as endowed reproducers rather than labouring producers was problematic to say the least. Schreiner herself had had some bitter personal experience of life on an allowance granted in view of her status as a female of marital age. Her brother Fred paid her an annual allowance until her marriage in 1894 and she complained to Havelock Ellis in that context, 'I can't live on dependence':

> Ah, freedom, freedom, freedom, that is the first great want of humanity. That is why I sympathise so much more with the Herbert Spencer school than with the Socialists, so called. If I thought Socialism would bring the subjection of the individual to the whole I would fight to the death . . . Better to die of cold or hunger or thirst than to be robbed of your freedom of action, of your feeling that you are an absolutely free and independent unit.[44]

Pearson's interpretation of socialism as an imperialist planned economy in which the female subject would be but the physical vessel of the future race ran counter to Schreiner's passionate belief that women had scarce yet gained a self to renounce. Her challenge was to find a means of demanding freedom and independence for women—and in particular, middle and upper class women aspiring to professional work—whilst thinking through the new ideas of collectivism offered by the socialist movement in the 1880s.

As Burdett has demonstrated, Pearson's pairing of evolutionism and the woman question was one that Schreiner was to tackle head-on in her article 'The Woman Question' (1899) and book *Woman and Labour* (1911).[45] But during the mid-1880s, Schreiner's friend, Eleanor Marx, a sometime visitor to the Men and Women's Club, offered her an alternative analysis of socialism and feminism. Marx reviewed the English translation of August Bebel's *Women in the Past, Present and Future* (1879) in Morris's Socialist League journal, *Commonweal*, in August 1885, a month after Pearson's paper 'The Woman Question' was circulated among interested parties.[46] A year later, an extended version of Marx's review emerged as *The Woman Question*, under the joint names of Edward and Eleanor Marx Aveling, which argued that the 'position of women rests, as everything in our complex modern society rests, on the question of economics'.[47] Although *The Woman Question* shared elements of the intellectual orthodoxy of evolutionism with Pearson's work, the former paper framed women themselves as active

---

[44] Olive Schreiner to Havelock Ellis, 29 March 1885, *Schreiner: Letters*, p. 63.
[45] Burdett, *Schreiner*, pp. 61–77.
[46] Kapp, *Eleanor Marx*, pp. 82–6.
[47] Eleanor and Edward Marx Aveling, *The Woman Question* (London: Swan Sonnenschein, 1886), p. 4.

agents in the process of social change.[48] Bebel's original work, like Friedrich Engels's *The Origin of the Family, Private Property and the State* (1884), had harnessed Bachofen's study of prehistoric 'mother-right' cultures to conclude that patriarchy was the foundation of private property and capitalism.[49] Bourgeois marriage and its necessary adjunct, the sexual exploitation of proletarian women, resulted from the capitalist imperative of augmenting and transmitting property down a 'pure' male bloodline. In a new socialist order, women could no longer be viewed as vehicles of inheritance and hence would be free to labour for the collective, repudiate the 'unhealthy and unholy . . . crime' of chastity, and join men in relations of free love, undeterred by fears of illegitimate children, indigence, or abandonment.[50] As 'oppressed classes' at present, both women and labourers 'must understand', the Marx Avelings conclude, 'that their emancipation must come from themselves'.[51] Progress in sexual relations could be achieved here and now by individual 'men and women . . . discuss[ing] the sexual question in all its bearings, looking frankly into each others' faces', whilst the new socialist era was advancing by the day.[52]

Eleanor Marx Aveling's analysis of socialism and the woman question was certainly more amenable to Schreiner than Pearson's reduction of women down to a single 'function of race reproduction'. Both Bebel and the Marx Avelings emphasize that women possess individual, desiring selves stifled under capitalism. Indeed, *The Woman Question* cites Lyndall, the heroine of Schreiner's *African Farm*, as an example of a woman who simply cannot develop in contemporary capitalist culture that sexually segregates education and commodifies women for the marriage market. Schreiner was unconvinced, however, by the theory that women's oppression was rooted in the prehistoric overthrow of a culture of mother-right and the emergence of private property. In her preface to *Woman and Labour*, Schreiner looks back to her childhood in South Africa to frame an oblique critique of such scientific socialist analyses of the woman question. Countering Bachofen's cultural anthropology with idealist evolutionism, Schreiner details the variety

---

[48] For a lucid analysis of Darwinism and Marx Aveling's *The Woman Question* see Emma Francis, 'Socialist Feminism and Sexual Instinct: Eleanor Marx and Amy Levy', in Stokes (ed.), *Eleanor Marx,* pp. 113–27. Francis argues convincingly that the Darwinian reading of sexual instinct in the work can be construed as Edward Aveling's contribution (pp. 124–7).

[49] Schreiner mentions her intention of reading Bebel's work to Havelock Ellis in Aug. 1884: *Schreiner: Letters,* p. 49. Ellis reviewed Bebel's work in *Today* (Nov. 1884). On Pearson's interest in Bachofen see Porter, *Karl Pearson,* p. 152.

[50] Marx Aveling, *The Woman Question,* p. 13.

[51] Ibid. 7.

[52] Ibid. 17.

and plasticity of sexual roles among species. 'Sex relationships', she argues, 'may assume almost any form on earth as the conditions of life vary' and the co-operative labour and reproduction of some species represent 'the realisation of the highest sexual ideal which haunts humanity'.[53] This haunting ideal of a possible future is contrasted with Schreiner's account of a conversation with 'a Kafir woman still in her untouched primitive condition', who, for Schreiner, represents an anthropological past. This 'person of genius' illuminates the pains of womanhood even without private property and convinces Schreiner that women as a collective will never rise against men or their position in society so thoroughly determined are they by the life and conditions of their race.[54] Materialism fixes women in maternity and a material revolution will leave this sex role unchanged. Schreiner implies rather that both men and women need to realize a new ideal of sexual relations by sharing the labour of production and of reproduction.

In the late 1880s, Schreiner encapsulated this thought in her allegory 'A Dream of Wild Bees' which she wrote for Pearson.[55] In this brief text, reproduced in the collection *Dreams*, a woman sits heavily pregnant with her ninth child, working through a pile of sewing which covers a potentially stimulating book besides her. She drifts into a dream in which the worker bees 'who make no honey' droning outside the window become men who proffer different talents to her unborn child.[56] Successive figures offer health, wealth, fame, love, and talent, but none stir the child like the final, nameless figure, who questions 'what *is* real' success in life? (96) The mother whose life has been absorbed into the materiality of race reproduction accepts his gift for her last child: '*This shall be thy reward—that the ideal shall be real to thee*' (96). Schreiner's commentary works here, as in so many of her writings, by analogy. The infertile male drone pollinates the 'antenatal thing' in the mother's womb with idealist fervour and the foetus's vision of hope is in itself a version of birth:

> In those eyes that had never seen the day, in that half-shaped brain was a sensation of light! Light—that it had never seen. Light—that perhaps it never should see. Light—that existed somewhere! (96)

Childbirth and maternity for Schreiner were never simply material race reproduction but the original analogy of idealism. Reading the birth of hope and creativity as reproduction and reproduction as the birth of hope

[53] Schreiner, *Woman and Labour*, pp. 13–14.
[54] Ibid. 14.
[55] See Burdett, *Schreiner*, pp. 85–7; Olive Schreiner to Karl Pearson, 23 Oct. 1886: *Schreiner: Letters*, p. 110.
[56] Olive Schreiner, *Dreams* (London: Fisher Unwin, 1890), p. 90.

and creativity enabled Schreiner to make maternity central to her feminist politics and avoid purely biological determinism.[57] Both men and women, whether father and mothers or not, become responsible for reproducing the race through the pollinating force of idealism in Schreiner's aesthetic analogy. In response to Pearson's separation of female reproduction from male production, Schreiner redefines maternity to encompass masculine creativity and abstract thought.

II

Schreiner's correspondence with Pearson came to an abrupt and seemingly traumatic halt shortly after her departure for the continent in January 1887. By 1888, the feminist activist Henrietta Müller confirmed to Schreiner that 'the [Men and Women's] Club is a piteous failure. The men lay down the law, the women resent in silence and submit in silence—there is no debate at all.'[58] Müller's experience led her to conclude that separatism was the only path for women's advancement and that, not just in the short term, but for 'a very long time it will be better that the less men have to do with women the better for women'.[59] The heterosocial first men and women's club, in which members such as Radford and Black had attempted to elide sexual difference in the name of fellowship, had given way to a new order of gender relations by the end of the decade which underlay the subsequent New Woman debates of the 1890s.

During the mid-1880s, however, Schreiner had become involved in another organization that had helped to form her hope for a communal socialist future in which idealism would both reshape the nature of sexual relations and encourage expressive individuality. In the midst of her fraught correspondence with Pearson concerning the Men and Women's Club, Schreiner issued regular invitations to him to join her at meetings of the Fellowship of the New Life. 'Would you care to come to a New Life meeting on the 21st [?]', she enquired in December 1885, '[Edward] Carpenter and Miss [Isabella] Ford will be there'.[60] It was, she informed him subsequently, after his non-appearance, 'very interesting. I wanted you to have

---

[57] Heilmann, *New Woman Strategies*, p. 148, provides an analysis of the juxtaposition of male creativity and female reproduction as the failure of women's art in Schreiner's posthumous novel *From Man to Man*.

[58] SCL Carpenter 359/19 (2), Henrietta Müller to Olive Schreiner, n.d. (1888).

[59] Ibid.

[60] UCL Pearson 840/4, Olive Schreiner to Karl Pearson, (n.d. Dec. 1885?). Schreiner's continued involvement in the FNL is often overlooked partly because these brief notes are not included in Rive's edition, *Schreiner: Letters*.

been there'.[61] The previous spring, Schreiner's new acquaintance, Havelock Ellis, had sent her the initial resolutions of the Fellowship which he had helped to found a few months earlier. Like Ellis, Schreiner noted at the time 'I sympathize with [socialism]', but worried that a mere redistribution of wealth would 'pass over with it the disease of which the rich are dying, the selfishness, the hardness of heart, the greed for material good . . . what we want is more love & more sympathy'.[62] On closer acquaintance however, Schreiner decided 'I like the "New Life", especially the clause on combining physical with mental labour'.[63] Unlike Pearson's analysis of 'labour' as a class of a certain type of male producers, labour in the New Life was always already part of an aesthetic continuum and was something to be eagerly embraced by all as communal weal and individual self-realization.

The Fellowship of the New Life aimed to create 'perfect character in each & all' by founding a 'communistic society' in which 'material things would be subordinated to spiritual things' and manual labour pursued 'in conjunction with intellectual pursuits'.[64] In the Fellowship's vision of a new society, old social divisions would be erased by holding wealth in common, but most importantly, by all members taking a turn in the fields with a spade after a few hours of mental labour. The Fellowship drew together many of those such as Ellis, his future wife Edith Lees, and Edward Carpenter, who were in the process of exploring, and living openly in, same-sex relationships and 'semi-detached' marriages.[65] The nature and tendencies of sexual desire were never assumed to be fixed by such members of the Fellowship, but viewed rather as a transitive force that only needed to be released from the forms of bourgeois society in order to bring a new future of social relations into being. The Fellowship provided an easy target for satire on the part of members of scientific socialist organizations such as the SDF, and indeed, its own former members such as Isabella Ford and Edith Lees Ellis in later years. But as Stanley Pierson argues, the organization exercised a disproportionate influence on the formation of the modern British labour movement and nowhere is this more palpable than in the Fellowship's focus on labour itself as a redemptive, communal activity that would be the ethical (and aesthetic) route to the New Life.[66]

[61] UCL Pearson 840/4, Olive Schreiner to Karl Pearson, 8 Jan. 1886.
[62] Olive Schreiner to Havelock Ellis, 2 May 1884, Draznin, *My Other Self*, p. 46.
[63] Ibid.
[64] BLPES archives, LSE, Fabian Collection C36, Fabian Society Meetings Minutes 1883–1888; 24 Oct. 1883.
[65] My thanks to Diana Maltz for an instructive discussion of this aspect of the FNL and for bringing this term to my attention.
[66] Stanley Pierson, *Marxism and the Origins of British Socialism: The Struggle for a New Consciousness* (Ithaca, NY: Cornell University Press, 1973), pp. 22–38, 75–80.

Schreiner, like Isabella Ford, as we have seen in the previous chapter, was worried that the experiment in communal living projected by the New Life placed little emphasis on women members working outside the home. 'I want to join the 'New Life'' she wrote to Ellis in 1884, 'but I hope they don't mean if we form a community that we are all to live together. It isn't living together but working together in heart that helps people. (I mean large bodies of people[.])'[67] Although Schreiner was fascinated by life lived in community, as was evident from her experience staying in a convent in Harrow in the mid-1880s, her belief was that work itself was the point of connection between disparate individuals and that both men and women were entitled to this form of productive self-development. Again and again Schreiner's letters from this period reflect her interest in the production of things—pots, sandals, books, poems, children—and how the act of creation always produces a surplus affect for the maker, beyond the physical presence of the thing made. For the members of the New Life, influenced by Carpenter's own experiments in smallholding life at Millthorpe, this excess affect was to be a route to social change. Never one to give up easily, Schreiner continued to press invitations to attend meetings of the Fellowship of the New Life onto Pearson so that he could witness this movement for social evolution through communalism. The Fellowship acquired 'a piece of ground' for their planned commune in Merstham, Surrey, in 1886 and Schreiner encouraged Pearson to join them there for tea and an address at the local working men's institute followed by an exploration of the site one Saturday afternoon in May.[68] Herbert Rix, a leading member of the Fellowship, reminded his audience that the prospect of labour close to nature offered a chance to reinvigorate the arts and crafts, opening the eyes of the Fellowship to (in a Ruskinian analysis) beauty of integrity rather than mere ornament.[69] Schreiner's friend Edith Lees, who was secretary of the Fellowship, encouraged more women to join the movement, arguing that women 'are chiefly responsible for [the] speedy or tardy' approach of a new, more equitable, simpler life.[70] But Lees's vision of the 'Womanhood of

---

[67] Olive Schreiner to Havelock Ellis, 15 October 1884. Draznin, *My Other Self*, p. 158.

[68] Olive Schreiner to Karl Pearson, UCL Pearson 840/4/60, 62: 21 May 1886. Meetings in this location became a regular occurrence as Katherine Bradley (one half of the poetic partnership 'Michael Field') notes, joining the Fellowship at a meeting there in May 1889. For a discussion of 'Michael Field' and the suburban context of the Fellowship see Ana Parejo Vadillo, *Women Poets and Urban Aestheticism: Passengers of Modernity* (Basingstoke: Palgrave, 2005), pp. 168–75.

[69] Herbert Rix, 'The Return to Nature: An Address delivered to the New Fellowship on the Occasion of a Country Excursion', *Seed-time: The Organ of the New Fellowship* (2 Oct. 1889), 1–2.

[70] Edith Lees, 'Women and the New Life', *Seed-time* (3 Jan. 1890), 6.

Tomorrow . . . free . . . and strong' standing 'shoulder to shoulder' with men 'as both fulfil their sex and work' is unlikely to have found favour with Pearson, however much such sentiments influenced Schreiner's own analysis in the later sections of *Woman and Labour*.[71]

In its early days the Fellowship was open to accusations of being a band of sentimental Luddites who thought to change the world by resigning from lucrative professions to become market gardeners. Certainly even the most cursory consideration of the original minute books, prior to the secession of some members to form the Fabian Society, reveals the Fellowship's extreme confusion about how exactly the planned creation of a new ethical and political order was to arise. But during the later 1880s and early 1890s, the Fellowship's journal, *Seed-time*, interspersed articles on Tolstoyan agrarian experiments and the instruction of children in secular ethics, with information regarding more immediate questions of the economic organization of society. Several prominent members of the Fellowship moved towards an increasingly critical analysis of the 'idleness', 'individualism', and sexual antagonism of the middle classes in contrast to the co-operative and productive relations of 'non-degraded' working-class men and women faced with the necessity of 'doing good honest work for [their] living'.[72]

By 1890, Clementina Black was using the pages of the journal to nudge members and friends of the Fellowship towards a more pragmatic response to such a perception of class division than aiming 'at weaving, spinning and dyeing for ourselves'. Far from sentimentalizing labour, Black's work with women's unions persuaded her that 'the modern commercial system needs to be abolished':

> we ought to pay, for the things we buy in shops, a price that covers the cost of their production and their distribution, allowing to every person engaged in these necessary processes a reasonable living wage, in the truest sense of the word.[73]

Although the Consumers' League for ethical shopping formed by Black was addressed to a politics of consumption she emphasized that such a campaign would allow a new state of labour to arise.[74] Black's work with the WTUL had convinced her that a certain amount of material security was

---

[71] Edith Lees, 'Women and the New Life', *Seed-time* (3 Jan. 1890), 6.
[72] Maurice Adams, 'The Mission of the New Fellowship', *Seed-time* (19 Jan. 1894), 1–2.
[73] Clementina Black, 'The Ethics of Shopping', *Seed-time* (6 Oct. 1890), 10–11.
[74] For an analysis of turn-of-the-century socialist feminism and the politics of consumption see June Hannam and Karen Hunt, *Socialist Women: Britain, 1880s–1920s* (London: Routledge, 2002), pp. 134–61.

necessary before women workers could engage in collective action and only some sort of co-operative production could ensure this security.

Like Black, Schreiner saw no simple solution to the question of woman and labour in the ideal of a simple life, free from what Carpenter termed the 'disease of modern civilisation'. Schreiner's 'The Woman Question' of 1899 is a text redolent of the heady modernity of the machine age: an age inevitably altered by the 'steam plough', the 'automatic reaper', the 'Krupp gun', and industrially baked bread delivered by motor-car. 'We do not ask', Schreiner wrote, 'that the wheels of time should reverse themselves, or the stream of life flow backwards . . . The past material conditions of life have gone forever.'[75] Schreiner had gained ample practical knowledge of the dehumanizing effects of labour on those women who did work under this late nineteenth-century capitalist system during her time in London and this knowledge prevented her easy assumption of utopianism in her socialist allegories composed during this period.

In the summer of 1887, Schreiner returned to London from Alassio and rented rooms in Gore Road overlooking Victoria Park in East London during one of the most momentous periods of labour activism which the city has ever witnessed.[76] The persistent misreading of Schreiner's brief residence in this salubrious row of grand houses—the acme of upward mobility for the East London lower–middle classes—as her living in the slums obscures the more complex nature of Schreiner's restless political iconoclasm.[77] As the park itself was the site of political rallies and speeches and the symbol of rational, respectable working-class leisure, Schreiner's brief stay distinguished her from sensation-seeking 'slummers' and earnest philanthropists at work further back down the tramline in Whitechapel. Here, as elsewhere, Schreiner's political engagements refused to conform to expected limits, not helping the 'residuum' but engaging with artisanal labour activists on their own territory through her long-standing friendship with Eleanor Marx and Margaret Harkness.

Marx herself became increasingly involved in labour organization after her experiences of that winter, commenting to Dollie Radford that 'in the streets here one sees so many starving people with hunger in every line of their faces that one cannot but be wretched' and turn that wretchedness into

---

[75] Schreiner, 'The Woman Question', p. 82.

[76] Schreiner wrote to Edward Carpenter on 8 June 1887, sending her new address at 50 Gore Road. A month later she left for a month-long trip to the North Yorkshire Moors, returning to Victoria Park again for less than a month before returning to Alassio. See SCL Carpenter, MSS 359/8–12.

[77] For examples of this misreading see Seth Koven, *Slumming: Sexual and Social Politics in Victorian London* (Princeton: Princeton University Press, 2004), p. 199.

action.[78] Whilst Schreiner differed from Marx in resisting a purely materialist solution to the inequities of capitalism, unlike the majority of her fellow
ethical idealists of the New Life in Bloomsbury boarding houses and cottages in Surrey, Schreiner's political consciousness took root in the particularities of place. Her socialism, like her feminism, was alert to the effects of
social and geographical location. Utopia was simply never enough of a
place for Schreiner.

Such consciousness of the geographical inscription of the inequalities of
capitalism is perhaps not surprising given Schreiner's own position in
Europe during the 1880s as a white South African woman born into a family that scraped by on the uncertain financial margins of the educated lower
middle classes. Schreiner's well-known restlessness, her constant search for
a place to call home during her time away from South Africa, reflects a
deeper sense of displacement from the social and geographical locations of
class and culture in 1880s Britain. It is, perhaps, this very dislocation which
enabled Schreiner to display such an unusual (and, for its recipients, frequently disturbing) passionate radical sympathy for the objects of her concern. Her intimacy with the Fabian socialist Edith Nesbit, which followed
the latter's revelations concerning her own, complex domestic situation, is
but one example of such personal identifications. Schreiner's drive to meet,
talk with, and reach out to women prostitutes in their homes is another case
of her political and emotional identification with those who embodied her
causes, coming to inhabit their places and imagine the lived experience of
such oppressions. The brief allegory 'I Thought I Stood', which Schreiner
composed during her time in Alassio, dramatizes this affective identification
between the woman of privilege and her 'sister, Woman . . . thrust . . . out
into the streets' by Man.[79] A woman goes to heaven to lodge a complaint
with God on behalf of her less fortunate sister, but he will not listen to her
at first. Although the narrator's robe is spotless, her feet are bloody from
walking over those beneath her in order to avoid the mire of the streets and
the angels cover their faces in shame. The narrator then returns to God's
throne a second time, hand in hand with the fallen woman, both covered in
the mire, and explains that 'I lay down by [my sister], and she put her arms
around my neck, and so I lifted her, and we two rose together' (128). It is
only after this moment of physical identification that God gives them both
the power to arraign their brother Man for his sexual predations.

For Karl Pearson, at least, such sentiments and passionate identifications
had no place in politics. In an address to the South Place Ethical Society in

---

[78] Eleanor Marx Aveling to Dollie Radford, 28 Dec. 1887, cit. Kapp, *Eleanor Marx*, p. 222.
[79] Schreiner, *Dreams*, p. 125.

1885, he had distinguished between two types of political enthusiasts and activists. The socialist state, he argued, needed to be ushered in by the efforts of the 'man of the study', gradually accruing knowledge of and political consensus for strategies such as the nationalization of capital. But, Pearson complained,

> how often does the man of the market-place rush by us proclaiming what he thinks an obvious truth, appealing to the blind passions of the ignorant mass of humanity, and drawing after him such a flood of popular energy that those germs of intellectual life and rational action which for years we may have been laboriously implanting disappear in the torrent![80]

Witnessing the increasing radicalization of labour in the East End during the late 1880s convinced Schreiner that her politics could never remain in this purely rational space of the study. In a letter to Havelock Ellis in January 1888, Schreiner explicitly identified herself with those 'enthusiasts of the marketplace' who had helped to move the masses in the labour demonstrations of the previous November: 'I want to go to Trafalgar Square and fight the enemies of Freedom of the hour wildly and get my head broken.'[81] Whilst Ellis and Pearson, she implied, might be happy sitting comfortably in the study working through the great social questions or 'grubbing out whether an old English dramatist put two dots over his *i*' when the 'world is *crashing* about you', this was not to be Schreiner's political mode.[82] 'In time of revolution' she decided, she would be in the marketplace with 'Eleanor' Marx, who had suffered considerable violence on 'Bloody Sunday' whilst leading a contingent from a Clerkenwell radical club to Trafalgar Square.[83] Writing to Mary Drew from Alassio in the midst of her composition of her socialist allegory 'The Sunlight Lay Across My Bed', Schreiner explicitly aligned herself with 'all my East End people' whom she felt 'so selfish to have left . . . & come here to the sunshine'.[84] Whilst Pearson and Ellis both moved further away from the question of labour which had appealed to them in the early 1880s, Schreiner's response to the labour demonstrations of the later 1880s was an increasing identification with that cause.

---

[80] Karl Pearson, *Enthusiasm of the Marketplace and of the Study: A Discourse delivered at South Place Chapel, Finsbury Sunday November 29th 1885* (South Place Religious Society, n.d. pamphlet), p. 10.

[81] Olive Schreiner to Havelock Ellis, 24 Jan. 1888. *Schreiner: Letters*, p. 133.

[82] Ibid.

[83] Ibid. Kapp, *Eleanor Marx*, pp. 224–34.

[84] Olive Schreiner to Mary Gladstone (Mrs Drew), BL Add. Mss. 46244 ff. 169. Letter dated 17 Nov. 1887, but internal evidence suggests that it should be dated Nov. 1888.

Schreiner's socialist allegories composed during this period grounded her politics in the affective power of the aesthetic. Pearson explicitly denigrated the aesthetic tendencies of the 'religion of socialism', scoffing at working towards an ideal that was merely 'some glorious poet-dreamed Utopia, the outcome of individual wishes, inspiration or prejudice'.[85] And yet by using the generic mode of allegory, rather than utopia, Schreiner created a work that both held out the affective vision of hope for a better future, and remained rooted in the particularities of the place of late nineteenth-century capitalism. Writing to Edward Carpenter, Schreiner commented: 'I feel if justice were done [Pearson] would have a share in any praise my work might have, even in the little dreams and allegories that seem so intensely unlike him, and which he might laugh at.'[86] Pearson argued that it was 'from the history of the past that the history of the immediate future must surely progress' and thus we must identify the socialist ideal.[87] Schreiner was, as Burdett has demonstrated so convincingly, deeply engaged with these evolutionary ideas of progress during the 1880s, but in 'The Sunlight Lay Across My Bed' she insisted upon the autonomy of the aesthetic ideal. If the highest human ideal of sexual and social relations was to be found anywhere then it was in the super-sensuous realm of the aesthetic.

III

As we have seen in the previous chapters the 'religion of socialism' in the 1880s and 1890s was articulated in a variety of non-realist literary forms such as romances, utopias, parables, and dreams. The use of parables and dreams created a formal link between the genres of socialism and the Christian religious tradition that the majority of socialist converts during this period had so painfully and recently left behind.[88] As numerous critics

---

[85] Pearson, 'Socialism and Sex', p. 429.

[86] Olive Schreiner to Edward Carpenter, 10 Jan. 1889. *Schreiner: Letters*, p. 146. Pearson himself seemed to acknowledge the place of such visionary work in political intervention, however, as he used an excerpt from Schreiner's 'The Lost Joy' as the epigraph to a reprinted version of his essay 'Socialism and Sex', p. 410. For Pearson's appreciation of the emotional truths of literature versus the true aesthetic satisfactions of science see Porter, *Karl Pearson*, pp. 45–6. Schreiner had published 'The Lost Joy' (composed in South Africa, before her departure for Europe) in the *New College Magazine*, Eastbourne. She reprinted it as the first allegory in *Dreams* (1890).

[87] Pearson, 'Socialism and Sex', p. 429.

[88] See, for example, a quasi-religious response to Schreiner's *Dreams* in the form of Dollie Radford's poem 'A Dream of "Dreams": To Olive Schreiner', in *A Light Load* (London: Elkin Matthews, 1891), pp. 63–4.

have pointed out, Schreiner herself adopted the cadences of her much-loved Bible in her own *Dreams* to harness the ancient form of prophetic discourse to new ends.[89] In 'The Sunlight Lay Across My Bed' Schreiner takes the form of the Christian allegorical dream tradition to explore something she could not represent at the time in rational prose argument and she only tentatively held together in *Woman and Labour* (1911). Whereas 'A Dream of Wild Bees' gives shape to an ideal of reproduction shared between the sexes, 'The Sunlight Lay Across My Bed' addresses the complicity of female desire with capitalist consumption and the need to reshape that desire itself for human progress.

Although Schreiner's text opens with the narrator falling asleep in contemporary London, what follows is not the total vision of a new world order familiar in utopias such as Morris's *News from Nowhere*. Instead a figure Schreiner calls God (writing to Carpenter she exclaimed 'if anyone can give me a better name for it I'll use it') shows the dreamer three visions of hell and three separate heavens.[90] The first hell is a place of stark gender divisions. Fair-seeming women draw down the branches of trees, appearing to kiss the fruit born upon them. But looking closer the narrator sees that the women are making 'a tiny wound in [the fruit] with their foreteeth', placing in poison which lies under their tongues and then closing the wound with their lips so that 'another may not eat'.[91] The origin of Schreiner's hell is thus woman's voracious erotic consumption: it is an allegorical gloss of the waking world of London at the very start of the text in which the dreamer hears wealthy women rolling home in their carriages and a prostitute laughing on the street corner at midnight. Whilst the women of hell foreshadow Schreiner's later biological analogy of female parasitism with the 'field-tick', as they suck and poison the fruit, the men seem to labour, but are merely digging concealed pitfalls for their fellows in an allusion to the world of competitive individualism.

The hell of capitalism is thus founded, in Schreiner's allegory, on privileged female consumption that poisons the fruits of labour so that others may not take their share. God only takes the dreamer on to the 'Banqueting

[89] See Laura Chrisman, 'Allegory, Feminist Thought and the Dreams of Olive Schreiner', in Tony Brown (ed.), *Edward Carpenter and Late Victorian Radicalism* (London: Frank Cass, 1990), pp. 126–51 (p. 127). Berkman, *Healing Imagination*; Rose Lovell Smith, 'Science and Religion in the Feminist Fin-de-Siècle and a New Reading of Olive Schreiner's *From Man to Man*', *Victorian Literature and Culture*, 29 (2001), 303–26.
[90] Olive Schreiner to Edward Carpenter, 1 April 1889. *Schreiner: Letters*, p. 153: 'I've got a little Socialist dream but you'll all say again it's not up to [the] mark because it's all about God. How can I help writing about God when there's nothing else in heaven or earth that I love and cling to? If anyone can give me another name for it I'll use it.'
[91] Schreiner, *Dreams*, p. 135.

House' of organized production after this first vision of the complicity of female consumption in sustaining capitalism. The Banqueting House is full of families drunk on the rich red wine that emerges from a press filled with the bodies of those who have not succeeded in the capitalist struggle. The drinkers refuse to see the welter of starving bodies scarce concealed from them behind a curtain and mystify the material basis of their vampiric feast. As one small white hand creeps from under the screen, the assembled drunkards stamp it out in an orgy of collective violence. Far from the consensual evolution advocated by Pearson, here Schreiner envisions the capitalist system as one founded on, and inevitably productive of, violent struggle between the parasitic bourgeoisie and the exploited proletariat. Laura Chrisman argues that Schreiner's use of the biological analogy of consumption in the allegory results in 'a kind of fetishism' which 'risks colluding with the very economy which it wishes to condemn'.[92] But Schreiner's interest in what Chrisman identifies as the 'superstructural effects' of the economy rather than the economy itself is an attempt to displace the stories of complacent benevolence through which her contemporaries lived with an alternative 'religion of socialism'.

In the final vision of hell God takes the dreamer on to witness the ruins of four former banqueting houses that still scar the landscape. Each is obliquely marked as a site of imperial domination: the first, with its 'seven hills', Rome; the second Athens; the third, with its grave marked by a 'crown of thorns', Jerusalem; the fourth, with its 'wide plain of sand', desert fox and broken, semi-legible monuments, an African empire reminiscent of Shelley's 'Ozymandias'. As Scott McCracken suggests, here Schreiner provides a remarkable insight into the interpolation of imperialism in the emergence of capitalism.[93] This is Schreiner's history: an allegory of how consumption and exploitation recuperate those very forces that once seemed ranged against it, whether in the shape of classical reason or Christian benevolence, to justify its renewed existence as 'progress'. In Schreiner's vision of contemporary British capitalist imperialism, Eve no longer eats the fruit of the tree of knowledge, but poisons it for others, Adam does not till the soil to bring forth goodness, but digs holes with evil intent. Those banqueting on surplus value conflate the feast at Cana with the Last Supper and ensure an endless supply of wine by drinking of the

---

[92] Chrisman, 'Allegory, Feminist Thought', p. 147.

[93] Scott McCracken, 'Stages of Sand and Blood: The Performance of Gendered Subjectivity in Olive Schreiner's Colonial Allegories', in Alice Jenkins and Juliet John (eds.), *Re-Reading Victorian Fiction* (London: Macmillan, 2000), pp. 145–59. McCracken reads the poem rather anachronistically as exploring the 'New Woman's experience of the city' in relation to colonialism (p. 146).

blood of their fellow men in an act of collective amnesia, rather than remembrance: 'Pour forth more wine upon us Lord', intone the feasters, 'More wine. More wine. More wine! Wine!! Wine!! Wine!!! Dear Lord!'(143).

If established Christianity has become part of the legitimating ritual of materialist consumption in nineteenth-century capitalism then Schreiner's route to heaven provides an alternative in ethical idealism. God shows the dreamer two bridges to heaven and mentions a third, invisible one, which leads 'straight upwards'. The names of the bridges are 'the Good, the True, the Beautiful' (159). The three heavens the dreamer encounters echo this idealist triad. In the first heaven men and women work together 'sometimes two men and sometimes two women, but mostly there was one man and one woman' (163), nurturing gardens with the light of their bodies and reverencing the maimed and the blind. In a celestial reworking of Edward Carpenter's ideals of a sexually radical agrarian commune, labouring in virtue and desiring comradeship brings forth the good of the earth. In the second heaven, by implication that of the True, men labour hard with picks to unearth bright stones from the earth, which they place into a gloriously beautiful crown of collective craft. The search for truth makes real wealth visible as the stones can only be seen by the light that labour itself brings to the brow of the working men. The dreamer is filled with desire to join this collective mining of truth:

> 'I too will work here; I too will set stones in the wonderful pattern; it shall grow beneath my hand. And if it be that, labouring here for years, I should not find one stone, at least I will be with the men that labour here' ... so great was my longing as I looked at the crown, I thought a faint light fell from my forehead also. (173)

In the aesthetic socialist visions of William Morris and Edward Carpenter, labour itself, even swinging a pickaxe and road-mending, as Morris suggests in *News from Nowhere,* becomes the somatic expression of the innate human desire to craft beauty from nature. But Schreiner's use of physical labour as an allegory for, rather than motive force of, social transformation addresses the gendered exclusions of the aesthetic of manly labour. It is not physical strength that enables these labourers to bring about a new world, but an earnest desire for truth: the woman scholar too can be a labourer in this heaven.

In the last heaven, that of the Beautiful, gender has been superseded. One figure stands alone and in an earlier version of the text, Schreiner underscored its transgressive, transgendered state as the phrase 'its breasts were the breasts of a woman' stood in place of the passage in brackets: 'Whether it were man or woman I could not tell; for [partly it seemed the

figure of a woman], but its limbs were the mighty limbs of a man'(175).[94]
Schreiner's intersexed ideal blurs reproduction and production in this heavenly body. Whilst the women of hell were defined by their mouths, sucking
the goods of the earth, in heaven the nurturing breasts of woman are married to the productive limbs of man: womanliness and manliness are con-
joined in this (re)productive ideal. God informs the dreamer that 'In the
least Heaven sex reigns supreme; in the higher it is not noticed; but in the
highest it does not exist'. The good works with and through liberated sexual desire; the search for truth transcends sex; the beautiful preserves its
absolute autonomy from such empirical categories. In the highest heaven
the product of labour differs from the visible goods of the previous two
heavens and is the model of the absolutely autonomous aesthetic, freed
from the material world. It is music that the final lone figure produces;
music of such unearthly beauty that it moves the dreamer to tears. Of all art
forms, music is that which cannot be reduced to the material of the sensuous world and is replete with unrepresentable affect.[95] Schreiner's heaven of
beauty is the home of the absolute sexless aesthetic and it retains its affective power and autonomy from the hell of capitalism. The dreamer, however, is unable to join in the song in heaven and returns to earth still
weeping.

It is that return to another day in London at the end of this allegory that
foregrounds Schreiner's use of literary form as a vehicle for a politicized aesthetic. For the very form of allegory, as opposed to utopia, is concerned with
the parallel mapping of the place of the abstract and the unfamiliar onto
daily experience; with finding the key that matches the reader's place and
destiny to the collective map of the allegory. Whilst utopias are by definition
concerned with embodying nowhere, allegories ask readers to interpret the
connections between an abstract ideal and their material daily experiences.
In revising *Dreams* for an American edition, Schreiner noted to her publisher that it was vital that the place of composition be noted at the end of
each allegory after a printer's error had omitted these from her first edition.[96] It was crucial, she felt, that 'Paris and London' stood at the end of
'The Sunlight Lay Across My Bed', placing the allegory in a specific time
and place: in two cities of high capitalist imperialism disturbed by the
return of the exiled Communards and the events of Bloody Sunday.

---

[94] BL Add. Mss. 70571, Havelock Ellis Papers, vol. xlviii A (printed version of *Dreams* with
author's emendations).
[95] On the place of music in 19th-cent. discussions of the aesthetic see Andrew Bowie,
Aesthetics and Subjectivity from Kant to Nietzsche, 2nd edn. (Manchester: Manchester
University Press, 2003), pp. 152–60, 221–45. More work remains to be done on Schreiner's
engagement with Hegelianism during this period.
[96] BL Add. Mss. 70571.

The final section of 'The Sunlight Lay Across My Bed' complements this insistence upon the material, historical location from which the allegory emerged. The dreamer wakes to hear the beat of hundreds of men and women's feet on their way to work: 'prostitutes, men and women, dragging their feet wearily after last night's debauch; artists with quick impatient footsteps; tradesmen for orders'. He wakes from the previous London night of feminized individual consumption to a world of labour (181). Together the feet beat a collective cry, 'We are seeking! We are seeking' and the cracked notes of a barrel organ in the street 'sobbed "The Beautiful, The Beautiful, the Beautiful"' (181–2). The dreamer recognizes this as the song from the highest heaven and, rather than mourn utopia, he laughs to see the streak of London sunlight on his bed.[97] He wakes to a world of labour in which he too can feel the affect of the beautiful and strive towards the good and the true with his fellows: 'I was glad the long day was before me' (182). That self which Schreiner felt too precious to renounce before the material demands of socialism can be freed into communal fellowship by the aesthetic ideal.

Pearson's vision of the socialist future during the 1880s had been one in which increasing sexual differentiation was accompanied by an acceptance that ethics and morality sprang from hereditary impulse and needed to be tutored by the study of science and history. Dismissing the idealist impulse of nineteenth-century philosophy on the basis that Kant and Hegel were 'petulant and irritable' individuals, whose ethics clearly did not inflect their personal morality, Pearson asserted that in his materialist ethics it was impossible for the ignorant and uneducated to be moral subjects.[98] Only the man of the study could pursue the knowledge that disclosed the future socialist state and develop a free-thinking rational morality. Schreiner's allegory rewrites Pearson's assertions at every level. The sexual division of labour that Pearson reads as race instinct Schreiner suggests is contingent upon the desiring organism of capitalism; the pursuit of the good, the true and the beautiful remains autonomous from the material world, available to all who can feel. The learned and the ignorant alike can join in Schreiner's ethical quest and the form of the allegory underscores this notion of an eth-ical and aesthetic democracy. As Liz Stanley suggests, for Schreiner, 'matters of genre and writing are also matters of principle, while her aesthetics are less about questions of ethics than they *are* her ethics; or, rather, her ethics

---

[97] Lovell-Smith points out that these same features of a ray of sunshine, a barrel organ, and a London street form the images of despair in Schreiner's novel, *From Man to Man*, but concludes that it is impossible to work out which scene is a rewriting of the other, given the revisions of this posthumously published work. 'Science and Religion', p. 320 n. 43.

[98] Pearson, *Enthusiasm of the Marketplace*, pp. 3–4.

and her aesthetics are each constitutive of the other'.[99] Schreiner's allegory frees the reading subject into the indeterminate space of interpretation and marks out that affective process as a politics in its own right. It demonstrates what Schreiner could not assert in her argumentative prose of the 1880s: that desire is subject to and an agent of political change; that the aesthetic will always retain some autonomy from material determinism; that individuals (especially women) will need to express a feeling self even in the midst of collective labour for a new world.

                                    IV

When Schreiner came to publish her extended essays 'The Woman Question' (1899) and *Woman and Labour* (1911), the brief allegory of female parasitism in 'The Sunlight Lay Across My Bed' had become the central plank of her analysis. The modern female parasite is a contingent creature in these essays, sucking off the juices of capitalist man to form a sink of non-productive wealth. Schreiner explores the uneasy complicity of female desire with capitalism and thus makes sexual desire seem itself to be a historically contingent force. By founding her argument on female parasitism, Schreiner's works construct a continuum between the prostitute, the desires of the idle dependent wife, and the accrual of unearned wealth under capitalism. Mutually reinforcing, Schreiner's vision of capitalism is of a feminized desiring organism, endlessly consuming and capable only of reproducing itself. It is precisely because of Schreiner's indictment of female sexuality under capitalism that her vision of the future in 'The Woman Question' is, in the end, so non-prescriptive. Schreiner's demand on behalf of woman, *'Give us labour and the training which fits us for labour!'*, marks the beginning of a process that should, for her, reshape the 'nature' of woman, liberating the contemporary determination of passive female sexual and economic consumption into as diverse an array of autonomous desiring subjects as there are forms of labour. For Schreiner, women needed to make selves through labour before their sexuality could be seen as a fact of nature, rather than a trick of capitalism.

In the later sections of *Woman and Labour* Schreiner attempts to redefine the meanings of 'labour' to offer a vision of 'virile' womanhood labouring side by side in community with men, in which men and women are both producers for and reproducers of the future race. 'The perfect ideal of that which the modern woman desires to be', she claims, is 'labouring and virile,

---

[99] Stanley, *Imperialism*, p. 135.

womanhood, free, strong, fearless and tender.'[100] History, Schreiner suggests, has not only successively deprived women of their creative involvement with the lesser arts of domestic life, turning them into mere sex-parasites, but also alienated women from their innate productivity. We must, she suggests—in a truly remarkable image—reclaim 'men's bodies as our woman's work of art'.[101]

As Regenia Gagnier argues, such a reclassification of women's biological reproduction as ethical and aesthetic production counters both the spectre of female 'sex parasitism' and the 'effeminate' aesthetics of consumption.[102] One of the most disturbing passages to appear in both 'The Woman Question' and *Woman and Labour* reflects some of the strain in Schreiner's attempts to construct such a continuum of virile womanhood, reproduction, and the aesthetics of production. Schreiner identifies the 'curled darling' of the drawing-room, 'scented and languid', with his delicate tastes as a 'repulsive . . . product of decay' born of parasitic womanhood: 'it is only the scent of his mother's boudoir that we smell in his hair'. Such a turn of argument should, as Sally Ledger has argued, alert us to the latent homophobia of Schreiner's analysis.[103] But there is an important distinction to be made here between Schreiner's emphasis upon production and labour and, for example, the Marx Avelings' argument that late marriage and homosocial culture led to the 'unnatural' 'horror' of the 'effeminate' man and the 'masculine woman'.[104] Schreiner attacks the effeminate dandy because he is a consuming pleasure-seeker, rather than a productive labourer: he is the metonym of a society—and crucially an aesthetic—that is founded on parasitic consumption rather than labouring production. The troubling excess of Schreiner's figuring of the effete man can thus be traced back to a concern at the heart of her own creative work. For Schreiner, female parasitism (re)produces the consumerist male aesthete and that aesthete threatens her conceptualization of the aesthetic as the symbol of morality, lying beyond sex, class, and the marketplace.

By the end of the nineteenth century the woman's movement and the labour movement seemed to Schreiner to present some parallels, but remained fundamentally distinct. Woman's problem was *a* labour problem, as she needed to determine herself by and shape her consciousness through productive independent labour, but it could not be assimilated with *the*

---

[100] Schreiner, *Woman and Labour*, p. 258.
[101] Ibid. 174.
[102] Regenia Gagnier, *The Insatiability of Human Wants: Economics and Aesthetics in Market Society* (Chicago: University of Chicago Press, 2000), p. 87.
[103] Sally Ledger, *The New Woman: Fiction and Feminism at the Fin de Siècle* (Manchester: Manchester University Press, 1997), p. 76.
[104] Marx Aveling, *The Woman Question*, p. 18.

labour problem. *Woman and Labour* neither elides the distinction between socialism and the woman question nor is it simply, as Gagnier suggests, 'the culmination of the liberal feminist or women's movement's appeal to put women on the market equally with men'.[105] A Pearsonian policy in favour of the protection of women as potential mothers, as Schreiner suggests in a short story from 1892, would inevitably leave them in a state of perpetual infantilism, whilst all around them others were sacrificed on the altar of their insularity.[106] The rising tide of support within the labour movement for restrictive employment practices and a so-called 'family wage' for the male breadwinner threatened to extend parasitism to 'millions of [working-class] women to-day leading healthy and active lives'.[107] On the other hand, Schreiner's passionate interestedness, her defence of woman's labour as both somatic production and the origin of idealism worked against the notion of the autonomous liberal subject at the heart of the nineteenth-century women's movement.

Schreiner returns to analogy in *Woman and Labour* to hold together the two terms of her title in the face of these tense relations between the woman's movement and socialism in the early twentieth century. Schreiner takes the equation of manhood, labour, and artistry so familiar to her from the socialist lectures and debates of the 1880s and uses it as a trope for exploring the situation of middle-class women intellectuals and political activists. Describing the efforts of feminist reformers over the previous decades, Schreiner allegorizes the medieval cathedral builders: an image which, as we have seen, is at the heart of both Morris's history of hope and that of his romantic radical forebears, Ruskin and Carlyle:

> [women reformers] labour on patiently year after year at some poor little gargoyle of a franchise bill . . . They carve away all their lives to produce a corbel of some new and beautiful condition in sexual relations, in the end to find it break under the chisel . . . It is through the labours of these myriad toil-ers, each working in her minute sphere, with her own small outlook, and out of endless failures and miscarriages, that at last the enwidened and beautiful relations of woman to life must rise.[108]

In these latter parts of *Woman and Labour*, Schreiner adopts and revises the socialist aesthetics of manly labour associated with Morris and Carpenter to provide a vital way into the vision of bodily toil for middle-class woman

---

[105] Gagnier, *Insatiability*, p. 84.

[106] 'The Policy in Favour of Protection' (1892) parallels the selfishness of a sheltered young woman in the marriage market with the Australian Colonies' decision to pursue a policy of economic protectionism.

[107] Schreiner, *Woman and Labour*, p. 119.

[108] Ibid. 143.

artists and intellectuals at work in the late nineteenth century. Paradoxical though it may seem, Morris's equation of the artist with the productive virile man provided a means for middle-class women artists to insert themselves into a history of productivity and engaged social action. If a working man breaking stones on the road could, under the right conditions of hopeful labour, be a producer of aesthetic pleasure and symbol of revolution, then the continuum, Schreiner suggests, could work the other way too. If through labour a man can participate in the transforming power of art, then through art and politics a woman can know the effortful labouring life that she seeks to transform.

It is no coincidence that in the later sections of *Woman and Labour* Schreiner incorporates several of these super-sensible aesthetic allegories which she could not assimilate into her 'sex book' during the 1880s. Bringing the aesthetic back into conjunction with politics—and marking that aesthetic as a space of production, rather than consumption—offered some hope of making a substantial alliance out of the uneasy analogies of progress offered by the socialist and woman's movements in the early twentieth century. Despite Schreiner's unbridled loathing for Edward Aveling, his early review of *The Story of an African Farm* might then hold some truth. Schreiner, too, had faith in the progress of modern science, but her science both was a 'dear Mistress' and a 'true god', generating moments of desire, vision, and transcendence as well as obedience to that contemporary Leviticus, Pearson's *The Grammar of Science*.

4

Socialism, Masculinity, and the 'Faddist' Sage: Edward Carpenter and George Bernard Shaw

In May 1907 a new series of the journal the *New Age* was launched under the editorship of two Fabian socialists, Alfred Orage and Holbrook Jackson. Under the banner of 'An Independent Socialist Review of Politics, Literature and Art', the weekly paper established an iconoclastic forum where established socialist thinkers such as Edward Carpenter and George Bernard Shaw found their work rubbing up against contributions from a new generation of writers including Ezra Pound, Katherine Mansfield, and John Middleton Murry.[1] In their eagerness to underline the fresh start marked by their relaunch (a fresh start seen by many present-day critics as the foundation of the genre of 'little magazines' of literary modernism), Orage and Jackson published a series of letters congratulating them on their venture.[2] One letter in particular recommended an editorial policy that would separate the journal definitively from the host of socialist literary periodicals that had sprung up and died away since the resurgence of British socialism in the early 1880s. 'Above all', wrote H. Hamilton Fyfe, 'don't let the paper be amateurish and faddy. Socialism wants a wider interpretation. It must not be associated with Jaeger clothing and vegetarianism.'[3]

Fyfe's comments could be read without too much difficulty as a pointed attack on George Bernard Shaw, who, as we shall see, combined his dominance of the literary marketplace of socialist criticism at this time with his

---

[1] See Ian Britain, *Fabianism and Culture: A Study in British Socialism and the Arts* (Cambridge: Cambridge University Press, 1982), pp. 168–72, for Orage, Jackson, and the Fabian Arts Group in the early 20th cent.; Tom Steele, *Alfred Orage and the Leeds Arts Club, 1893–1923* (Aldershot: Scolar, 1990), p. 137. See also the digitized text and resources of the Modernist Journals Project, Brown University: http://www.modjourn.brown.edu.

[2] Ann Ardis, *Modernism and Cultural Conflict, 1880–1922* (Cambridge: Cambridge University Press, 2002), pp. 143–71; Wallace Martin, *The New Age under Orage: Chapters in English Cultural History* (Manchester: Manchester University Press, 1967).

[3] H. H. Fyfe, letter in *The New Age*, 1 n.s. (1907), 19.

carefully staged iconography as poster-boy for Dr Jaeger's Sanitary Woollen Clothing System and the benefits of vegetarian living. But when the repeated jibes aimed at sandal-wearing, 'Jaegerism', and vegetarianism which are scattered elsewhere in the pages of the *New Age* during the period 1907–14 are added up it seems that there was something wider at stake here than an *ad hominem* criticism of one figure in the socialist landscape. The tag of 'faddism' had come to mark off the particular type of idealist ethical socialism home-grown during the 1880s which, as we have seen, had such an influence upon writers such as Olive Schreiner. This radical idealism was left in the years before the First World War standing uncomfortably between pragmatic and increasingly dominant Labourism on the one hand, and 'scientific' socialism on the other. In this chapter I explore here how the ethical socialist movement of this earlier period opened out spaces for the exploration and discussion of the masculine body through such 'fads': spaces that were closed off within socialist discourse and became embarrassed silences with the rise of Marxist scientific materialism in the early twentieth century. Whilst the aesthetics of labour offered Schreiner the means to dream of 'virile' feminine production and artistry, this chapter examines how the 'fads' associated with late nineteenth-century socialists offered a means for male writers to negotiate the tensions between their political beliefs and their profession as men of letters.

Understanding how and why socialism became intertwined with the belief systems and practices of vegetarianism, 'Jaegerism', and sandal-wearing in the first place leads back to the context of what Stephen Yeo has characterized as the 'religion of socialism' at the end of the nineteenth century.[4] During the period from around 1883 to about 1896 membership flourished within newly established socialist organizations such as the Social Democratic Federation, the Clarion movement, the Fabian Society, William Morris's Socialist League, and the Fellowship of the New Life. As Yeo argues, this period of socialist activism did not just prefigure the later formation of the Labour Party, but possessed 'its own special dynamism' in which the concerns for the ethical transformation of the individual and the aesthetic rejuvenation of the arts shared platform space with—and for thinkers such as Morris and Carpenter, were indivisible from—economic analysis.[5] The concerns that brought the Black and Ford sisters and Olive Schreiner through the culture of metropolitan club life into political engagement emerged, as we have seen, from both such ethical ideals and the all-too-evident inequities of the capitalist system. In this epoch of the 'religion

---

[4] Stephen Yeo, 'A New Life: The Religion of Socialism in Britain, 1883–1896', *History Workshop Journal*, 4 (1977), 5–55.
[5] Ibid. 7.

of socialism', looking inwards to the effects of capitalist modernity on the individuated subject through the lens of romantic philosophical idealism was coupled together with a growing acceptance that the organization of the means of production and distribution was the engine of historical change.

I

It was only around 1882 that individuals and societies which had clustered together around such disparate interests as secularism, Henry George's proposal for land nationalization, Ruskinian criticisms of the 'illth' of capitalism, and the works of American transcendentalists such as Ralph Waldo Emerson, found a new way forward under a banner of socialism. There was an ecstatic idealism prevalent in the movement and its new converts that stemmed from its origins in romanticist thought: a belief that casting off the false accretions of capitalism and returning to honest labour with nature was the only hope for the future.[6] With this idealism went a new conviction that the great change was bound to come soon in the face of the industrial unrest of the latter half of the 1880s—a conviction that arose from the dissemination of Marxist historical materialism through the agency of H. M. Hyndman's Social Democratic Federation and its journals.

For some believers at this moment 'when we were all socialists more or less', as the Independent Labour Party activist Isabella Ford put it in her tellingly titled novel *On the Threshold*, the prospect of utopia as a result of the reorganization of production and distribution meant that all more individual, embodied issues could be deferred:[7]

> I remember once recommending a friend of mine, who was very full of the Socialism of the early eighties, to set to work & qualify himself in medicine & surgery. He replied that he had thought of it, but as the period of qualification was four years, and he was convinced that 'the revolution' would come within eighteen months, he had given up the idea as impracticable. When I pointed out to him that even under Socialism we should still need surgeons, he was taken aback, post-revolutionary socialism having presented itself to his imagination as a condition in which no more needs or difficulties would exist—in short a *heavenly* condition.[8]

---

[6] On the debt of British socialism to American transcendentalism see Mark Bevir, 'British Socialism and American Romanticism', *English Historical Review*, 110 (1995), 878–901.

[7] Isabella Ford, *On the Threshold* (London: Edward Arnold, 1895), p. 29.

[8] *Bernard Shaw: Collected Letters*, ed. Dan H. Laurence, 4 vols. (London: Max Reinhardt, 1965–88), ii. 145. Subsequent references to *Shaw: CL*.

Even by 1900 Shaw could happily mock the millenarianism of 1880s social-ism. But when, for instance, the mission of the ethical socialists who formed the Fellowship of the New Life in the early 1880s is given a less conde-scending reading, a rather different story emerges. Far from the health of the body being a minor issue to be resolved with all else after the revolution, questions of embodiment—and especially of the embodiment of bourgeois masculinity—were central to the inquiry into revolutionary social change. As James Ramsay MacDonald (the future Labour Prime Minister) empha-sized in his editorial for the Fellowship's journal, *Seed-time*, standing 'some-what aloof, although in sympathy with the ideals of the [other] Socialist societies', the Fellowship 'felt that it had to insist upon the necessity of moral reform, as well as political and economic reform'.[9] Moreover MacDonald was convinced that the Fellowship's insistence upon individual ethical reform in the present, as well as economic revolution and reform in the future, was gaining increasing ground within the socialist movement as a whole towards the end of the century.

For many socialists associated with the Fellowship, vegetarianism and dress reform were a tangible means of acting upon this ethical reformist agenda of the 'religion of socialism'. Where the Fellowship's founding father, Thomas Davidson, exhorted his readers to pursue the higher goods of altruism and the simple life, members renouncing meat, wearing sandals, or Jaeger's loosely structured woollen garments, visibly dismantled the ornate structures of bourgeois domestic life and signalled a reaching out beyond the self to comradeship with others. Such practices were framed as a means of unravelling the boundaries between man and animal nature by planting one's feet firmly in the soil of the earth and absorbing in new life through the extra pores of stockinette woollens. H. S. Salt, who had been forced to resign his post as a master at Eton for his socialist activities, claimed that vegetarianism in particular was 'inter-locked and inter-dependent' with the socialist movement's struggle for freedom.[10] Vegetarianism, he asserted was nothing less than 'Progressiveness in diet', freeing man from the cravings for meat consequent upon advanced capitalism and returning him to the humane farinaceous diet of the peasants of the past.[11]

It was Edward Carpenter, the former clergyman who had adopted the simple life on a Derbyshire smallholding in the early 1880s, who became the most articulate voice within the Fellowship for this view of the body and its

[9] James Ramsay MacDonald, 'The New Fellowship', *Seed-time*, 12 (1892), 1–3 (p. 1).
[10] H. S. Salt, *The Logic of Vegetarianism* (London: Ideal Publishing Union, 1899), p. 104; Stephen Winsten, *Salt and his Circle with a Preface by George Bernard Shaw* (London: Hutchinson, 1951).
[11] Salt, *Logic*, pp. 107, 14.

relationship to socialism. For Carpenter, advanced capitalist civilization itself was a form of disease, slowly killing the body by encasing and invading it with 'enfeeblement, obscuration, duplicity'.[12] 'As for the feet which have been condemned to their leathern coffins so long that we are almost ashamed to look at them', he concluded at the tail end of his lecture to the Fellowship in January 1886, 'there is still surely a resurrection possible for them'. Going barefoot 'as the Irish do', or wearing sandals, was a means of bringing revolutionary new life to the body and identifying with the outcast and rejected, for 'Democracy which redeems the lowest and most despised of the people, must redeem also the most menial and despised members and organs of the body'. 'Effeminated as our feet are', he added, there was still hope that naked contact with the pleasures of the soil would restore them to freedom, 'and so the little toe, like the proverbial worm, though nearly crushed, may at last turn and revenge itself on a civilisation whose oppression it has too long endured'.[13] The sexual class politics of Carpenter's revolution of the toes receives due attention shortly. First, however, it is worth placing Carpenter alongside another socialist, vegetarian dress reformer of the 1880s who has a very different critical history.

During the late 1880s George Bernard Shaw regularly escaped the rigours of the life of journalism in London for weekends in the Surrey hills. He went to stay with his friends, fellow 'Shelleyans and Humanitarians' and convinced vegetarians Kate and Henry S. Salt in their cottage in Tilford.[14] Another frequent visitor there was Edward Carpenter. Sporting the sandals made by Carpenter's friend George Adams, the two visitors would sit and play 'piano duets . . . making a fearful noise with Wagner' and acting as '"Sunday husbands" to [Kate Salt]'.[15] In later years Shaw wrote dismissively to Salt of 'that ultra-civilized impostor, the ex-Clergyman of Millthorpe' and sought to distinguish his own brand of Fabian socialist thought from that of the 'Noble Savage' Carpenter as far as possible.[16] A few years earlier though, the two as with so many others of the metropolitan middle-class socialist circle converged, upon the surface at least, in the display of radical political identity through dress and diet. Whilst Carpenter's sandals liberated the feet on a pattern imported from India, Shaw's Jaeger suit, sold to

---

[12] Edward Carpenter, *Civilisation: Its Cause and Cure and Other Essays* (London: Swan Sonnenschein, 1889), p. 14.

[13] Edward Carpenter, *England's Ideal and Other Papers on Social Subjects* (London: Swan Sonnenschein, 1887), p. 94.

[14] Winsten, *Salt*, p. 9; George Bernard Shaw, 'A Sunday in the Surrey Hills', *Pall Mall Gazette* (1888).

[15] Winsten, *Salt*, p. 10.

[16] *Shaw: CL*, ii. 348.

Figure 1. Edward Carpenter in the porch at Millthorpe, wearing sandals. Photograph by Emery Walker, 1905. Sheffield City Libraries, Carpenter Collection Box 8/31a.

him by Austrian political refugee Andreas Scheu, fulfilled his desire for all-over bodily 'cleanliness and porousness'.[17] So Shaw rose to prominence in the London political and literary scene in the late 1880s as a 'Jaegerized butterfly', resembling, as Frank Harris recalled, 'nothing but a forked radish in a worsted bifurcated stocking'.[18]

For the Salts, Shaw, and Carpenter, experimenting with vegetarianism was in part a means of identifying themselves with a well-established nineteenth-century radical tradition. H. S. Salt drew together a pantheon of vegetarian thinkers in the preface to his essays reprinted from the *Vegetarian* as a means of commending the diet to his readers' serious consideration. 'Thoreau, Wagner and Tolstoy' featured as the more modish later nineteenth-century examples, but it was Shelley who headed the list.[19] Salt's own biography of Shelley, 'Poet and Pioneer', did its utmost to reclaim a virile, radical vegetarian Shelley as a driving force behind what one recent critic has termed 'the revolution of taste' of the early nineteenth century.[20] Shaw, too, claimed that he first came to vegetarianism through reading Shelley on the subject in 1881, whilst he circulated between radical liberal and Christian socialist debating societies in London.[21]

Although scarcely acknowledged by either Salt or Shaw, vegetarianism had remained a significant force in radical non-conformist circles throughout the nineteenth century. Kathryn Gleadle's recent work has disclosed how women's involvement with, for example, the Manchester-based Vegetarian Society in the middle decades of the nineteenth century sustained a radical political education in middle-class dissenting homes in the fallow years that followed the decline of Chartism.[22] Vegetarianism, anti-vivisection, and the temperance movement were closely allied avenues through which middle-class women asserted the need for reform in the public sphere also: it was a fleshless diet, several authors asserted in the 1870s, that would douse down excessive passions, encourage sympathy with our

---

[17] *Shaw CL*, i. 840.

[18] Frank Harris, *Bernard Shaw: An Unauthorized Biography Based on First-Hand Information* (New York: Simon & Schuster, 1931), p. 103.

[19] Salt, *Logic*, p. ii.

[20] Henry Stephens Salt, *Percy Bysshe Shelley: Poet and Pioneer* (London: W. Reeves, 1896); Timothy Morton, *Shelley and the Revolution in Taste: The Body and the Natural World* (Cambridge: Cambridge University Press, 1994).

[21] Michael Holroyd, *Bernard Shaw*, i. *1856–1898: The Search for Love* (London: Chatto & Windus, 1988), p. 84.

[22] Kathryn Gleadle, 'The Age of Physiological Reformers: Rethinking Women and Domesticity in the Age of Reform', in A. Burns and J. Innes (eds.), *Rethinking the Age of Reform: Britain, 1780–1850* (Cambridge: Cambridge University Press, 2003).

fellow creatures, and thus prove 'the Radical Cure for Intemperance' and other ills of modern urban society.[23] But Shaw was careful to distinguish his vegetarian beliefs from a feminized, compassionate strand of thought. According to Salt, Shaw 'disliked vegetarians of the flowery and sentimental sort; for instance, [Dr] Anna Kingsford', who claimed to have cured herself of tuberculosis through vegetarianism and whose thesis, 'The Perfect Way in Diet', combined theosophy and Pasteurism in advocating this universal panacea.[24]

Both Carpenter and Shaw styled their 'fads' as forms of virility in opposition to such 'sentimentalism', negotiating late nineteenth-century anxieties of bourgeois masculinity in the process.[25] As middle-class men, as writers and critics, and, perhaps above all, as self-declared socialists, Carpenter and Shaw worked within a complex of competing models of masculinity in the last decades of the nineteenth century. Numerous recent studies have argued that the works of many male writers in the post-romantic period display an unease as to whether intellectual labour qualified as quite manly enough for the age of progress.[26] The dominant nineteenth-century understanding of middle-class manliness and 'character' emphasized accumulation and action, self-denial and foresight: a continual striving in the world of work to provide for the space of private affections at home.[27] Such a model of manliness was difficult to reconcile with the life of letters. James Eli Adams's

[23] Henry Fowler, *Vegetarianism the Radical Cure for Intemperance* (New York: n.publ., 1879); see also Brian Harrison, *Peaceable Kingdom: Stability and Change in Modern Britain* (Oxford: Oxford University Press, 1982), ch. 2.

[24] Winsten, *Salt*, p. 216. See also Anon., 'Obituary: Dr Anna Kingsford', *The Vegetarian Messenger and Dietetic Reformer*, 1 n.s. (1887), 98–100. Kingsford's remarkable career included presidency of the Theosophical Society in 1883. Annie Besant, a one-time close ally of Shaw's in the London socialist scene and a fellow Fabian, also became a theosophist in the early 1890s and her work on vegetarianism and theosophy contains a similar fusion of materialist microbial theory and a belief in the magnetic powers of fear and pain in animals to affect human subjects' health: see Annie Besant, *Vegetarianism in the Light of Theosophy* (Benares: Theosophical Society, 1895). Vegetarianism as a cure for tuberculosis found a new promoter in the shape of Dr Paul Carton in early 20th-cent. France, although he distanced himself from any radical tradition of dissenting thought: see Arouna Ouedraogo, 'Food and the Purification of Society: Dr Paul Carton and Vegetarianism in Interwar France', *Social History of Medicine*, 14 (2001), 223–45.

[25] For an analysis of the class and gender dynamics of the broader vegetarian movement in this period see James Gregory, 'The Vegetarian Movement in Britain, 1840–1901' (unpublished doctoral thesis, University of Southampton, 2002), ch. 6.

[26] See, for example, James Eli Adams, *Dandies and Desert Saints: Styles of Victorian Masculinity* (Ithaca, NY: Cornell University Press, 1995); Frederick Kirchoff, *William Morris: The Construction of a Male Self, 1856–1872* (Athens, Ohio: Ohio University Press, 1990).

[27] Stefan Collini, *Public Moralists: Political Thought and Intellectual Life in Britain, 1850–1930* (Oxford: Clarendon, 1991), pp. 186–96.

influential work has suggested that as a reaction against this unease a disparate array of nineteenth-century male writers were rhetorically affiliated: such diverse figures as Charles Kingsley and Walter Pater, he suggests, converged in the construction of their vocation in the arts as an 'ascetic regime' and as a distinctively masculine self-discipline.[28]

Edward Carpenter's theory that asceticism in diet and dress would open out a new life of aesthetics grounded on homosexual 'comradeship' with a 'lusty, unpresentable pal' is thus in certain respects, as I shall argue, the offspring of the affinity Eli Adams identifies between Kingsley's muscular Christianity and Pater's Hellenistic aestheticism.[29] A new life of art and beauty awaited those who schooled their bodies with desire for virile labouring manhood. When it comes to rigorous asceticism, few could ever want to rival Shaw in the 1880s and 1890s, who during those years carefully orchestrated the public performance of both his spartan gruel-centred diet and his subsequent necrosis in 1898 brought on by excessive work. Yet the very performative iteration of this self-discipline by Shaw was a dandification of the ascetic regime in itself, begging an audience to appreciate the aesthetic quality of such 'manly' self-denial and self-suppression.[30] In the final section of this chapter I will explore how this performance of asceticism twined together with Shaw's biological interpretation of the 'earnestness' embodied by an earlier generation of cultural critics and thus modified the rhetoric of the 'manly' sage in the last decades of the century.

It is in the context of Shaw and Carpenter's socialist beliefs, however, that competing representations of masculine embodiment are most visible and striking. The spread of socialism amongst artists and writers in the 1880s and 1890s laid a new stress on the body of the labouring man as the grounds both of political analysis and of hope for aesthetic regeneration. Thomas Carlyle and John Ruskin had both drawn upon the figures of medieval hand craftsmen as a means of exploring manly artistic labour outside capitalism and criticizing the effects of the age of progress earlier in the century. It was, however, the series of lectures that William Morris delivered after his conversion to socialism that figured a return to the 'definite sensuous pleasure' of the labour of the hand as a utopian hope for the future of aesthetics after the revolution, rather than a site of nostalgic return.[31] For

---

[28] Adams, *Dandies*, p. 2.

[29] Ibid. 150–4.

[30] See Diana Maltz, *British Aestheticism and the Urban Working Classes, 1870–1900: Beauty for the People* (Basingstoke: Palgrave, 2005), pp. 93–6, for a parallel example of the aestheticization of ascetism.

[31] William Morris, 'The Aims of Art', CW, xxiii. 84.

Morris, as we have seen, all art under present capitalist organization was pretty much doomed: mere 'sham' 'carried on by dilettanti fine gentlemen and ladies' in 'the carefully guarded interiors of our aesthetic drawing-rooms, unreal and foolish'.[32] The only hope for the arts—and for free manhood—lay in a complete transformation of the means of production and distribution when all would take their part in the labour of the commonwealth. The nastier the work, the more vividly would the individual be reborn into a manly world of art through the pleasure of physical labour. As we saw in Chapter 1, Morris thus constructs an aesthetic continuum which places the muscular, manly labour of the road-mender on the same scale (if at the opposite end) as the artist.

Within the socialist circles of Shaw and Carpenter in the 1880s, therefore, masculinity, labour, artistry, and embodiment were bound up together at the heart of the cause. Whilst their own manliness was under question as the idle effeminated bourgeois production of capitalism, the muscular labouring bodies of working men were held up as the proletarian engine of revolution and the rebirth of the arts. Ascetic regimes conceived as an intellectual discipline, leaving the body to one side, were no longer sufficient to affirm the manliness of the middle-class socialist man of letters in the 1880s and 1890s. Instead, faddism provided a means of theorizing and working through the body itself in reframing radical masculinity. For both Carpenter and Shaw, as we shall see, vegetarianism and dress reform offered a means of positioning their embodiment in relation to the effortful muscular struggle of the labouring man. These practices were imagined in the context of Lamarckian evolutionary theory as labours of the will; acts of intellectual desire, which nevertheless were seen to have material effects on the bodies of future generations.

II

'The Stupid Old Body'
Do not pay too much attention to the stupid old Body.
. . .
Why, then instead of the body becoming like you, you will become like the body—
Incredibly stupid and unformed—going back in the path of evolution—you too with fish-mouth and toad-belly, and imprisoned in your own members, as it were an Ariel in a blundering Caliban.

---

[32] Ibid. 91, 93.

> Therefore quite lightly and decisively at each turning point in the path
> leave your body a little behind—
> With its hungers and sleeps, and funny little needs and vanities—pay-
> ing no attention to them;
> Slipping out at least a few steps in advance, till it catch you up again,
> Absolutely determined not to be finally bound or weighted down by it,
> Or fossilized into one set form—
> Which alone after all is Death.[33]

Edward Carpenter's role in rethinking sexual embodiment and theorizing homosexuality—or 'Uranism' as he termed it—has received welcome attention in the past few decades. The republication of his works by the Gay Men's Press and enlightening studies by the likes of Sheila Rowbotham and Jeffrey Weeks in the late 1970s and early 1980s coincided with the decline of Marxist orthodoxy as attention shifted to alternative radical histories—of gender and sexuality—within the academy and beyond.[34] To some extent, however, these recuperative studies have displaced Carpenter from the central role he played in promulgating such theories of the body to a widespread socialist audience in the 1880s and 1890s. For example, Scott McCracken's otherwise enlightening reading of Carpenter's poem *Towards Democracy* argues that it should be interpreted as primarily a closed 'discourse between men', elaborating the representations of male same-sex desire explored by Carpenter in his private correspondence with Walt Whitman and John Addington Symonds.[35] This reading is difficult to reconcile with the fact that sections of *Towards Democracy*, like that one cited above, were chanted communally and responded to ecstatically at socialist gatherings mixed by sex and class nationwide during the 1880s and 1890s.[36] Carpenter's writings on desire are striking precisely because his explorations of sexualities are not couched in secrecy: even after the passing of Labouchere amendment outlawing homosexual acts in 1885 and the trial of Oscar Wilde in 1895, his lectures on 'homogenic' love, among other subjects, reached a wide audience. In later years Carpenter seemed somewhat bemused that he was considered the 'special prey' of 'faddists of all sorts and kinds' as a result, who would make pilgrimages to his smallholding and insist on him 'join-

---

[33] Edward Carpenter, *Towards Democracy* (London: Swan Sonnenschein, 1892).
[34] Sheila Rowbotham and Jeffrey Weeks, *Socialism and the New Life: The Personal and Sexual Politics of Edward Carpenter and Havelock Ellis* (London: Pluto, 1977); Tony Brown (ed.), *Edward Carpenter and Late Victorian Radicalism* (London: Frank Cass, 1990), p. 14.
[35] Scott McCracken, 'Writing the Body: Edward Carpenter, George Gissing and Late-Nineteenth Century Realism', in Brown (ed.), *Carpenter*, pp. 178–204 (p. 183).
[36] Yeo, 'New Life', pp. 12, 29.

ing their crusades', but the appeal of Carpenter's representation of the body to a wide array of such causes lay in its very plasticity.[37]

Carpenter's discussion of the 'Urning' or 'intermediate sex' was central to his representation of the desiring body and hence his vision of the social-ist future, as I shall argue shortly. However, it was his aestheticization of a Lamarckian model of evolution that led primarily to his adulation within the 'religion of socialism'. The simplification of diet and dress was nothing less than the primary means of allowing the desires of the individual to reshape the future race into a more transparent vehicle of the 'cosmic con-sciousness', of shattering the 'chrysalis' that was modern material man and releasing the potential of the ideal 'imago' of the human trapped within.[38] The fads which are all too easily brushed over as 'alternative lifestyles' tacked on to the important business of socialism, were in fact perceived as an important means by which individual ethical actions could pave the way to a new society. Far removed as they might be by class and gender from the proletarian struggle, readers of Carpenter's works were exhorted that they too could set their wills to work on their 'stupid old body', reshaping it to give birth to the new order, rather than waiting for historical processes beyond their own control.

Rejecting the purely material determinism of Darwinism and 'modern science', Carpenter provided his own selective interpretation of Lamarck, the 'true poet' of evolution, in which the desiring self took centre stage in the development of the race.[39] By translating Lamarck's *besoin*, or need—the driving force behind species modification—as desire, Carpenter was able to sketch out a thoroughly intentionalist and idealist model of development. Change of any sort, Carpenter argued, was 'not accretive, but exfoliatory', beginning in the 'mental region' and moving from 'desire, gradually taking form in thought' passing into the 'bodily region', expressing itself in action, and only then 'solidifying itself in organisation and structure'.[40] Wanting to have a certain form, thinking of the self a certain way brought that body into being. 'Who shall say', Carpenter argued, that 'the forms of the shark or of the gazelle are not the long-stored results of character leaning always in certain directions, as much as the forms of the miser or the libertine among men?'[41] That character and will shaped the individual to the virtual exclusion of all other factors was a truism for thinkers across the political

---

[37] Edward Carpenter, *My Days and Dreams: Being Autobiographical Notes* (London: George Allen & Unwin, 1916), p. 167.
[38] Carpenter, *Civilisation*, pp. 44, 35–6.
[39] Ibid. 140.
[40] Ibid. 138.
[41] Ibid. 135.

spectrum in the 1880s and 1890s and it is important to recognize that the popularity of such neo-Lamarckian theories was therefore in keeping with the widespread (and underrated) idealism of much late nineteenth-century social thought.[42] Carpenter's interpretation of Lamarck in particular played down the utilitarian idea that acquired characteristics developed as adaptations to changing environments. Instead, he veered close to the vitalist version of Lamarckism popularized by his contemporary, Samuel Butler, in placing the desiring self with power to wield change over the body through habit at the centre of his evolutionary narrative.[43]

Though never pausing to be too specific about how such acquired characteristics were transmitted from generation to generation, the earliest version of Carpenter's prose-poem *Towards Democracy* hymned the dangers that lay in the descent of the bourgeoisie:

> Do you talk of the Future of Society, and is it possible you are begetting children with tainted blood, and handing down to them the refuse of dinner-parties and the insides of committee rooms and hansom cabs, and impressions of pamphlets on their retinas and stove-pipe hats on their brows, and bad teeth and foul breath?[44]

The boundaries between inside and outside, the aesthetic impression and the biological effect, the individual and the species, here are broken down just as the communal lyric voice of Carpenter's prose-poem refuses the conventional regulation of poetic form in impassioned flow. In later writings Carpenter sketched out his theory that individual desires and the changes these wrought on character were stored as additions and alteration to the Platonic ideal of humankind and hence passed on to the species. Yet if, as Carpenter argued, evolution was a Lamarckian ideal creation rather than a Darwinian material 'Machine', the poet's vision of truth was of more importance than any mechanistic explanation of how, exactly, the impress of stove-pipe hats was passed from father to son.[45] For creation itself in this scheme was 'a stupendous and perpetually renewed work of Art', unfolding from dim feelings within an individual to structured visible form in the world.[46] The poet in Carpenter's Lamarckian aesthetic was therefore nothing less than a catalyst of evolutionary change, arousing desire in his read-

---

[42] Peter Bowler, *The Eclipse of Darwinism: Anti Darwinian Evolution Theories in the Decades around 1900* (Baltimore: Johns Hopkins University Press, 1983); Collini, *Public Moralists*, pp. 82–3.

[43] Bowler, *Eclipse of Darwinism*, p. 73.

[44] Edward Carpenter, *Towards Democracy* (Manchester: John Heywood, 1883), LXIV.

[45] Edward Carpenter, *The Art of Creation: Essays on the Self and its Powers* (London: George Allen, 1904), pp. 10, 33.

[46] Ibid. 33.

ers who modified themselves and the coming generations as a result. Poetic identity and a vocation in the world of letters was the force of creation and progress itself in microcosm. This was a world away from the anxious nego-tiations of the threat of effeminacy and poetic identity visible in William Morris's work two decades earlier, in which the 'Dreamer of dreams' remained barren in a materialist world as 'The idle singer of an empty day'.[47] Carpenter's Lamarckian aesthetic reimagined the man of letters as the agent of production, breaking open the 'coffin' of conventions that encased respectable manhood and unleashing the desires that would bring forth new developments in the species.

For all the radical drive of Carpenter's criticism of the 'disease' of advanced bourgeois civilization and the habitual constraints on sexual identity that accompanied it, his representation of the forces needed to overcome this were familiar ones to a late nineteenth-century readership. The rituals of courtship and self-restraint in the landscape of 'death'—the modern drawing-room—were a husk that needed to be shrugged off by both men and women to bring forth the new life. The forces within that would bring about this metamorphosis, however, were nothing less than those much praised virtues associated with middle-class manliness in the later nineteenth century: self-help, character, determination. Whilst Carpenter admitted that the 'external' forces of evolution theorized by Darwin played some part in modification, these were mere 'easy success won by an accident of birth'. Up against this representation of natural selection as an arbitrarily imposed aristocracy of variations, was a Lamarckian democracy, in which species change was the result of 'the uphill fight of a nature that has grown inwardly and wins expression for itself in spite of external obstacles'.[48] Carpenter's very phraseology here could have been lifted straight from Samuel Smiles's exhortations to the literate manhood of the lower middle classes on the power of 'character' and will to propel the individual upwards just as far as he aspired.[49]

Carpenter's works, however, turned the logic of such manly success manuals on its head. Whilst Smiles's work in particular recommended asce-tic regimes of self-denial and a focus on ideal characteristics as best calcu-lated to achieve material advancement and a fixed place for the individual higher up the social hierarchy, Carpenter's ascetic regimes aimed to dis-mantle the material trappings of manly success by working through the body. Only when this 'external and momentary' individual self of man had

[47] William Morris, 'Prologue: The Earthly Paradise', *Selected Poems* (Manchester: Carcanet, 1992), p. 88.
[48] Carpenter, *Civilisation*, p. 136.
[49] Samuel Smiles, *Character* (London: John Murray, 1871).

been discarded would a new life emerge from the newly disclosed 'more universal and incorruptible part' of humanity: the communal, Neoplatonic idea of manhood. His readers and listeners were to strive towards a new communal virility of the spirit by setting to work on their bodies.

Carpenter's main practical advice to his listeners was that they eat less meat and wear fewer clothes, and this may appear rather difficult to reconcile with their own response that 'the earth reborn to beauty and joy' was consequently within reach just around the corner.[50] However, Carpenter's biological idealism carefully constructed a relationship between the individual body and the communal body politic that made social transformation the necessary result of dietary and dress reform. Rejecting Marxist materialism, Carpenter argued that the desires at work in the individual could set off a change in the body that would be reciprocated in an alteration in the communal ideal of mankind itself and hence its material organization. The body social was therefore itself a neo-Lamarckian organism that could acquire radically different structures and change its appearance within a generation if communal desires and habits willed it so. For what was modern capitalism itself but the disordered appetite of man written on the communal body? 'England is full of . . . undigested wealth', Carpenter asserted, 'and while her upper classes are suffering a chronic indigestion from this accumulation of dead matter upon them . . . her poor are dying for mere want of nourishment.'[51] Property, like food, Carpenter argued, should move freely through the social body, nourishing and stimulating it. However, in the current terminally 'congested' state of society, no 'gilded pill' could free the system up: only a truly heroic revolutionary purgative could restore the social body to health, 'a drastic bolus plowing its way through the very frame of "society", not without groans and horrible noises'.[52]

The appetite for property, Carpenter argued, coincided with the fall of man from a pre-lapsarian unselfconscious unity of mind and body and the entry into a culture of shame. For Carpenter, unlike Friedrich Engels whose *Origin of the Family, Private Property and the State* he drew upon, it was not the division of labour within the family that triggered the 'fall' into modern civilization. Rather, the struggle within the family reflected that within the individual himself, as original unity was lost and 'the stomach . . . started the original idea of becoming itself the centre of the human system'.[53] As the disease of complex civilization developed, so the stomach and its companion rebel, the sexual organs, formed competing desires, 'threats,

---

[50] Yeo, 'New Life', p. 12.
[51] Carpenter, *England's Ideal*, p. 128.
[52] Ibid. 141.
[53] Carpenter, *Civilisation*, p. 15.

menaces against the central authority—against Man himself', ruling that man should 'make pulps of all his victuals' and enervating the stomach in degenerate luxury.[54] In succumbing to these desires consequent upon modernity 'man inevitably weakens his own Manhood . . . and he falls prey to his own organs'.[55] Advanced capitalist civilization was bound to bring about its own end, overcome by the very forces of accumulation that had enabled its development. Marx himself strayed into a rare instance of biological metaphor in discussing this inevitable eruption in *Das Kapital*, arguing that 'centralization of the means of production and socialization of labour at last reach a point where they become incompatible with their capitalist integument'. The over-stretched skin of capitalism can no longer contain this negation and 'is burst asunder'.[56]

What was a contingent metaphor for Marx was an allegorical truth for Carpenter. His dietary advice aimed at disciplining this greed-driven body, in which effeminated organs and limbs had consumed the essential ideal core that was Man himself. Flesh eating might be tolerated in moderation, but it was an external 'stimulant' that man had come to 'lean on for support', rendering his own system 'passive'.[57] Manly independence decayed as the individual allowed his body to be built up by such 'external' forces of the 'non-ego'.[58] The solution was to feed the body foods that could not but set the idle organs to work in effortful labour, resulting in a self no longer parasitic upon the energy-value of other beings. 'Shovel in the curry and the rice', Carpenter urged, and let the body get back to work.[59] Food with roughage, as that grotesque metaphor of eating as manual work with a shovel suggests, was a return to virile rough labour from the inside out. If enough people concentrated their desires on this end, then the effeminate, diseased social body, constipated with property, would be purged and purified as a result.

Although Carpenter's analogy between the health of the individual body and the social body is one with a pedigree stretching back over millennia to the very first works of political theory, his formula for the liberation of the desiring body marks a distinct turn in nineteenth-century thought. What

---

[54] Ibid. 26.

[55] Ibid. 27.

[56] *Karl Marx: Selected Works*, ed. David McLellan (Oxford: Oxford University Press, 2000), p. 525.

[57] Carpenter, *England's Ideal*, p. 84; Carpenter, *Art of Creation*, p. 247.

[58] Carpenter, *The Art of Creation*, p. 247.

[59] Ibid. Carpenter's interest in Indian and Sri Lankan philosophy and culture was developing during this period, informed by the interests of Annie Besant and his own travels. Carpenter also corresponded with M. K. Gandhi and the two-way flow of ideas that resulted invites further research.

distinguishes Carpenter's formula from, for example, the 'Muscular Christianity' preached by Charles Kingsley a few decades earlier, is the question of whose body and what style of masculinity is being held up as the hope for the regeneration of the body social. And in Carpenter's case, the type of body which we must school our desires towards is that of the working-class labourer. Carpenter's advice on dress and diet suggested that a move towards the perceived naturalness of the life of working-class labourers was the route towards the healthful rebirth of society. The very suppressions and repressions of instinct, the 'wrapping' and 'swathing' of the body in the 'coffin' of 'layers upon layers of stiff buckram-like clothing', led to the unhealthy dominance of the 'head' alone in representing 'the little finnikin, intellectual, self-conscious man' of the educated classes of nineteenth-century civilization.[60] Health was to be restored to the body social by a process of unwrapping and casting off such 'strait-waistcoats' of bourgeois bodily repression. Carpenter himself lovingly recalled the new possibilities of life he felt after meeting his companion, the scythe and rivet-maker, Albert Fearnehough, 'the one "powerful and uneducated" natural person I had, as yet, met'.[61] Life among the workers on Carpenter's small-holding was 'so native, so unrestrained', with manual labour in 'elementary' woollen clothing next to the skin and sandals on the feet allowing light and energy to the 'vital organs'.[62]

   The potent naked body of the labouring man writ large was the very emblem of democracy for Carpenter. This democracy had little to do with constitutional government, but was a coming utopia of primitive communism, foreshadowed by desire for 'The thick-thighed hot coarse fleshed young bricklayer with the strap around his waist' and deified as:

> Gigantic Thou, with head aureoled by the sun—wild among the mountains—
> Thy huge limbs naked and stalwart erected member,
> Thy lawless gait and rank untameable laughter[.][63]

These icons of priapic labour were more than just the aestheticized visions of the honest working man, visible from Ford Madox Brown's *Work* through to Soviet era statuary as hymns to the principle of production. In Carpenter's writings the embodiment of working-class masculinity is both

---

[60] Carpenter, *England's Ideal*, p. 44; Carpenter, *Civilisation*, p. 93.

[61] Carpenter, *My Days*, p. 103. Carpenter here slightly misquotes the single writer who had the most direct influence over his thinking and poetic form, Walt Whitman: 'go freely with powerful uneducated people . . . and your very flesh shall be a great poem', 'Preface', *Leaves of Grass* (1855).

[62] Carpenter, *My Days*, p. 105; Carpenter, *England's Ideal*, p. 36.

[63] Carpenter, *Towards Democracy* (1883), LIV.

a productive and reproductive state. Desire for and contact with the labouring man was another way of bringing forth the new life.[64] As the 'effeminated' little toe was to be stimulated into revolutionary action once released from shoes into naked contact with the earth, as the enervated stomach would be disciplined by shovelling through rice and curry, so too the future development of society rested 'more firmly than anywhere else' on relations between those 'of good position and breeding' and 'rougher types, as of manual workers'.[65] 'Uranians' or the 'intermediate sex' were to engender a new life for the social body through 'Eros . . . the great leveller'. Carpenter's reworking of Lamarckian theory enabled him to refigure desire itself as a type of ideal labour going to work on the individual body and transforming future generations as a result. Species change and new societies were to be born through the effects of desire within the individual, rather than through the drive to copulate initiated by those insurgent sexual organs that threatened to consume manhood itself.

Carpenter's vision of the new life of socialism was therefore a community of desire in which embodied experience was at the centre of political transformation. It was to involve a radical negotiation of bourgeois masculinity, whereby the overheated mind of one class would be rebalanced by desire for the aestheticized body of the labourer. But at the same time this revision of masculinity was founded on pervasive nineteenth-century anxieties: the rejection of effeminacy and the need for hardening, striving, and asceticism as a means to the higher virtues.

III

THE SHE-ANCIENT: The body was the slave of the vortex; but the slave has become the master; and we must free ourselves from that tyranny. It is this stuff [*indicating her body*], this flesh and blood and bone and all the rest of it, that is intolerable. Even prehistoric man dreamed of what he called an astral body, and asked who would deliver him from the body of this death.[66]

In 1921 Shaw's 'Metabiological Pentateuch', *Back to Methuselah*, returned to that preoccupation with the dialectical 'tyranny of the flesh' over the will

---

[64] For the interplay between Carpenter's pastoral sexual dissidence and contemporary urban homosexual culture and reform see Matt Cook, *London and the Culture of Homosexuality, 1885–1914* (Cambridge: Cambridge University Press, 2003), pp. 133–42.

[65] Edward Carpenter, *The Intermediate Sex: A Study of Some Transitional Types* (London: Swan Sonnenschein, 1908), p. 115.

[66] George Bernard Shaw, *Back to Methuselah: A Metabiological Pentateuch* (New York: Brentano, 1921), p. 293.

which the playwright had explored on stage first in his *Man and Superman* of 1903.[67] In his typically trenchant and lengthy preface to the cycle of five plays, Shaw constructed an intellectual history of evolutionary thought which asserted that 'Neo-Darwinist . . . Mechanists' were 'practically running current Science' by the beginning of the twentieth century. In 1921, however, all was changed. Emerging 'under the title of Creative Evolution' was 'a genuinely scientific religion for which all wise men are now anxiously looking'.[68] In the preface and the plays that followed, Shaw pulled out the strands of this initial apparent paradox of a scientific religion to fine-drawn strings of logic. Bringing Lamarck's natural history together with its 'metaphysical complement', Schopenhauer's *World as Will*, Shaw retold the story of Genesis.[69] Only this time around the Serpent does not tempt Eve, but shares the secret he has learnt from Lilith: 'that imagination is the beginning of creation. You imagine what you desire; you will what you imagine; and at last you create what you will'.[70] The miracles and parables that unfold in the sequence of metabiological plays that follow instruct the believer that a properly rigorous will to live enables the individual to mature to a decent age of 300 or more and engender a future race free from the prison of the body altogether. Creative evolution, in Shaw's formula, is therefore a belief system—both an evolutionary system that can only be brought into existence by sustained acts of belief and willing and a deification of the superhuman force of vitalism. For Shaw, creative evolution had already taken its place as the religion of the twentieth century: it was a religion in which the flesh was death and the will was the life force that would produce the eventual superman.

To find such confident assertions of the demise of natural selection ('a chapter of accidents') and the coming rule of Lamarckism (or Shavianism) as late as 1921 is a little unexpected.[71] Peter Bowler concludes that, for all Shaw's brilliance in expounding his theory, by this date such Lamarckian thought 'was no longer fashionable, even outside science'.[72] It is precisely this longevity of Shaw's preoccupation with the struggle between flesh and will and with the liberation of intellect by ascetic bodily regimes that has made this aspect of his thought and his life such a rich source of speculation among contemporary critics. Whilst Edward Carpenter's idealist communism of desiring bodies was off even

---

[67] George Bernard Shaw, *Man and Superman: A Comedy and a Philosophy* (1903; repr. Harmondsworth: Penguin, 1972), p. 139.
[68] Shaw, *Methuselah*, p. xix.
[69] Ibid., p. xxxiv.
[70] Ibid. 10.
[71] Ibid., p. xxxv.
[72] Bowler, *Eclipse of Darwinism*, p. 105.

the margins of socialist debate by the First World War, Shaw's role as one of the chief propagandists of the Fabian Society guaranteed that his political analyses exerted influence on the left mainstream into the twentieth century. Indeed, as Gareth Griffith has shown, Shaw's works were an acknowledged and formative influence on socialist thinkers and Labour politicians well after the Second World War, even if, by this stage, his fads appeared to be eccentric oddities.[73] Carpenter's body politics has been exhumed recently within its cultural and historical context, but the very vitality of Shaw's performance of ascetic virility during the twentieth century has obscured its origins in late nineteenth-century models of masculinity and 'faddism'.

There is a seeming paradox in that, despite being the best-known vegetarian in twentieth-century Britain, with his own cookbook to match, despite featuring prominently in the (by then, rather more stylish than sanitary) Jaeger Co. history of 1950, the very self-publicizing consistency of his performance of radical faddism has been read by biographers from the notorious Frank Harris onwards as evidence of a secret, sexually conflicted self or 'darker side'.[74] In the final section of this chapter I will examine Shaw's fads in the context in which they took shape in the 1880s and argue that his ascetic bodily regimes were intimately connected with his evolutionary thought. Whilst his philosophy of wool-wearing and a meatless diet thus appear as part of his individuated quest for the superman's triumph of intellect over the flesh, it is important to recognize the extent to which this self-styled secular saint also took up and developed the rhetoric of earnest, embodied masculinity used by an earlier generation of Victorian 'sages' and cultural critics.

In amongst Shaw's letters from the Austrian political refugee, Andreas Scheu, concerning the splits and schisms within the British socialist movement in the mid-1880s is one with three pages of urgent laundry instructions.[75] In his other guise as a travelling salesman for Dr Jaeger's Sanitary Woollen System British franchise, Scheu was guiding his friend on the best techniques of washing, mangling, and ironing new Jaeger garments to maintain their optimum porosity. Shaw was far from alone in his fabric anxiety in the last decades of the nineteenth century. Moved to write an article on the 'great underclothing question', S. William Beck remarked that the debate on dress reform was so widespread that 'it is not difficult to imagine

---

[73] Gareth Griffith, *Socialism and Superior Brains: The Political Thought of George Bernard Shaw* (London: Routledge, 1993), p. 1.

[74] Harris, *Bernard Shaw*, p. 107; Alfred Silver, *Bernard Shaw: The Darker Side* (Stanford, Calif.: Stanford University Press, 1982).

[75] BL Add. Mss. 50511.

the future historian thinking that there must be some social significance in this sudden solicitude about skin clothing, and setting to work to ascertain the full extent of it'.[76] The Jaeger system, as Beck acknowledged, took chief place amongst the many clothing gospels evangelized in continental hygienist spas and sanitoria in the last decades of the nineteenth century: Dr Lahmann had patented a cotton waffle fabric, Pastor Sebastien Kneipp, a sanitary flax one, and 'Professor Pettenkofer of Cologne' a 'Patent Invigorating Net Cloth Vest'.[77] At the heart of all these systems was a belief in the hygienic value of fresh air, freely circulating around the skin and enabling the exhalation of the body's natural poisons.

Edward Carpenter's advocacy of sandals evidently owed much to this first strand of hygienic thought: the body must be invigorated by the forces outside it and open to the rougher elements. Yet Shaw's discussion of his Jaegerism—and indeed 'Dr Jaeger's London Representative', Lewis Tomalin's own writings—place a nearly exclusive emphasis on the concept of exhalation. The flesh was inevitably in a state of poisonous decay and 'dead vegetable fibre' surrounding the body would 'greedily take up the malodorous emanations': only Jaeger's live wool would throw off an 'impure atmosphere' adequately.[78] Whilst Carpenter's utopian socialism rested upon the liberation of the self through an invigorated and desiring body, there is a sense in Shaw's writing that the best such faddism could achieve would be to mitigate an individual's thrall to his embodiment by pacifying it: 'I want my body to breathe', he pleaded to Ellen Terry, in an attempt to explain his 'much ridiculed Jaegerism'.[79]

It is this sense of an individuated struggle between mind and body— rather than between self and environment—that distinguishes Shaw from his contemporary faddists, Carpenter and Salt. Carpenter's aestheticization of the labouring body owes much to the neo-classical Hellenism and the idea of *mens sana in corpore sano* that permeated cultural criticism during his years at Cambridge in the 1860s and 1870s. For Carpenter, the effeminating environment of 'civilization' had to be set aside in order rediscover the integrity of desire in the balance between body and mind. Shaw, on the other hand, represented his Jaegerism and vegetarianism in terms that fused Lamarckian thought with a Puritan suspicion of the tendencies of the flesh: 'man may have his opinion as to the relative impor-

---

[76] S. William Beck, 'The Great Underclothing Question', *New Review*, 11 (1894), 534–42 (p. 536).

[77] W. M. Green, 'Dr Lahmann's Sanitorium', *Vegetarian Messenger and Health Review* (1904), 277–80 (p. 278); Beck, 'Underclothing', p. 538.

[78] Lewis Tomalin, 'The Great Underclothing Question—A Rejoinder', *New Review*, 11 (1894), 606–11 (p. 608).

[79] *Shaw: CL*, i. 840.

tance of feeding his body and nourishing his soul', Shaw argued, but once the body was past the point of hunger, the two appetites worked against each other.[80] As director of the London Jaeger franchise, Tomalin certainly had no hesitation in suggesting that the unique selling point of his goods was their ability to limit the spread of sin from body to mind. Jaeger nightwear was particularly important, he argued, as this was the time when 'the brain no longer acts as the body's sentinel, and the sleeper is particularly exposed to unwholesome influences'.[81]

Shaw was keen to argue that this belief in the tendency of the body to pull down the progress of the mind was something quite distinct from mere prudery. In the 'Revolutionist's Handbook' he appended to the published version of *Man and Superman*, Shaw anticipated an aspect of Michel Foucault's dissection of nineteenth-century 'repression' in arguing that prudery and ribaldry were the same thing.[82] The two resulted from the lack of appropriate language for discussing the body and the necessary 'absence of cleanliness' in modern cities, with the result that 'many of the natural conditions of life become offensive and noxious':

> at last the association of uncleanliness with these natural conditions become so overpowering that among civilized people (that is, people massed in the labyrinth of slums we call cities), half their bodily life becomes a guilty secret . . . In short, popular prudery is only a mere incident of popular squalor.[83]

Shaw's Jaegerist faddism worked against the prudery/ribaldry dyad on two levels. First, the scientized language of hygienic dress reform offered one path to the 'decent' 'technical vocabulary' needed to situate the discussion of the body and the relations of the sexes in mainstream discourse.[84] Second, at a more figurative level, the cleanliness and porosity that Shaw attributed to Jaeger's loose-knit woollens opened up and expired the grubby, guilty secrets of the body. Out walking, his 'smart-looking stockinette . . . stridulating so frightfully as the wearer's arms swung against his sides', Shaw's body was all visible (and audible) surface: Jaegerism enabled Shaw to negate the assumption—in his case, at least—that it was the body that held secrets.[85]

Whilst exceptional geniuses might release the odours and prudish secrets of the body through acts of conscious will and reformed dress, Shaw

---

[80] Ibid. ii. 146.
[81] Tomalin, 'Rejoinder', p. 609.
[82] Michel Foucault, *The History of Sexuality*, 1 (1976; repr. Harmondsworth: Penguin, 1990), p. 18.
[83] Shaw, *Man and Superman*, pp. 229–30.
[84] Ibid.
[85] Harris, *Bernard Shaw*, p. 104.

Figure 2. George Bernard Shaw in Jaeger clothing c. 1888. Jaeger Company Archives, City of Westminster Archives Centre, Acc. 1431/ Box 3.

accepted that the majority would have to wait for gradual socialist reforms to cleanse their environments instead. Unlike Carpenter, Shaw argued consistently that faddism itself—'the simple life, the aesthetic life'—was, quite simply, the privilege of those who had a surfeit of goods and pleasures to turn away from.[86] '"Cease to be slaves, in order that you may become cranks" is not a very inspiring call to arms', he concluded, 'nor is it really improved by substituting saints for cranks. Both terms denote men of genius; and the common man does not want to live the life of a saint or a man of genius'.[87] As chief propagandist of the Fabian Society, Shaw was perhaps pre-eminently responsible for separating out this association of socialist politics and the aestheticization of manly labour that so shaped his own development in the 1880s. The working man, Shaw argued, could never act as an aesthetic source or resource because of the material constraints that shaped him. Asking the working man to 'fight for the difference' between popular journals such as the *Illustrated London News*, or as he updated it in later editions, the *Picture Post,* and Morris's luscious hand-printed Kelmscott Chaucer was simply 'silly': he will always prefer publications like the *ILN* or *Post*. Here therefore, in *Major Barbara* (first performed in 1905), Shaw's pragmatic Fabian socialism countered both Carpenter's romanticist vision of working-class labourers, the latter's reading of Lamarck, and the wider aesthetic radicalism associated with Morris. As long as capitalism dictated that the masses lived in poverty and squalor, so shame and want entrapped them in the body and enabled them to aspire only to 'costly vulgarities'.[88] The 'Gospel' of Shaw's model armaments manufacturer 'St Andrew Undershaft' asserted that only exceptional men of individualist will could break away from the constraints of poverty in and of themselves: the common people would have to wait for external forces to relieve them of the new 'seven deadly sins':

> UNDERSHAFT: . . . Food, clothing, firing, rent, taxes, respectability and children. Nothing can lift those seven millstones from Man's neck but money; and the spirit cannot soar until the millstones are lifted.[89]

Working-class masculine embodiment was not therefore a productive site of restoration, recuperation, and evolutionary sexual desire for Shaw, but rather a set of limiting material needs that barred the 'common man' from finding his 'own dreams' and taking part in the development of the 'Life Force'.[90]

---

[86] George Bernard Shaw, *Major Barbara* (1905; repr. London: Penguin, 1945), p. xii.
[87] Ibid.
[88] Ibid., p. xi.
[89] Ibid. 158.
[90] Ibid. 157.

Cranks and saints, prophets and geniuses: these oddities were the driving forces needed to bring forth the superman in Shaw's evolutionary theory; 'men selected by Nature to carry on the work of building up an
intellectual consciousness of her own instinctive purpose'.[91] Throughout
Shaw's writings these exceptional beings tend towards disembodiment,
from the seamless flow of rhetoric from the would-be Superman, Jack
Tanner, that is finally swallowed up by the procreative life force of Anne
Whitefield to the ancient bodies without organs who anticipate a final liberation from the flesh in the end sequence of *Back to Methuselah*. The man
of genius (who was occasionally, Shaw noted, a woman) must be constantly
alert to the master/slave dialectic between his intellect and his body, and vegetarianism was one means of keeping this in check. 'I do not eat flesh, fish
or fowl', Shaw responded to one correspondent:

> It does not greatly matter what most people eat or drink because they are not
> working to the limit of their capacity in either quality or quantity. To the few
> who are working on the finest edge of their utmost powers it matters a great
> deal. You can be Sancho Panza on any food providing there is enough of it. If
> you want to be Pythagoras, you have to be more careful.[92]

The benefits of vegetarianism were, Shaw argued, mostly indirect and
derived from that fact that the practice forced people to think about their
diets and reshape long-held, embodied, childhood habits.[93] At the same
time, then, as Carpenter preached vegetarianism as a means to bring new
life to the body by increasing the virile labour of the organs, Shaw practised
dietary asceticism as a means of minimizing the body and letting the mind
get to work.

There is a sense of triumphant vindication of such mental mastery in
Shaw's letter to Beatrice Webb recounting the tragi-comic series of accidents and operations that precipitated his marriage to Charlotte Payne
Townshend in 1898. Lacing his boots too tightly one morning, Shaw was
too busy attending the theatre, writing his reviews, and cycling to socialist
meetings across London to attend to the slight pain which then accumulated
over the next few days. By the time he got round to taking his massively
swollen foot to the doctor, Shaw wrote, 'I was in an almost superhuman
condition—fleshless, bloodless, vaporous, ethereal, and stupendous in literary efficiency . . . When [the surgeon] cut into the foot he not only found
no blood—"only some wretched sort of ichor" he said—but the bone was

---

[91] Shaw, *Man and Superman*, p. 20.
[92] *Shaw: CL*, iii. 672.
[93] Ibid. ii. 954.

Figure 3.   George Bernard Shaw, 'The Dying Vegetarian', 1898. British Library of Economic and Political Science, LSE, Archives, Shaw Photographs, Box 1.

necrosed'.[94] Rejecting the doctors' suggestions that he could only be saved by steak and port wine, Shaw framed the incident as proof of the efficiency of his intellect in feeding off his flesh. Vegetarianism freed the mind of the genius from the distasteful business of eating murdered animals and

[94] Ibid. 66.

subjugated the body to his needs: this, not Carpenter's somatic economy of desire, was the manner in which faddism was to usher in the new life. While Carpenter's Lamarckism rested upon an idea of the self and the social as a set of organs connected to each other and evolving each other through desire, Shaw set the individuated intellectual will against the body and against the world, at the heart of his evolutionary narratives.

There is a paradox inherent in all this discussion of ascetic fads and the disciplining of the body on Shaw's part: one highly visible in Shaw's article for the *Saturday Review*, 'GBS Vivisected', which followed his operation and in the several photographs Shaw posed for during his lengthy convalescence.[95] In a series of photographs Shaw staged and submitted to the *Academy*, the Jaeger-clad author stares out at his viewers from a bath chair, foot raised and entombed in miles of bandages, belying the magazine's caption, 'the dying vegetarian'.[96] The paradox is that Shaw's ascetic regimes simultaneously displayed and drew attention to his body whilst claiming to be disciplining and subjugating it.

Shaw's was the dandyism of the social critic, the prophet who marks his distinction from the world and its material criteria, whilst at the same time needing an audience in that world to receive and reflect back his great thoughts. When refusing a dinner invitation from Mrs Humphry Ward, one of the best connected (if rather fusty) figures of late nineteenth-century literary London, Shaw declined on the grounds that once he started dining out he would become 'a lost man':

> The very first thing you would do would be to ask me to take down some lady whose invitations I had scorned on pretence of not going into society, always dressing like a navvy, and not being fit company for ladies and gentlemen. Or else it will be somebody I don't know and don't want to know; and I shall have to sit sipping a glass of water & talking to her whilst she eats murdered animals.[97]

Despite refusing the invitation and remaining outside 'society', Shaw could not but dramatize the critique his bodily habits would have offered to the spectators at Ward's salon if he had gone. It is in this respect, I want to suggest, that Shaw's public performance of rigorous asceticism and the 'ferocity' of 'temper' he attributed to vegetarianism draws close to Thomas Carlyle's notion of the critic and man of letters as a hero 'savage' against the world.[98] James Eli Adams argues that Carlyle's attack on dandyism in *Sartor Resartus* (1833) barely veils the extent to which his seemingly antithetical

---

[95] George Bernard Shaw, 'G.B.S. Vivisected', *Saturday Review* (14 May 1898).
[96] *Academy*, 55 (15 Oct. 1898).
[97] *Shaw: CL*, i. 824.
[98] Holroyd, *Bernard Shaw*, p. 87.

concept of the manly, ascetic hero also depends upon an audience for completion and validation. Masculinity is in both these models, Adams argues, 'always a spectacle exposed to the public gaze'.[99]

Shaw's debt to this earlier Carlylean model of the man of letters as an exceptional prophet who labours in ascetic self-forgetfulness to bring about a new life against the world is nowhere clearer than in his exposition of 'Creative Evolution'. Disciples of creative evolution,

> have observed the simple fact that the will to do anything can and does, at a certain pitch of intensity set up by conviction of its necessity, create and organize new tissue to do it with . . . If the weight lifter, under the trivial stimulus of an athletic competition, can 'put up a muscle', it seems reasonable to believe that an equally earnest and convinced philosopher could 'put up a brain'.[100]

Will, intensity, earnestness, conviction: here then, Shaw attempts to bring new life to (and through) the paradigmatic virtues of Carlylean manly heroism. The earnest manly prophet on the margins of this world can become the superman who determines the next one. Yet Shaw's biological extrapolation of the ideal of 'earnestness' collapses entirely Carlyle's fragile distinction between saints, cranks, prophets, and geniuses on the one hand, and dandies on the other: the former concerned with an audience for their inwardness and self-forgetfulness, the latter with displaying the importance of being bodily surface. Shaw's creative evolution dictates that the hero-philosopher too must now display himself through embodiment. As the weight lifter develops and displays his muscles and presents himself as bodily spectacle to his audience, so too the earnest philosopher must perform and signal the creative evolution of his brain and its advanced mastery of the body. Ascetic fads thus figure as a means of acting out the evolutionary truth that the body is ultimately a contingent and dispensable surface that can be superseded by will and 'superior brains'.

IV

In Carpenter's organic socialist utopia, the reshaping of bourgeois masculinity through desire for the 'people' integrated body and politics. The 'New Life' was to be born through the somaticization of labour and the rejection of intellect. Although Carpenter's politics of embodiment brought him many devoted female followers, it took the astute criticism of his friend,

---

[99] Adams, *Dandies*, p. 25.
[100] Shaw, *Methuselah,* p. xiii.

Olive Schreiner, to point out that such a vision of the future was all very well for one who had spent a decade at Cambridge, but quite at odds with the desires of women who had been confined to this realm of the body, desire, and (re)production for all too long.[101] By the early years of the twentieth century Carpenter's 'romantic anti-intellectualism', as Laura Chrisman terms it, seemed increasingly distant from the intellectual and political concerns of the socialist and labour movements.[102] Alfred Orage, the editor of the *New Age* who had been inspired into socialist activism as a young man by Carpenter's works, came to reject his ideas as mere sentimentalism and, regardless of Carpenter's careful negotiations, effeminacy. But as we shall see in the final chapter, Carpenter's attempts to fuse a radical rethinking of sexual embodiment with utopian socialist politics found a receptive readership among writers such as Roger Fry and Rupert Brooke. Carpenter's 'simple life' thus influenced the experiments in living of the Bloomsbury Group, even if such radical idealism of the 1880s was stripped of its commitment to communalism in the early twentieth century.

Shaw's resistance to Carpenter's utopian socialism seems to have strengthened during the 1890s as he became more deeply involved with the 'scientific' investigative agenda of the Fabian Society. The Fabian Society itself had drawn away conclusively from its origins in the 'religion of socialism' of the 1880s by the beginning of the twentieth century.[103] Its members advocated gradual welfare state provision for the many, guided by elite intellectual leadership: 'the people' were no longer a site of romantic return and political revolution. The ideal citizen of the future for Shaw was the new universal 'gentleman' who demanded a state that allowed him to live as a fully cultured human being and in turn strived to return more to his country.[104] The people, in fact, were simply not evolved far enough for a utopia of Carpenter's sort to be a possibility:

> poets who plan Utopias and prove that nothing is necessary for their realization but that Man should will them, perceive at last . . . that the fact to be faced is that Man does not effectively will them. And he never will until he becomes Superman.[105]

There was, for Shaw, no hope, no desire, no will to be found in the bodies of the mass of men prior to the political transformation of society. Yet

---

[101] *Olive Schreiner: Letters*, ed. Richard Rive (Oxford: Oxford University Press, 1988), p. 147.
[102] Laura Chrisman, 'Allegory, Feminist Thought and the Dreams of Olive Schreiner', in Brown (ed.), *Edward Carpenter*, pp. 126–51 (p. 128).
[103] But for a useful revisionist account of this period see Mark Bevir, 'Fabianism, Permeation and Independent Labour', *Historical Journal*, 39 (1996), 179–96.
[104] Griffith, *Socialism and Superior Brains*, p. 104.
[105] Shaw, *Man and Superman*, p. 245.

whilst his political analysis shaped the pragmatism of the mainstream left into the twentieth century, his continued ascetic fads displayed his debt to the belief in progress through the body so central to the utopian 'religion of socialism' of the 1880s.

All socialism could aim to do, Shaw concluded, was to end the one greatest crime, that of poverty, and leave working men to 'find their own dreams'. Shaw—the second-best self-publicist of the period—claimed that Wilde's 'Soul of Man under Socialism' was largely influenced by his Fabian lectures and certainly we find an echo here of Wilde's article.[106] Both Wilde and Shaw insist that the prime concern of socialism can only be to reshape the material basis of society. The individual artist has a role in bringing about this change and, in turn, the communal ownership of the means of production will encourage the artist in new directions. The boundary between individual artist and communal political reorganization, however, is marked down carefully: the one may tease, delight, and educate the many, but his gift is that of the individual genius without the resources of the people. Shaw's Fabian vision that shaped so much of twentieth-century British history on the left, then, was concerned with the production of autonomous socialist subjects, freed from material inequality to choose vulgarity if they wished, but free nevertheless.

---

[106] Lawrence Danson, *Wilde's Intentions: The Artist in his Criticism* (Oxford: Clarendon Press, 1997), p. 162.

5

Dollie Radford and the Ethical Aesthetics of Fin-de-Siècle Poetry

> I got your poems, my dear Dollie. They made me sad. They make me think of the small birds in the twilight, whistling brief little tunes, but so clear, they seem almost like little lights in the twilight, such clear vivid sounds. I do think you make fine, exquisite verse . . . I hear your voice so plainly in these, so like a bird too, they are, the same detachment.[1]

A little bird, singing her song of personal subjectivity, 'exquisite verse', rather than estimable poetry, a sprinkling of lights too dim to be true stars, detached from the world and all fading away into the twilight of a new age. There is little difference between this appreciative letter of 1916 and the reviews of Dollie Radford's volumes of verse that appeared on their publication in the 1890s. As LeeAnne Richardson has pointed out in her recent reconsideration of Radford's work, Radford's *A Light Load* (1891) and *Songs and Other Verses* (1895) were greeted with similarly decorous tepidity by reviewers at the time. The 'trill and flutter of a song bird' the *Athenaeum* decreed, 'slight', 'simple', 'pretty', 'feminine', 'spontaneous', 'a tiny, fragile load indeed', Arthur Symons concluded for the *Academy*.[2] At barely over six stone, that 'pretty Dollie Radford' who crops up on the margins of so many memoirs of the fin de siècle could stand as a case in point of the 'poetess' being written into her verses by the eyes of the reviewers.[3] Radford herself was only too aware of—but interestingly, not that unhappy about—this persistent compression of women's poetry into the feminine body. As we shall see, Radford's works continually negotiated the circum-

---

[1] D. H. Lawrence to Dollie Radford, [27 Jan. 1916], in *The Letters of D. H. Lawrence,* ed. James T. Boulton and others, 8 vols. (Cambridge: Cambridge University Press, 1979–2000), ii. 515–16.
[2] LeeAnne Marie Richardson, 'Naturally Radical: The Subversive Poetics of Dollie Radford', *Victorian Poetry,* 38 (2000), 109–24; 'Recent Verse', *Athenaeum* (8 Aug. 1891), 189–90; review Dollie Radford 'Songs and Other Verses', and Ernest Radford 'Old and New', *Athenaeum* (21 Sept. 1895), 378; Arthur Symons, review 'A Light Load' by Dollie Radford, *Academy* (13 June 1891).
[3] Yvonne Kapp, *Eleanor Marx,* ii (London: Virago, 1972), p. 193.

scribed identity of the 'poetess' and explored an alternative possibility for a woman poet at the turn of the century: that of a socially engaged yet feminized lyricism. On receiving her author's copies of *A Light Load* she concluded, rather archly, that it was 'A very nice little book. I think I should be quite pleased with it if I met it unawares', only adding to this imagined drawing-room encounter with her proper little body of work: 'I wish it were not *so* small'.[4] Her fears were confirmed when a few days later she received a letter from her friend Symons letting her know of his review and adding how much he liked her '*small* volume'.[5]

Feminist scholarship over the past two decades has ensured that the tepid enthusiasm shown for Radford's works by D. H. Lawrence and Symons can be read as part of a wider story about the fate of the late nineteenth-century woman poet in the era of early literary modernism. The reception of Radford's work can thus be read as representative of the erasure of nineteenth-century women's poetry in the twentieth century's acts of literary remembrance.[6] During the years of the 1914–18 war, whilst Lawrence struggled to publish his early novels, his practical difficulties were lightened by Radford, who arranged deliveries from London to Lawrence's Cornish outpost and then loaned Lawrence her Berkshire cottage for most of 1918.[7] Lawrence and Frieda only eventually relocated when faced with the prospect of Radford arriving with her mentally unstable husband Ernest, 'the madman', as Lawrence put it.[8] Meanwhile the twilight of D. H. Lawrence's moment of modernism put out the little lights of the verse of Radford and her peers, and declared such lyrics spontaneous, feminine, and essentially trivial: verses that were self-concerned but did not self-consciously reflect on the nature of that lyric selfhood.

---

[4] Dollie Radford Diary 1891–1900, MSR 126 M3, William Andrews Clark Memorial Library, UCLA. Entry dated 15 April 1891 (emphasis in original).

[5] Radford Diary, 21 April 1891 (my emphasis).

[6] For a recent reflection on the literary politics of the neglect and recovery of 19th-cent. women's poetry see the editors' preface to Isobel Armstrong and Virginia Blain (eds.), *Women's Poetry: Late Romantic to Late Victorian* (Houndmills: Macmillan, 1999), pp. vii–xiv. See also Isobel Armstrong, 'Msrepresentations: Codes of Affect and Politics in Nineteenth-Century Women's Poetry', ibid. 3–32 (pp. 3–6) and Cynthia Scheinberg, *Women's Poetry and Religion in Victorian England* (Cambridge: Cambridge University Press, 2002), pp. 41–4, for two varied critiques of the 'Whiggish' and 'androcentric' critical models deployed by earlier feminist accounts of 19th-cent. women's poetry.

[7] Lawrence and Frieda were resident at Chapel Farm Cottage, Hermitage, Berks, from 18 Dec. 1917 to 2 May 1918 and then again from April to July 1919, troubled on this later occasion by the Radford's younger daughter Margaret, an aspiring poet who also suffered from mental instability.

[8] D. H. Lawrence to S. S. Koteliansky [25 Feb. 1918], *Lawrence: Letters*, iii. 218.

The story does not have to be told like this, however, and such a retrospective literary history in which all goes into the dark or under the hill of
modernism underplays the extent to which Radford's poetics emerged from
a structure of feeling particular to the late nineteenth century. Starting over
again from the early 1880s places Radford's slender canon of verse within
the radical socialist moment of aesthetic production in which she participated. It was a moment that instilled itself in the remembrance of the
younger generation of modernist writers such as Lawrence, even if the specific political energies of the 1880s were dissipated by the early twentieth
century. Of all the writers examined in this book who became involved with
the socialist movement in the early 1880s, Dollie Radford was the one most
intimately involved with the late and last flowering of aestheticism in the
1890s and the aesthetic innovations of the early twentieth century. Radford's
life and works challenge the easy critical ascription of an opposition
between aestheticism and political commitment, the individuated pleasures
of taste and the communal struggle for social change at the fin de siècle. She
was both an active member of the revolutionary Socialist League in the
1880s and a poet whose publications with John Lane and contributions to
the *Yellow Book* in the 1890s have led Talia Schaffer to identify her as a 'forgotten female aesthete'.[9] Her work thus sheds light on the tension between
socialism and aestheticism at the fin de siècle whilst underscoring the possibility of unlooked-for pluralism: politics and aesthetics might work in this
case as a both/and rather than an either/or.

Trace Radford to the 1880s and 1890s and she is to be found sitting
under two distinct signs: a political banner and the careful engraving of an
aesthetic frontispiece. She appears in a photograph taken in 1887 of the
Hammersmith Branch of the revolutionary Socialist League, led by William
Morris. There, in the front row between May and Jenny Morris, sits the tiny
figure of Dollie Radford. Radford had been convinced of the 'seriousness
and beauty of the socialistic movement', along with her friends the sisters
Clementina, Constance, and Grace Black, after hearing Morris's lecture
'How we Live and How we Might Live' in 1884.[10] The following year
Radford and her husband Ernest moved to Hammersmith from their former
home in Bloomsbury largely in order to participate in Morris's socialist
organization; this was a political commitment they maintained alongside

---

[9] Talia Schaffer, *The Forgotten Female Aesthetes: Literary Culture in Late Victorian England*
(Charlottesville, Va.: University Press of Virginia, 2000), pp. 24–5. Schaffer's account of the
construction of feminine aestheticism in the works of the poet Alice Meynell, however, provides both common ground and an instructive contrast with Radford's negotiation of
lyricism, pp. 159–96.
[10] Radford Diaries, entry dated 30 Nov. 1884.

Figure 4. Photograph of Socialist League, Hammersmith, 1887. Dollie Radford sits third from left, facing forwards between Jenny and May Morris. People's History Museum.

active membership of the ideologically distinct Fabian Society. The second illustration reproduced here is a copy of the frontispiece to Radford's volume of poetry, *Songs and Other Verses*, published in the high aesthetic imprint of John Lane, at the sign of the Bodley Head in 1895. This, her second collection of poetry, was produced at a time of considerable strain for Radford. Ernest Radford suffered a severe nervous breakdown in 1892 from which he seemingly never fully recovered, leaving the couple (and their three children) to scrape a living from writing and the goodwill of their extended families as best they could. Here again we see Dollie Radford, but this time rendered as a pastoral woman poet with her lyre and puffy aesthetic sleeves. Hemmed in by the intertwining boughs of the border, the portrait emphasizes the solipsistic pleasure of individuated lyric poetry. There are no signs of revolutionary socialism here: even her footwear, which might be seen as a witty allusion to the sandal-wearing championed by Edward Carpenter and other fin-de-siècle socialists, seems to be modelled on a classical pattern rather than any more radical fad.

It would be easy to speculate from these two signs that Dollie Radford abandoned her earnest commitment to collective radical politics in the mid-1880s for the individuated pleasures of aestheticism in the 1890s. But Radford's political reflections in her diary, in addition to her continuing membership of the Fabian Society, suggest that she maintained her socialist beliefs alongside her growing confidence in her identity as a poet. Radford's lyrics and ballads continue to negotiate the tension between aesthetics and politics during the 1890s. This tension is all the more palpable in Radford's work because what I have termed as the communal socialist aesthetic, disseminated by writers such as William Morris and Edward Carpenter during the 1880s, laid such an emphasis on productive, manly labour.[11] Both the communal meetings of the Hammersmith Socialist League and the aesthetes gathered under the sign of the Bodley Head thus proved problematic for Radford during the late 1880s and 1890s in terms of their articulation of opposed, gendered aesthetics. Whilst aestheticism was underpinned by what Regenia Gagnier has termed an aesthetic of consumption and located in a sphere of strategically feminized taste, delectation, and individual responsiveness, the aesthetic disseminated by Morris within the socialist movement emphasized production, manly labour, and the effortful struggle to create communal subjects for the socialist era.[12] Radford may have moved freely from the meeting hall to the salon, but her works reflect upon the

---

[11] Ruth Livesey, 'Morris, Carpenter, Wilde and the Political Aesthetics of Labor', *Victorian Literature and Culture*, 32 (2004), 601–16.
[12] Regenia Gagnier, *The Insatiability of Human Wants: Economics and Aesthetics in Market Society* (Chicago: University of Chicago Press, 2000), p. 13.

Figure 5. Frontispiece to *Songs and Other Verses* (1895). British Library, shelfmark 011652.ee.48.

inadequacy of either space to provide a form of poetry which gave a home to engaged yet feminized aesthetic production. This chapter examines the extent to which Radford's poetics can be seen as an attempt to challenge this gendered opposition. Whilst several of Radford's lyrics explore how manly communal socialism overwrites a feminized sphere of individual affect and sympathy, others foreground the inadequacy of beauty and solitary contemplation in the long struggle for social change.

I

Radford's first significant success in publishing her verse in 1883 was inextricably linked to the world of free-thinking ethical clubs and debating societies in Bloomsbury from which the socialist movement later drew many of its most prominent activists. Thanks to her friendship with Eleanor Marx and Clementina Black, Radford (or Caroline Maitland, her name in this period before her marriage) was increasingly drawn into the debates on atheism and ethics generated by the Progressive Association and G. W. Foote's radical secularist journal *Progress*. During the early 1880s Black and Radford drew this debate into their own circle of acquaintances, inviting several speakers to address the men and women's discussion club they organized on the question of the coming ethical order in the new age of agnosticism.[13] In 1883 Radford herself delivered a paper to the club entitled 'To the Progressive Soul, true friendships are momentary' which seems to have applied the extreme subjectivism and temporality of Walter Pater's aestheticism to the sphere of ethics and human relations.[14]

If the radical flavour of such subjects of debate seems slightly dulled now, the fact of G. W. Foote's imprisonment for twelve months on a count of blasphemy during 1883 probably did something to clarify the edgy political position of the secularist movement to its members in the early 1880s. Edward Aveling, who was to become Eleanor Marx's common-law husband in 1884, served as interim editor of *Progress* during Foote's unavoidable absence and it was in his term of office that nine of Radford's poems appeared in the journal.[15] As Caroline Maitland or 'C.M.' Radford's poems

---

[13] See Ch. 3 for the Men and Women's Club. For an account of the club which replaced this see Judith Walkowitz, *City of Dreadful Delight* (London: Virago, 1992), pp. 135–70, and Lucy Bland, *Banishing the Beast: English Feminism and Sexual Morality* (Harmondsworth: Penguin, 1995).

[14] Radford Diaries, 15 May 1883.

[15] The very public and acrimonious debate between the Marxist H. M. Hyndman of the Social Democratic Federation and the free-thinking secularist Charles Bradlaugh in summer 1884 is often seen as the point of definitive break between an older radical tradition and

Figure 6. Emma Black (Keriman Mahomed), *Dollie Radford*, exh. R.A. 1883. Photograph from Archive Department, National Portrait Gallery.

were published along with contributions from, among others, Ernest Radford and Eleanor Marx in a journal which liberally interspersed verse with crusading articles on the necessity of atheism and the disestablishment of the Church of England.[16]

Although *Progress* was a relatively new journal, its founding editor, Foote, looked back with some pride on the conjunction of secularist publishing and radical poetics in the later nineteenth century. He became a staunch defender, for example, of the atheistic legacy of James Thomson, whose *City of Dreadful Night* was first published in Charles Bradlaugh and Annie Besant's free-thinking *National Reformer* in 1874. *Progress* secured permission to publish Thomson's literary remains from his executors, and, from Foote's return as editor in April 1884, Thomson's poetry and essays came to dominate the literary component of the journal. In a break with the older radical tradition of Chartist poetry however, the pages of *Progress* generally devoted considerable space to lyric poetry and relatively little to explicitly politicized hymns and ballads. Anne Janowitz has recently situated the radical poetry associated with the Chartist movement in a (long) nineteenth-century field of romanticism and argued that many such works embody a formal dialectic between the labouring-class oral tradition of the ballad and the bourgeois interiority of the individuated lyric.[17] In contrast to such radical dialectic of the individual and communal—a dialectic poetics that was, as we shall see, sustained in many of the works published in contemporary socialist journals—the poetry in *Progress* was content to explore the parameters of subjectivity and individualism in conventional lyric form. This formal preference was, I argue, inextricably linked to the editors' ethical secularist agendas.

In the course of an extended review of Philip Bourke Marston's volume of poetry, *Wind Voices*, published in *Progress* in 1884, Edward Aveling concluded that 'in this age of transition [to atheism] the task of the imaginative writer is difficult. He has to teach the great lesson of godlessness. But he has also to describe human beings.'[18] Lyric poetry, so inalienably associated with reflection and interiority during the nineteenth century, thus assumed a particularly significant role in the age of secularization. Such a form of imaginative writing was not merely a vehicle for

---

'scientific' socialism. To underscore the pluralism of socialist thought in the 1880s, however, Edward Aveling (perhaps in a characteristic act of bigamy) continued to combine his commitment to Foote's *Progress* with work for his newer, scientific socialist interest, the magazine, *Today* throughout the 1880s.

[16] Radford selected five of these nine poems for *A Light Load* eight years later.

[17] Anne Janowitz, *Lyric and Labour in the Romantic Tradition* (Cambridge: Cambridge University Press, 1998), pp. 28–31, 133–59.

[18] Edward Aveling, '"Wind Voices": Second Notice', *Progress,* 4/3 (Sept. 1884), 134–9 (p. 135).

the description of human beings, but a means of inscribing secular subjectivity. Lyric poetry, Aveling implied, could serve the new dissident belief
system of atheism as humbly as it had established religion throughout the
nineteenth century. In examining the intertwining of theology and poetics in the nineteenth century Cynthia Scheinberg has concluded that such
interdependence not only framed poetry as the 'handmaid' of religion but
also disseminated an ideal of the 'poetic heart' as 'a realm that privileges
female and Christian identity'.[19] The private virtues of Christian humility
preached by poet-theologians such as John Keble, Scheinberg argues, are
not only heavily coded as feminine within the nineteenth-century logic of
gender, but also concur with the affective language of the poetry of the
heart. Whilst Foote's editorial policy was noted for its misogyny, as acting editor Aveling oversaw the publication of numerous lyrics by women
poets, including Radford, that can be read as secular negotiations of this
Christian tradition of the feminized 'poetic heart'.

Dollie Radford's poem 'The Starlight has Gladdened the River', published in *Progress* in October 1883 and not reprinted in her later collections,
is typical of this secularized affective lyric. In the first stanza the lyric
speaker reflects on her alienation from the beauty of the natural world
around her:

> The starlight has gladdened the river,
> The moonbeams have silvered the sea,
> But lonely I stand in the midnight,
> No beacon has brightened for me.

The light shining down on the lyric speaker in this first stanza invokes a
Christian poetic tradition in which the heavens above provides transcendent inspiration and the animating touch of some greater force, sparking
the solid human clay on earth into spiritual life. Sparse and simplistic as it
is, however, Radford's poem subverts this conventional order of things.
The speaker does not yearn for heavenly light, but a humble 'beacon'. That
beacon's parity with the speaker's subject position is emphasized by the
internal rhyme which yokes it to the heavily endstopped 'me' at the end of
the line. The light of inspiration and love that completes the beauty of the
earth is found in humanity, not in the heavens. In the second and third
stanzas of the poem this reading is extended by exploring and denying the
possibility that the 'music' of the stars and the 'poetry' of the moonlight
might complete 'the beauty' that is wanting in the speaker's vision of the
evening.

---

[19] Scheinberg, *Women's Poetry*, p. 51.

The poem closes with a stanza that seems to typify the affective domestic realm prescribed for the nineteenth-century woman poet and this, in addition to some clumsy prosody in the final line, might indicate why Radford decided not to include the poem in her later collections. Nevertheless, the text gives a good indication of Radford's subtle subversions of even the most trite poetic conventions with the radical intellectual currents of her Bloomsbury circle.

> But I think in my own little valley,
> With the faces and scenes that I love,
> I shall there find the light that is wanting
> To perfect the beauty above.

The lyric subject returns to the firmly non-transcendental world of affective relations in which she finds perfection and completion. But the familiar domestic sentiments here should not obscure the important inversion of the conventional religious positioning of the giver and receiver of light, inspiration, and beauty. Whilst the natural world 'glows with a softened delight' thanks to the beneficent light from above, in the materially specified, remembered and populated world of the valley, the light of inspiration is generated from below and shines from human community. An ethical affect emanating from humanity completes the limited beauty of the naturalized heavens. As Martin Priestman has suggested, in a rather different context, within an atheist poetics 'nature' accretes a new set of referents as an autonomous material system rather than as a source of some spirit more deeply interfused in its matter.[20] Radford's poem denies that lyric subjectivity is inspired from above and thus teaches the 'great lesson of godlessness', as Aveling recommended. But Radford's alternative ideal is far from that of a self-authorizing subject: her lyric shadows forth an idea of aesthetic creativity embedded in the affective heart of human(ist) community. The verse combines conventional feminized lyrical affect with a new secular ethical subjectivity.

Dollie and Ernest Radford's ventures in secularism stopped short of a wholehearted advocacy of rationalist atheism and, like many of their peers at the fin de siècle, the couple explored alternative belief systems to supplement the spiritual void.[21] The particular form taken by the developing socialist movement in the early 1880s offered one such alternative in an age of agnosticism. During this period the 'religion of socialism' entwined the

---

[20] Martin Priestman, *Romantic Atheism: Poetry and Freethought, 1780–1830* (Cambridge: Cambridge University Press, 1999), p. 7.

[21] See Ch. 3 for the exchange between Ernest Radford and Eleanor Marx in the pages of *Progress* in late 1883 concerning absolute atheism.

prospect of material revolution with a millenarian belief in a new life of ideal beauty outside capitalism.[22] With poets such as William Morris and Edward Carpenter as its prophets, this aspect of the wider movement proved particularly attractive to the aesthetic secularist circles of 1880s Bloomsbury. Yet Dollie Radford was initially resistant to socialism, perhaps, paradoxically, because it numbered some of her oldest friends among its most eminent advocates. It was Karl Marx who first observed the young Caroline Maitland paying 'fearful court' to Ernest Radford at his daughter's play-reading club in 1881 and Eleanor Marx continued to keep Dollie Radford abreast of developments in the socialist movement during sociable outings to the Turkish Baths in the early 1880s.[23] Thanks to her friendship with Eleanor Marx, Dollie Radford was introduced to the editorial team of a new 'scientific' socialist journal, *Today*. As members of the avowedly Marxist Social Democratic Federation, Ernest Belfort Bax and James Leigh Joynes aimed to create a very different forum from Aveling and Foote's radical secularist journal, but Radford was pained by the group's lack of charitableness and aesthetic sensibility.

Radford turned her mind to producing some verses for *Today*, despite her ambivalent attitude to 'scientific socialism', after an encouraging meeting with Bax and Joynes in Eleanor Marx's rooms in January 1884. Even in these early months of the rebirth of the socialist movement in Britain, however, Radford was aware that her philanthropic social observations and unsystematic sense of social injustice marked her out from Marx's other visitors. Bax, in particular, was a notorious misogynist who claimed that women were simply incapable of turning their attention from their own love affairs to great social questions.[24] He directed his ire at what he termed 'sentimental socialists' who were merely a manifestation of the 'morbid self-consciousness of our Christian and middle-class civilisation run to seed': a solipsistic indulgence of young men and women who required a 'stimulus' of some sort.[25] Radford was all too aware of how likely Bax was to reject her work on such grounds and her first step was to work through her sense of political dislocation with some humour in her diary.

---

[22] Stephen Yeo, 'A New Life: The Religion of Socialism in Britain, 1883–1896', *History Workshop Journal*, 4 (1977), 5–50.

[23] Karl Marx to Jenny Longuet, 11 April 1881, *Karl Marx and Friedrich Engels Correspondence, 1846–1895* (London: Martin Lawrence, 1934), pp. 389–90; Radford Diary, 25 May 1883.

[24] Ernest Belfort Bax, 'Some Heterodox Notes on the Woman Question', *Today*, 8 (1887), 25–7.

[25] Ernest Belfort Bax, *The Religion of Socialism: Essays in Modern Criticism* (London: Swan Sonnenschein, 1887), pp. 92, 100.

I have some verses in my head
As many have, but then
What is the use; I wish instead
The same were in my pen.
Oh I would write such stirring lines
About the great To-morrow,
And send them to the owners of
'To-day' to ease their sorrow.

What idle dreams! My simple writing lacks
All qualities that Messrs Joynes & Bax
Would most approve: in intimate relation
I've been with Nihilists of every station
And German socialists of every plan,
But never have I known a working man.[26]

Ever an astute judge of the periodical press and its editorial expectations, Radford anticipated that the sort of poetry required for *Today* would be very different from the secular affective lyrics published in *Progress*. It was not that *Today* was wholeheartedly devoted to expositions of *Das Kapital,* despite the journal's rather stern subtitle, 'The Monthly Magazine of Scientific Socialism'. The first volume contained the serialization of George Bernard Shaw's *An Unsocial Socialist*, William Morris's 'Art under Plutocracy', Edward Carpenter's *England's Ideal*, Edward Aveling on Ibsen, essays by Walt Whitman, Edith Simcox, Eliza Lynn Linton, Eleanor Marx, and poems by Ernest Radford and Havelock Ellis in addition to nihilist novels and socialist essays by the usual suspects such as Stepniak. It was rather that the journal required a vigorously material aesthetic in which poetry performed a triumphant march towards a future of labour. Idealist dreams evoking the 'religion of socialism', such as Edward Carpenter's contributions to the journal, lacked sufficient rigour for Bax and Joynes and were published with an editorial disclaimer, disavowing the content as unscientific.

Despite Bax's own misogyny, *Today* had a far higher proportion of female contributors than the increasingly intellectually chauvinist *Progress* ever did. It was in this forum that the Fabian socialist E. Nesbit and her half-sister Saretta Green or 'Caris Brooke' published a considerable number of socialist hymns and topical dramatic lyrics such as 'The Husband of Today: The Wife of all Ages'.[27] Nesbit asserted that in contrast to her 'published

---

[26] Radford Diary, 23 Jan. 1884.
[27] *Today,* 4 (1885), 403. We might read the title of the former poem as a not-so-subtle pun in this context, given that Nesbit's husband, Hubert Bland, was soon to take over the editorship of *Today* himself. In the later 1880s, under the influence of the Blands, *Today* edged away

poems' which were 'nearly all *dramatic lyrics*', only her 'socialist poems are *real me*, and not drama'.[28] But as Nesbit in retrospect felt her 'real' self to be sufficient for *Today*'s needs, so at the time, Dollie Radford felt herself absurdly lacking in what the editors required. That affective discourse of the feminized poetic heart could not be further from the embodied labour of the 'working man' that so eluded Radford's limited field of acquaintance in the radical drawing-rooms of Bloomsbury. Nevertheless, Radford laboured on trying to produce something suitable, toying with a 'Socialists' Hymn', during early 1884.[29] I want to consider her 'Two Songs' from *A Light Load*, which according to her diary she completed during this period, as a response to this pressure and the anti-affective thrust of scientific socialism she associated with Bax and the SDF.[30]

> Winds blow cold in the bright March weather,
> Yet I heard her sing in the street to-day,
> And the tattered garments scarce hung together
> Round her tiny form as she turned away.
> She was too little to know or care
> Why she and her mother were singing there.
>
> Skies are fair when the buds are springing,
> When the March sun rises up fresh and strong,
> And a little maid, with her mother, singing,
> Smiled in my face as she skipped along,
> She was too happy to wonder why
> She laughed and sang as she passed me by.
>
> Stars are bright, and the moon rejoices
> To pierce the clouds with her broken light,
> But the air is heavy with childish voices,
> Two songs ring through the clear March night –
> Songs which the night with burning tears
> Sings out again to the coming years.[31]

Radford's 'Two Songs' draws a motif of revolutionary poetics from the work of a writer to whom Radford 'felt nearer than any' during the early 1880s, Percy Bysshe Shelley, and uses that motif to question the limits of

---

from supporting the revolutionary socialism of the SDF towards the state socialism of the Fabian Society.

[28] E. Nesbit, cit Julia Briggs, *A Woman of Passion: The Life of E. Nesbit* (New York: New Amsterdam, 1987), p. 71.

[29] Radford Diary, 18 April 1884.

[30] Radford Diary, 5 March 1884.

[31] Dollie Radford, 'Two Songs', in *A Light Load* (London: Elkin Matthews, 1891).

heroic masculine radicalism.[32] Shelley's 'Ode to the West Wind' frames the autumnal West Wind as a dialectic 'Destroyer and preserver' which drives the seeds of future life to the ground, 'Each like a corpse within its grave, until / Thine azure sister of the Spring shall blow / Her clarion o'er the dreaming earth . . .' Radford's 'Two Songs' returns upon Shelley's ode by opening in that promised spring which closes his poem; but in 'Two Songs' this is a spring that brings to light only urban fragmentation. In Shelley's text the dense interlocking of terza rima propels a turn from figuring the wind as the natural force of seasonal death and rebirth to the inspiration of a poetics of tangible social effects: 'Be through my lips to unawakened earth / The trumpet of a prophecy!' Yet in Radford's urban spring of modernity, the March wind of the first stanza heedlessly blows past the singer on the pavement as an uncaring force of inevitable material change.

Radford's 'Two Songs' reworks the conventional radical poetic association of the masculinized wind with a message of hope in political transformation by contrasting the impersonal force of March with the vulnerable, ignorant singer in the first stanza. The singer is no longer the unencumbered lyric self of Shelley's ode, but rather a child rooted in the marketplace, singing spontaneously, but singing for her supper nevertheless. The speaker of the first two stanzas observes the street singers at the level of the pavement and rather than aspiring to join the onward sweep of the March wind, couches a description of the scene in language that harks back to an earlier nineteenth-century tradition of women's philanthropic poetry; Radford's rendering of the tiny, vulnerable child forced to sing thus owes something to Elizabeth Barrett Browning's 'The Cry of the Children'. In this instance, however, the type of child labour being criticized is in itself uncomfortably close to the recuperation of the aesthetic by capitalism. The child singing on the pavement for money is closer to the woman poet selling her verses to indifferent editors than the factory children, indentured to the iron wheel of manufacture, that form the subject of Barrett Browning's poem. 'Tiny', 'little', 'singing', 'happy', and unknowing, the spontaneous child singers in 'Two Songs' echo the familiar critical terminology of the spontaneous feminized 'poetess' applied to Radford by her contemporaries and underscore the passivity of such a role. The two songs of the first two contrasting sesta rima stanzas are those of girl children in radically different social positions: the indigent beggar child and the happy 'little maid' out for a walk with her mother. Yet the final stanza suggests that both these singers will be condemned to join in chorus but still remain unheard in the long cycle of 'the coming years'. Radford might not know the working man, but here the lyric

---

[32] Radford Diary, July 1883.

voice elides the distance between the woman poet and the working-class girl child under capitalism in order to examine the consequences of really not knowing why one is singing in public; of merely babbling meaningless song in the capitalist marketplace. I want to suggest that by means of this strategic identification the poem re-examines socialist hopes of change and questions the persistent deferral of the question of women's sexual exploitation within the movement.

The oppositional reworking of radical poetics can be traced through the dialectic of forms of time at work in the poem. In the second stanza the virile sun of early spring, 'fresh and strong', encourages the little feminine buds of the 'happy' little maid to blossom into precocious maturity just as the March wind exposes and penetrates the body of the 'tiny form' of the working-class girl in the previous stanza. Despite the cyclical logic of the seasons, March here is linear, progressive, and developmental. In the final stanza, however, there is a very different form of time at work. Gravid assonance displaces the tripping consonance of the first two stanzas and the straining anapaests foreground that odd juxtaposition of 'childish' and 'heavy'. The feminine moon rejoices, but is not to be looked to as an alternative source of authority to that of the 'strong' March sun: she, perhaps like the late nineteenth-century woman poet, is 'broken' by her attempts to pierce the obscurity and lighten the streets below. In this nocturnal streetscape the two voices of the ignorant girl children have become one with the night itself, condemned to weep 'burning tears'. Given the public concern with prostitution and the sexual exploitation of children in London during the mid-1880s, it is possible to read these 'burning tears' as an allusion to the physical hazards of women taking to the streets at night in the form of venereal disease. This heavy fruit of sexual knowledge is shared by women of all classes for endless 'coming years', whilst the revolutionary promise of the March wind is implicated by its absence from this female cycle of sexual performance and commerce.

Almost exactly a year after Radford drafted 'Two Songs', William Morris composed the opening poem of his epic *The Pilgrims of Hope*, 'The Message of the March Wind'.[33] Anne Janowitz has recently restated the significance of 'The Message of the March Wind' in the face of a critical tradition of apology and neglect by placing it within a radical dialectic of romanticism. Morris's debt to Shelley is, Janowitz argues, 'recuperative and revitalising' and 'brings a poetic of lyric solidarity to bear upon the complex punctual and inward self of liberal hegemony'.[34] If Morris's recuperative

---

[33] *The Collected Letters of William Morris*, ed. Norman Kelvin, 4 vols. (Princeton: Princeton University Press, 1984–96), ii. 386.
[34] Janowitz, *Lyric and Labour*, p. 31.

aesthetic endows the romantic dialectic with new vigour, Radford's poem interrogates the limitations of a radical poetics that does not engage with the realm of the heart and sweeps past the charitable object of sympathy on the street, unable to carry her message in its haste to the bright communal future. The sequence in which Radford republished 'Two Songs' in *A Light Load* in 1891 emphasizes this subjective critique. The preceding poem, 'Why seems the world so fair, / Why do I sing?' explores the resources of the aesthetic in preparing for a world of hope in a future 'Spring' and LeeAnne Richardson has analysed the poem that follows 'Two Songs', 'What song shall I sing to you / Now that the wee ones are in bed', as a consideration of the domestic limitation of women poets.[35] Read between these two lyrics, 'Two Songs' gains an even sharper political resonance. The lyric voice abruptly breaks off its affective rhapsody of hopeful domesticity in the surrounding poems, to listen to another tune. After this, the following poem's vision of children 'tucked away on a pillow white / All snug and cosy for the night' reads as anxious overstatement in the face of the material basis of affective domesticity.

Several months after she composed 'Two Songs' Radford was convinced by William Morris that she was indeed a socialist. She had, she realized, been left cold by other leaders of the movement, such as Aveling and H. M. Hyndman, because they were incapable of giving form to the beauty as well as the seriousness of socialism.[36] As the mother of three young children during the rise of socialist activism in the 1880s and early 1890s, Radford was well aware of the limits to her own engagement in the movement. Whilst her friends Eleanor Marx, Grace, Constance, and Clementina Black all went to the East End and made various attempts to organize labour and foster socialist discussion, Radford's involvement remained limited to the drawing-room meetings of Bloomsbury and Hammersmith. Yet that peculiarly aesthetic and idealist flavour of the 'religion of socialism' during the 1880s enabled Radford to figure her own work as a contribution to the greater cause, providing the hope of beauty that was in itself a revolutionary force according to Morris. Inviting as Morris's aesthetic socialism was for Radford and her husband, however, the productivist communal ideal of socialist art disseminated by Morris sat awkwardly with Radford's attenuated lyrics and songs. The spaces of Morris's aesthetic socialism proved inhospitable to the individuated, feminized lyric voice and her second collection of poems negotiates its way through the communal political imper-

---

[35] Richardson, 'Naturally Radical', p. 112.
[36] Radford Diary, 30 Nov. 1884.

ative of Morris's manly socialism and the highly wrought autonomy of aesthetic poetry.

II

Whilst Morris's socialist lectures, collected and published as *Signs of Change* in 1888 provide the clearest formulation of his productivist, communal aesthetic, his utopian fiction *News from Nowhere* (1891) works through these theories and provides exempla of anti-individualist, post-revolutionary art. As Patrick Brantlinger suggests, *News from Nowhere* is a text preoccupied by the effects of communal socialism on aesthetic expression.[37] The narrative form reflects a concern with the types of art and creative subjectivity that will be possible under socialism. Lyric poetry is nowhere to be found and the realist novel has disappeared along with its precondition of bourgeois individualism. In Nowhere the environment has become 'our books in these days'. Novels speak only of the sorrowful past of individualism in which 'the hero and heroine [live] on an island of bliss' and work their way through 'a long series of sham troubles . . . illustrated by dreary introspective nonsense' whilst the world labours on around them.[38] As the text rejects bourgeois individualist interiority as a repository of aesthetic truth, architecture takes up the narrative function of emotional complexity and embodied history: communal space displaces individual depth. 'I console myself', Morris wrote in *Signs of Change*, 'with visions of the noble communal hall of the future' when confronting the vulgar possessive individualism of the 1880s.[39] Ellen, the most carefully realized (and interestingly eroticized) inhabitant of Nowhere, reaffirms her earlier contentions regarding the incomprehensibility of realist fiction when she reaches out to embrace the lichened wall of Kelmscott Manor towards the end of the novel. Rather than a conventional union between hero and heroine in defence against the world, the heroine's 'shapely sun browned hand and arm' stretches out to a union with the world in the form of the house that has 'waited for these happy days, and held in it the gathered crumbs of happiness of the confused and turbulent past'.[40] There is no chance of such a clinch for the visitor to utopia, William Guest, the unmistakable bourgeois individual product of high capitalism, for Ellen's love is for 'the earth . . .

---

[37] Patrick Brantlinger, 'News from Nowhere: Morris's Socialist Anti-Novel', *Victorian Studies*, 19 (1975), 35–49.
[38] William Morris, *News from Nowhere* (London: Routledge, 1970), p. 129.
[39] William Morris, *Signs of Change* (London: Longmans, 1888), p. 32.
[40] Morris, *News from Nowhere*, p. 174.

and all things that deal with it and grow out of it'. At the end of the novel, then, Kelmscott Manor displaces the old individualism and interiority of romance and the heart is given over to the commonweal.

But it is not only the old private realm of romance that is displaced by communal architecture in *News from Nowhere*. Politics, too, is unindividuated in this utopia and what Kelmscott Manor does for romance at the end of the novel, the site of Morris's Kelmscott House in Hammersmith does for politics at the beginning. As the narrator eats his breakfast after waking up in the guest hall, his eye is caught by 'a carved and gilded inscription on the panelling' in the hall. It is the only instance of the written word that Guest encounters directly in Nowhere and he is 'much . . . moved' by its simple statement: 'Guests and neighbours, on the site of this Guest-hall once stood the lecture room of the Hammersmith Socialists. Drink a glass to the memory! May 1962'.[41] The guest hall articulates a history that the younger inhabitants of Nowhere are unconcerned with, if not actively hostile towards. The space of socialist argument and education has become a place of pleasurable labour, but only the building memorializes the efforts of past individuals to bring about this new communal life. The inhabitants of Nowhere have no need to look forwards or backwards in a world in which history has come to rest in utopia. However, the eloquence of space in *News from Nowhere* works by drawing out the contrasts between present and future whilst at the same time offering a parallel of spatial practices under capitalism and primitive communism: a parallel of which the inhabitants of Nowhere, with their lack of history, are unconscious. As the ancient church in Oxfordshire is used for a harvest celebration and the Houses of Parliament are linked by a naughty metonymy to their use in Nowhere as a dung market, so the guest hall echoes the past: this is a utopian transformation of the meetings of the Hammersmith branch of the Socialist League.

Dollie Radford's record of evenings at the Hammersmith meeting hall provides a sense of the communal fellowship that Morris aimed to suffuse through his fellow socialists. The converted coach-house became a place of performance and celebration, with Morris himself as master of ceremonies:

> The 'At Home' of the Hammersmith Branch of the Socialist League. We went around to Mr Morris's and aided in putting the room in order . . . It was a very informal meeting—music—and recitations. Miss Morris sang to her guitar, & looked very beautiful, Ernest recited 'Hiawatha' . . . with much success. I played 'Chacone' & sang 'Little Binks' with moderate success. A gentleman recited half of 'The Revenge' & then broke down, another gentleman sang a song inviting the proletariat to revolt, & so on.—A very young

[41] Morris, *News from Nowhere*, p. 12.

socialistic babe was present. I wish **Mr Morris** were less noisy, his presence is so boisterous I feel its [sic] over**powering** . . . Walter Crane is a member of the League & sent some of his pictures to adorn the walls . . . we sent them our cups & silver spoons! . . . In bed very late.[42]

After joining the Hammersmith Branch of the Socialist League in January 1886 Radford's chief involvement lay with the educational and social side of the organization. The fact that Radford did not take part in more active campaigns may not have been a choice on her part. The minute books of the branch make it clear that a gendered division of labour was in force in the organization.[43] Whilst Morris, Emery Walker, Sidney Cockerell, and other men were in regular attendance at the Sunday evening meetings, Morris's daughter, May, was the only one of a considerable number of female members who participated at this level. It was May Morris who first suggested that the branch hold social entertainments every few months and she formed part of a largely female committee responsible for organizing these and other events.

Written in the cold light of day and feeling 'rather seedy' the next morning, Radford's account of her evening out emphasizes the very undomestic nature of the Hammersmith Socialist League 'At Home'. The working space of the coach-house is filled by other people's possessions in a fiction of communality, the open invitation for all to contribute to the pleasure of the evening sets an uneven tone between concert and conversation, and Morris's physical enthusiasm that all embrace this experience of fellowship sets the 'socialistic babe' crying. Yet as Morris's vision of pleasurable existence in *News from Nowhere* suggests, the future of revolutionary socialism lies precisely in being 'At Home' in such communal halls, mixed by age, class, and gender. Morris's efforts to imagine the future of art under socialism continually returned to the idea of the workshop populated by parties of 'merry young men and maids' finding a means to artistic expression without individualism through tradition and the pleasurable labour of the hand.

If Radford's attempt to class Morris's communal aesthetic as an 'At Home' sits at odds with this noisy celebration of revolutionary socialism, then other socialist organizations in the capital did offer a mode of politics closer to such middle-class salon culture. The Fabian Society, of which Radford was also a member, developed its political strategy through the culture of the 'At Home'. The society's drawing-room meetings, emphasis upon political reform through permeation, and gentle manipulation of prominent politicians cannot but provide a partial explanation of the

---

[42] Radford Diaries, 6 Feb. 1886.
[43] Minutes and Papers of the Hammersmith Socialist Society, BL Add. Mss. 45891.

prominence of women such as Annie Besant, Charlotte Wilson, and Emma Brooke on the society executive during the 1880s. By 1892 female Fabians were confident enough of their own standing to press for women-only shortlists and Radford's old friend Constance Garnett (née Black) served on the executive in 1894.[44]

With considerable ideological sleight of hand, George Bernard Shaw argued that it was the very nature of these Fabian Society drawing-rooms that led to Morris's refusal to join the society. They simply never offered the aesthetic resources of hope so necessary for his revolutionary socialism. Morris, Shaw argued, 'was an ungovernable man in the drawingroom [sic]' and would have been more out of place there 'than in any gang of manual labourers or craftsmen'.

> The furniture would have driven him mad; and the discussions would have ended in his dashing out of the room in a rage, and damning us all for a parcel of half baked, shortsighted suburban snobs, as ugly in our ideas as in our lives.[45]

Despite the amenability of the Fabian Society to middle-class women activists and writers like Emma Brooke and Edith Nesbit, by the early 1890s Radford's own aesthetic interests had drawn away from those of the increasingly research-driven Fabian Society. Ernest Radford served as secretary to the Arts and Crafts Exhibition Society from 1888 until 1892 and, thanks to this post and his membership of the Rhymers' Club, Dollie Radford's cultural life shifted towards the late flowering of aesthetes rooted in the publishing houses of John Lane and Elkin Matthews.[46] Yet although Radford's diary records her increasing interest in intellectual exchanges with her fellow poets, including Arthur Symons, 'Michael Field', and W. B. Yeats, her aesthetic Sunday salons were also attended by her fellow socialists. The utopian socialists and sexual radicals Edward Carpenter, Kate and Henry Salt, for instance, joined in one of 'Willie Yeats' . . . hypnotic experiments after supper' one evening in 1891.[47] If merely holding hands across the void seems insufficient evidence of the developing co-articulation of socialism and aestheticism for Radford, then her continued reflections on Morris's

---

[44] *Fabian News*, 2/3 (May 1892), 2–4. Emma Brooke opposed the motion for a quota of women on the executive.

[45] George Bernard Shaw, 'Morris as I Knew Him', in May Morris, *William Morris: Artist, Writer, Socialist*, 2 vols. (Oxford: Blackwell, 1936), ii, p. xviii.

[46] See Peter Stansky, *Redesigning the World: William Morris, the 1880s and the Arts and Crafts* (Princeton: Princeton University Press, 1985), pp. 171–262, for the Arts and Crafts Exhibitions Society. Ernest Radford was appointed secretary of the Society in April 1888 for a salary of £175 p.a. He was replaced by Sidney Cockerell in 1893.

[47] Radford Diary, 12 April 1891.

work underscores that intellectual debt which Bruce Gardiner argues was shared by all members of this Rhymers' Club generation in the 1890s.[48]

Radford was filled with gratitude by the kind reception the Hammersmith socialists gave Ernest on his first visit after leaving the asylum in March 1893 and stated more clearly than ever her commitment to the socialist productivist aesthetic she saw at work in Morris's home:

> it is new life to find again the intensity & joy of art work. How much I wish every one could make one thing . . . that might live for always . . . I do know many people—sad and hopeless—creeping through their lives in a shell— shut up & withered—If they could have painted one picture—made one song—or done one little thing of their very own I think they would have awakened. It is all in [Edward Carpenter's poem] 'Towards Democracy'. Edward Carpenter understands well.[49]

Although Radford could see a clear connection between the crafting of beauty and the future political ideal, both the communal space of the Hammersmith Socialist Society and the executive meetings of the Fabian Society became an increasingly ill fit to her circumstances and interests. By the mid-1890s Beatrice Webb decided that 'aesthetic middle-class' women socialists such as Radford's sister-in-law, Ada Wallas (née Radford), with their 'yellow-green sloppy garments . . . worn *on principle*' were distinctly 'old fashioned' in the context of the sleek investigative machinery of the Fabian Society.[50] Whilst Ernest Radford was able to develop the aesthetic and idealist aspect of Morris's socialism with his fellow socialist peers within the Rhymers' Club, Radford's separation from the site of labour proved problematic in her attempt to situate her poetics in the context of her productivist aesthetic socialist beliefs. As we have seen, some women socialist writers of the period, such as Olive Schreiner, found a means to refigure their work as 'virile' (re)productive labour in response to the aesthetic model outlined by Morris, but Radford's attenuated lyrics proved less amenable to the aesthetic of communal production. As Janowitz has pointed out, the designation of so much of Morris's poetry as song and chant during the period alludes to a poetic mode outwith the individualism and inwardness associated with lyric subjectivity: poetic form was in this sense politicized during the period.[51]

---

[48] Bruce Gardiner, *The Rhymer's Club: A Social and Intellectual History* (New York: Garland, 1988), p. 36. See also Norman Alford, *The Rhymer's Club: Poets of the Tragic Generation* (Houndmills: Macmillan, 1994).

[49] Radford Diary, 23 March 1893.

[50] *The Diaries of Beatrice Webb*, ed. Norman and Jeanne MacKenzie, 4 vols. (London: Virago, 1982–5), ii. 129. Entry dated 21 Jan. 1898.

[51] Janowitz, *Lyric and Labour*, pp. 216–32.

III

Two of Radford's poems from her 1895 collection *Songs and Other Verses* negotiate this tension between the individuated form of the lyric and the communal productive aesthetic of socialism. The first, 'If you will sing the songs I play', falls within a cycle of short lyrics in *Songs and Other Verses*, addressing the fate of creativity when the love that sustained it is rejected. It is tempting, of course, to read such lyrics autobiographically in the light of Ernest Radford's serious mental breakdown in April 1892 and subsequent periodic institutionalization. But I want to suggest that in this particular poem Radford counterposes the individualism of the lyric with the status of song as a historicized, communal endeavour which so animated the verse of other poets of the socialist movement.

> If you will sing the songs I play,
> Then you shall be my dear,
> And I will cherish you alway,
> And love you far and near;
> If you will, in sweet singing, say
> The songs I play.
>
> And if to all my deeper strain
> A golden rhyme you learn,
> Ah me, to what a rich refrain
> My striving chords shall turn;
> If you will learn the deeper strain,
> The great refrain.[52]

'If you will sing' reflects Radford's increasing interest in, and proficiency with, experimentation in verse forms in her second volume of poetry. The poem's ostensible subject matter of the changing relationship between singer and song is matched by a stanzaic structure which echoes the *rentrement* of the medieval rondeau, traditionally sung to a musical accompaniment. In this case, however, each stanza adopts its own rhyme scheme and refrain which underscores the movement of the poem between two alternative models of the relation between singer and accompanist, or, by extension, poet and muse, in the making of song. The first stanza could be read as a troubling love lyric in which love itself is conditional upon the 'sweet' singer's compliance with the accompaniment of the speaker. The speaker will love the singer only if she follows his or her tune and this might be

---

[52] Dollie Radford, 'If you will sing the songs I play', *Songs and Other Verses* (London: John Lane, 1895).

another reflection on the limitations imposed on the woman poet by her audience.

The second stanza turns outwards from this narcissistic demand for love (and art) as self-reflection, however, and figures the lyric speaker not as lover, but as a lyre, trembling under the breeze of a 'deeper strain' and striving towards a 'rich refrain'. The production of song in the second stanza moves from being the result of a sweet singer mouthing the tune of an accompanist to a collaborative endeavour in which both learn from each other and participate in 'The great refrain'. Although initially the lyric speaker marks his ownership of such deeper and richer music, 'strain' and 'refrain' are repeated in the *rentrement* without the possessive pronoun. Moreover, the refrain is modified from being an individual 'rich' aesthetic good in the third line, into a site of collective chant with 'The great refrain' at the end. The 'great refrain' here—and indeed, in the formal structure of the text—alludes to the work of art as a communal endeavour for truth and beauty that repeats itself throughout history. If the singer finds 'golden rhymes' to match the music of the speaker then both will participate in the communal aesthetic of '*the* deeper strain', '*the* great refrain'. Whilst the first stanza proffers a poetics of compliance in which the sweet singer will be cherished for matching the tune of the times, the second stanza insists that a higher alternative involves the singer joining the historic, choric 'great refrain' even at the cost of losing the fleeting sweet songs of her individual voice.

In Radford's poem 'Comrades' this ongoing struggle between the individuated affective figure of the woman poet and the demands of the greater communal refrain is given a sharp political inflection by the title of the work. It was during the 1880s and 1890s that the term 'Comrades' gained a particular association with revolutionary socialism as a non-hierarchical, unsexed denotation of fellow travellers, suggestive of a future ideal of fellowship. Morris's 1885 collection, *Chants for Socialists*, for instance, included the rowdy drinking song 'Down among the Dead Men' that insists 'Come, comrades, come, your glasses clink; / Up with your hands a health to drink' and condemns all 'that will this health deny' to lie down among the dead men in the chorus.[53] As Morris's *Chants* were frequently sung at meetings of the Socialist League and Hammersmith Socialist Society, Radford was doubtlessly aware of this vigorous celebration of 'strife in hope while lasteth breath / And brotherhood in life and death'. Against such collective, martial masculinity, the individual lyric speaker of Radford's

---

[53] William Morris, *Chants for Socialists* (London: Socialist League, 1885).

poem hears from 'afar the dire refrain' which beats upon the heart and brain of her distant comrades.

> What shall I do when you pass by
> And gaze at me so quietly,
> What shall I give of all my store,
> To help you to your joy once more!
>
> Some jewelled gift, some treasured thing,
> I had not meant for offering;
> Shall I not bid you take the whole
> Of what I prize, to heal your soul!
>
> For I have seen the lonely track,
> The cruel chasms, bitter black,
> The stony roads no pastures meet,
> Which you have pressed with bleeding feet.
>
> . . .
>
> What shall I give you, what shall I say
> To help you on your lonely way,
> A kindly hand, a smile or so,
> A gentler glance—for all I know?
>
> May be a tender word or two,
> At most a prayer, or tear for you,
> And strength to tell you help is vain,
> Dead joys do never rise again.

Whereas Morris's 'Down among the Dead Men' invokes a communal oral tradition with its double-couplet long metre, Radford's 'Comrades' uses the same measure to probe the tensions between collective experience and aesthetic form. In an echo of Radford's earlier admission 'never have I known a working man', the lyric speaker is at an enforced distance from the onward march of these sufferers and reflects upon her own limited capacity to contribute to the remedy. The speaker's 'store' of goods that she can offer the comrades reads almost as the stock in trade of the female aesthete: 'Some jewelled gift, some treasured thing' prized as an object of taste. But these individuated goods of the aesthetic movement are rejected as insufficient defence against the 'relentless days' ahead of the comrades. That aesthete's store of beauty does not, however, prevent her from identifying with the collective concerns of the comrades. The four central stanzas of this poem provide a sustained examination of four different means of access this feminized lyric subject has to the greater cause: she has 'seen the lonely track' of poverty; she has 'heard from afar the dire refrain' of historically recurrent strife; she has 'known the tears' which waste the 'gold of life' from the individual; she has 'pictured the relentless days' of a struggle 'Stretching before you like a sea'.

The final stanzas return to explore the resources of the lyric subject in alleviating the process of struggle. Rather than the aesthetic goods of the opening two stanzas, however, the text considers the value of sympathy and sentiment at its close and revisits the nineteenth-century tradition of feminine affective poetics. The first line of the penultimate stanza invokes the devotional tradition of the 'gift', echoing, for example, Christina Rossetti's 'In the Bleak Midwinter' and the first line of its final stanza, 'What can I give Him / Poor as I am'.[54] Rossetti's poem concludes, 'Yet what I can I give Him / Give my heart' but it is this very feminized Christian realm of the heart that is emphatically absent from the conclusion of Radford's verse. Tender words, prayers, and tears of poetic affect are alluded to as the inevitable, ineffective accompaniment of speech. That speech, however, must deconstruct the feminine poetic tradition of sympathy for the downtrodden: 'help is vain' and the comrades must move onwards through their own struggles without the palliative hope of the better resurrection of 'dead joys'. In many ways this conclusion that 'Dead joys do never rise again' reflects the decline of a millenarian spirit within the socialist movement in the early 1890s. The great demonstrations and strikes in London during the late 1880s had not, as so many activists like Morris and the Radfords hoped, led to a complete reorganization of society five years later. Socialism, as we saw in Chapter 2, could no longer be viewed as a romance in which desire for the beautiful would bring forth a second summer for the medieval guild system, a new life of communalism. The 'strength' to tell the truth that 'help is vain', that consciousness and long struggle alone could bring about social change, is a quality that resonates with twentieth-century socialism. It is an analysis of the future struggle which also does something to explain why the publication of poetry in socialist journals tailed off in the modernist era as politics and aesthetics became increasingly distinct categories.

Radford's most substantial contribution to that carefully wrought product of fin-de-siècle aestheticism, John Lane's *Yellow Book*, also works through this opposition of individuated feminine affect and the greater communal struggle that preoccupied 'Comrades'. 'A Ballad of Victory' appeared in the *Yellow Book* in April 1896 and the circumstances under which Radford was asked to contribute to the periodical serve as a reminder that socialism and aestheticism were never that distant from each other in

---

[54] 'In the Bleak Midwinter' was the first text in the 'Devotional Poems' section of Rossetti's collection *Poems* (London: Macmillan, 1875).

the late nineteenth-century metropolis.[55] Radford encountered Lane at the first night of George Bernard Shaw's *Arms and the Man* which she attended with Constance Garnett and a party of fellow Fabians. In between gawping at the 'real Bulgarian admiral' in the Stepniaks' box and critiquing Shaw's play, Radford agreed to send the requested 'lyric' for the next edition of Lane's volume.[56] 'A Ballad of Victory' was Radford's third contribution to the *Yellow Book* and by its very title it announces its formal divergence from the lyrics Lane commissioned from her. The ballad employs the same trope of pilgrims, journeying the rough roads of suffering with bruised feet, that structured Radford's poem, 'Comrades'. But the allegorical nature of 'A Ballad of Victory' enables, or even requires, an inversion of the relationship between the individual and the communal, subject and object, that structured the earlier poem and thus strives to find a means by which politics and aesthetics can continue to inform each other.

The formal properties of Radford's ballad invoke the customary culture of the oral tradition in which verse speaks from and for the commune. The narrative of 'A Ballad of Victory' is thus carried by a collective voice of legend, rather than by an individual lyric speaker, and concludes with a dialogue between and old woman and a young man. Radford's accomplished prosody is evident in the very restraint of this sustained exercise in the ballad form. Despite its publication in the *Yellow Book*, the poem refuses to call attention to itself as aesthetic artifice, focusing instead on the process of discovery in the narrative. The inhabitants of the walled market-town in the mountains marvel at the 'tender ways' and 'patient eyes' of a scarred traveller who visits their market. She is from distant lands but she refuses to share in the goods of their 'bounteous days' and must move ever onwards in her journey.

> With quiet step and gentle face,
> With tattered cloak and empty hands,
> She came into the marketplace,
> A traveller from many lands.[57]

The commune comes together to speculate on the identity of the lone female traveller after her departure and unravel the contradiction between the marks on her body of 'wounds so deep and old / The cruel scars on her

---

[55] Radford's works in the *Yellow Book* comprise 'I could not through the burning day', 2 (July 1894), 116; 'Outside a hedge of roses', 6 (July 1895), 121–2; 'A Ballad of Victory', 9 (April 1896), 227–9.

[56] Radford Diary, 21 April 1894.

[57] Dollie Radford, 'A Ballad of Victory', *A Ballad of Victory and other Poems* (London: Alston Rivers, 1907).

breast' and her 'steadfast air'. In the process of discovering her route and her name the townspeople construct a shared understanding that they too are fellow travellers on her road.

> And in their midst a woman rose,
> And said, 'I do not know her name,
> Nor whose the land to which she goes,
> But well the roads by which she came.'

The very refusal of the female pilgrim to identify herself and leave any trace other than the lingering affect of her love, requires the townspeople to inter-pret her self-abnegation for themselves. The answer is found by one 'youth' gifted 'With clearer eyes and wiser heart'.

> 'But stronger than the years that roll,
> Than travail past, or yet to be,
> She presses to her hidden goal,
> A crownless, unknown Victory.'

Like the contemporaneous allegorical figure of George Frederick Watts's painting *Hope* (1886), Radford's Victory consists in a transitive state against all odds. Victory, like Hope, is not a final destination in Radford's work, but a process of becoming. The very act of interpreting this feminine suffering body as Victory makes it so, on the part of the commune. In one sense, then, it is possible to read Radford's 'A Ballad of Victory' as a poem that restates the ethical affect of the aesthetic in an era increasingly hostile to such analy-ses. Through the act of seeing, reading, and interpreting a single woman's narrative of struggle, the commune can reconstruct their individual experi-ences as shared victory-in-process. Morris's 'Pilgrims of Hope' turned to epic and history to explore the self and the commune in the transitive journey of revolution in the pages of the socialist journal *Commonweal*. Radford's allegorical ballad carried forward that question of the coming into being of communal consciousness through the process of struggle in the midst of the *Yellow Book*.

IV

Although the *Yellow Book* is so often deployed as a shorthand notation for the particularities of decadent aestheticism in the 1890s, a closer study reveals a more complex aesthetic at work. Linda Hughes has recently pro-duced a valuable revisionist account of the 'literary and sexual politics' of the *Yellow Book* that foregrounds what she terms 'New Women' poets' use of the periodical 'to intervene in contemporary debates via individual poems'.[58] The stylistic diversity of the *Yellow Book* also requires some reassessment of the broad church of Lane's aesthetic interests. Radford's 'A Ballad of Victory' in the *Yellow Book, 9* (April 1896), for instance, is followed by the characteristically precious fragments of Richard Le Gallienne's 'Four Prose Fancies' and framed by Sydney Meteyard's decadent painting, 'Cupid'. T. Baron Russell's short story that precedes her ballad, however, is entitled 'A Guardian of the Poor' and is closer to a sentimentalized George Gissing than any aestheticist work. John Lane's diverse mix of iconoclastic aestheticism and social realism thus offered Radford more space to work through her ethical aesthetics than might be expected from that confining rendition of her as poetess-aesthete on the frontispiece of Lane's *Songs and Other Verses* (1895).

Writing in her diary in 1893, Radford affirmed that she wanted to teach her children 'to be socialists':

> But that must come with serious thought—to belong to the struggling ones, & those who are at a disadvantage—to be true as light, tender & sweet as flowers—strong & firm as rock.[59]

Ernest Belfort Bax dismissed what he termed such 'Sentimental socialism' as nothing other than the 'morbid self-consciousness' which, in other eras would be stimulated by 'languishing and vapouring on art' rather than social reconstruction.[60] Yet Radford's ethical aesthetic refused to separate political consciousness from aesthetic receptivity, socialism from ethical affect. In the face of the increasing inscription of proto-modernist aesthetic autonomy and scientific socialism Radford sought to marry the 'rock' of material determinism and the 'sweetness' of ethical affect.

[58] Linda Hughes, 'Women Poets and Contested Spaces in the *Yellow Book*', *Studies in English Literature*, 44 (2004), 849–72 (p. 866).
[59] Radford Diary, 3 April 1893.
[60] Bax, *Religion of Socialism*, p. 92.

6

Engendering a New Age:
Isabella Ford and Alfred Orage

Dear Edward Carpenter,
. . . Perhaps you may have seen in the 'Labour Leader' some bookish notes under the heading, 'A Bookish Causerie', and if you have you will see that I have been attempting, though with much less success than I had hoped, to read modern literature in the light of the new old conception you & Whitman have done so much to spread. And I want, if it be in my power, to go still further and more persistently into what inwardly I feel to be the deepest need of thousands like myself,—the need for a secure foundation in one's own soul for the more or less superficial & transitory beliefs, intellectual, physical and ethical.[1]

By 1896 Edward Carpenter had accustomed himself to the fact that his writings on socialism, sex-love, the simple life, and Neoplatonic evolutionism had made him the 'special prey' of enthusiasts on various 'crusades' who sought his approval either in person on pilgrimages to his smallholding or, as in this case, by post.[2] The 23-year-old teacher in Leeds who sent this particular letter, however, was to do more than any other admirer to continue the intertwining of Carpenter's own interests in esoteric philosophies of self-development, an artistic renaissance, and a communal socialist future. Alfred Orage's biography might be read as a paradigm of late Victorian self-help and character. The son of an indigent widow, Orage forged his way (thanks to a combination of old-fashioned local patronage and modern municipal provision) through teacher-training college into the world of journalism to edit one of the most influential modernist journals of the early twentieth century.[3] In 1896 he was already combining a full-time teaching post at Harehills Board School and his column in the *Labour Leader*

---

[1] Sheffield City Library, Carpenter Collection MSS 386/63, Alfred Orage to Edward Carpenter, 3 Feb. 1896.
[2] Edward Carpenter, *My Day and Dreams* (London: Allen & Unwin, 1916), p. 167.
[3] See Tom Steele, *Alfred Orage and the Leeds Arts Club, 1893–1923* (Aldershot: Scolar, 1990), pp. 25–42.

with producing propaganda material for the Leeds branch of the Independent Labour Party (ILP) alongside Isabella Ford and acting as de facto editor of the radical local paper, *Forward*.[4] Despite his own success story, Orage himself became increasingly critical of such blithe narratives of nineteenth-century progress during his years as editor of the *New Age* (1907–22). Orage's beliefs and the organizations with which he allied himself—the ILP, the Theosophical Society, the Leeds Arts Club, his personal mission to disseminate Nietzscheism, the Fabian Arts Group, guild socialism—encapsulate the diverse tendencies and forces held together by socialists during the 1880s; forces which for Orage were never simply those of progress, but of critical conflict and creative destruction in pursuit of utopia.

Like many of his predecessors in the socialist movement, Orage scrutinized the relationship between capitalist society and the current state of the arts and speculated about the aesthetic capacities of the 'beyond man' under socialism within the pages of the *New Age*. By the time he assumed editorship of that journal in 1907, however, Orage had become sceptical of the Liberal reformist political solutions advanced by the Parliamentary Labour Party, the Fabian Society, and even the avowedly socialist ILP which he had joined in its (and his) youth in Leeds in 1894. The flowering of late nineteenth-century idealism that led so many middle-class socialists to aspire to self-sacrifice and self-deadness in efforts for the cause of labour looked withered and dated in a new age in which, according to Orage, the elected representatives of Labour had 'perverted the conception of the commonwealth to a repugnant picture of a community dominated by themselves'.[5] Orage's response to this perception was twofold. First, he insisted that the socialist members of the ILP dissociate themselves from trade union representatives in Parliament and hence dismantle the uneasy alliance that was the Parliamentary Labour Party in favour of a new Socialist Party. Second, Orage espoused the cause of guild socialism which, in contrast to the centralizing tendencies of Lib–Lab social reform policies, sought to revolutionize the economic organization of society into a multitude of workplace-based, self-governing guilds which would provide welfare for their members and goods for the commonwealth in return for paying tax—or charter fee—to a radically limited central state.

In a recent study of the *New Age*, Ann Ardis has suggested that Orage's interest in guild socialism should unsettle the prevalent characterization of

---

[4] Steele, *Alfred Orage*, pp. 32–3.
[5] A. R. Orage, 'What is the Future of Socialism?', *Leeds and Yorkshire Mercury* (6 March 1907), 4; repr. Steele, *Orage*, pp. 269–70.

the journal as one in which emergent literary and visual modernism displaced an earlier preoccupation with realism and socialist politics.[6] Wallace Martin, for example, quite rightly identifies a shift in the aesthetic agenda of the journal after 1911, away from the Edwardian realism of Arnold Bennett and the propagandizing of the journal's early sponsor, George Bernard Shaw, towards the 'new directions' of Vorticism and Futurism. But Ardis concludes that Orage's continued (and increasing) commitment to guild socialism after this point in time represents a critique of the avant-garde aesthetic manifestos published alongside his political argument in the *New Age*.[7] Ardis argues that there is a 'crucial distinction between the journal's modernist style of presentation and its socialist politics which are insistently and consistently differentiated from modernism's by the editors'.[8] The existing literary history of modernism, Ardis suggests, cannot contain the complexity of a journal that offered a materialist critique of the modernist avant-garde and its complicity with consumer culture at the same time as it nurtured the careers of these very same writers and artists.

This chapter re-examines the relationship between guild socialism and modernism by tracing the development of Orage's political and aesthetic interests, from his early work with Isabella Ford for the ILP and Leeds Arts Club to the peak of his influence as editor of the *New Age* in 1914. Orage's dissatisfaction with the socialism of his youth was matched by his rejection of 1890s aestheticism and Edwardian literary realism: movements that had captured his interest at their heights. By 1913 he extended this criticism to the work of Ezra Pound and other early modernist writers published in the *New Age*. When Orage was himself criticized for publishing a parody of Ezra Pound's essays on recent French poetry whilst the latter works were still appearing in the *New Age*, he defended the journal's right to a distinct editorial line. 'Nobody . . . thinks it odd that Mr Belloc should write in the *New Age* in criticism of the National Guilds System', Orage countered, 'and nobody will think it odd if the editorial exponents of that system reply either currently or at the conclusion of the series.'[9] Publishing a critical parody of that 'enemy of the *New Age*', Ezra Pound, was no different:

[6] Ann Ardis, '"Life is Not Composed of Watertight Compartments": The *New Age*'s Critique of Modernist Literary Specialization', in *Modernism and Cultural Conflict, 1880–1922* (Cambridge: Cambridge University Press, 2002), pp. 143–72. Ardis's chapter responds to the framing of the invaluable online digital archive of the *New Age* by Brown University's Modernist Journals Project: http://www.modjourn.brown.edu/MJP_NA.htm.

[7] Wallace Martin, *The New Age under Orage: Chapters in English Cultural History* (Manchester: Manchester University Press, 1967), pp. 108–20.

[8] Ardis, *Modernism*, p. 146.

[9] 'R.H.C.' (Alfred Orage), 'Readers and Writers', *New Age*, 14 (13 Nov. 1913), 51.

> We have, as discerning readers know, as serious and well-considered a 'prop-
> aganda' in literature as in economics or politics. Why should it be supposed
> that the economic writers are jealous to maintain their views and discredit
> their perversions or antitheses; and the critics of literature be indifferent? It
> will be found, if we live long enough, that every part of the *New Age* hangs
> together; and that the literature we despise is associated with the economics
> we hate as the literature we love is associated with the form of society we
> would assist in creating.[10]

Orage's robust defence of the holistic integration of his aesthetic and political beliefs should not obscure just how different these were from the
aesthetics of the religion of socialism of his youth. Orage's rejection of
aestheticism and early modernism stemmed from his identification of both
as effeminate and decadent: the products of high capitalism in which part
was valued over the whole. Yet at the same time as the politics of guild
socialism spoke of collective production and Orage's aesthetic argument
called for a new national art, Orage promoted heroic individuality and an
increasingly aristocratic and individuated notion of aesthetic responsiveness. In his letter to Carpenter in 1896 Orage was evidently already formu-
lating this political aesthetic: that 'new old conception' in which the
individual soul and the material life of the collective, modernity, and tradition needed to be balanced. Despite his careful attention to dismantling the
capitalist system, Orage's later repulsion from mass culture, class politics,
and parliamentary democracy thus created a surprisingly fitting stage for
the politically conservative aesthetic iconoclasts of the early modernist
generation published in the *New Age*.

Unlike his near contemporaries in the Bloomsbury Group, Orage's politics were never, to use Raymond Williams's term, 'a matter of conscience'.[11]
Orage's materialist critique of the avant-garde prevents him, as Tom Steele
suggests, from representing a 'fraction' merely prefiguring a later mutation
of the taken-for-granted tastes and interests of the intellectual middle
class.[12] Sympathy and the sense of class-based duty towards less fortunate
others which, as we shall see in the next chapter, played an important part
in the contest between aesthetics and politics in the works of Virginia Woolf
and Roger Fry, had no place in Orage's mature beliefs. In part, of course,
Orage's own origins meant that no remnant of noblesse oblige could structure his feelings towards a working class from which he himself had
emerged. But Orage's late rejection of sentiment in political discussion was

[10] 'R.H.C.' (Alfred Orage), 'Readers and Writers', *New Age*, 14 (13 Nov. 1913), 51.
[11] Raymond Williams, 'The Bloomsbury Fraction', in *Problems in Materialism and Culture*
(London: Verso, 1980), pp. 148–69 (p. 155).
[12] Steele, *Orage*, pp. 17–18.

also part of a wider turn away from ethical idealism in British socialism in the early twentieth century.[13] What Orage retained from this early affiliation was a resolute belief in the autonomy of the aesthetic; its capacity to function as a symbol of potential social freedom in its moments of ecstasy; the power of the ideal to drive forward the development of man.

'Man' is used advisedly here. If Morris's rhetoric of labour in fellowship enabled women socialists like Isabella Ford to figure themselves as craftswomen of a new life, Orage's attempts to fuse Nietzsche onto such a legacy left women behind, implacably rooted in the material world and the embodied impulses of the 'will to life'. It is no coincidence that one of the founding manifestos of the National Guilds League, the Storrington Document (1914), combines a unanimous Morrisite commitment to communal craft ideals and individual self-realization through labour with an irreconcilable rift on the question of women's place in the guild socialist state. Whilst the majority report on the latter issue insisted on the economic equality of men and women and the irrelevance of sex to socialist democracy, the minority report argued for the exclusion of women from industry. The inclusion of women in this basic unit of socialist organization would involve, the minority report suggested, 'the lowering of the standard of Guild workmanship to meet the peculiar disabilities of women'. 'The relation of women to the State', it concluded, 'is not an essential part of Guild Socialist doctrine in the strict sense'.[14] Orage's own increasing misogyny in the era of a renewed campaign for female suffrage by women socialists like Ford underscores the parallel path of his political commitments and the emergence of a self-consciously virile aesthetic in the pages of the *New Age* and beyond. It was a politics and an aesthetics that repudiated the progressive idealism of the 1880s and 1890s as complicit with effeminate decadence whilst obscuring its, and Orage's, own roots in that very past.

I

In the aftermath of her work organizing the Leeds tailoresses' strike in 1889, Isabella Ford found herself increasingly frustrated by the attitude of existing political parties towards her dual interests in socialism and the 'woman question'. During the strikes she had, she recalled some years later,

[13] See Stanley Pierson, 'The Exhaustion of Ethical Socialism', in *British Socialists: The Journey from Fantasy to Politics* (Cambridge, Mass.: Harvard University Press, 1979), pp. 157–226.

[14] 'Guild Socialism: The Storrington Document' (1914); repr. in Asa Briggs and John Saville (eds.), *Essays in Labour History*, 2 vols (London: Macmillan, 1967–71), ii. 332–49 (p. 349).

found that it was quite impossible to obtain any help, politically, from either of the two [political] parties ... There was no room for women anywhere. The insolent tone in which the working women who were daring to strike and daring to join Unions were referred to showed that sex hatred or what is even worse, 'sex-contempt' on the part of men towards women, was underlying our social structure.[15]

For Ford, the Independent Labour Party, and the particular inflection of the Leeds branches under the guidance of Tom Maguire in the early 1890s, seemed to fulfil the need of women (and potential union members) for 'some deeper teaching, something which would make them know that they were men's equals as human beings'.[16] A truly successful socialist movement would have to overcome the widespread inculcation of submission as a mark of moral respectability for the working-class woman. Writing in the *Women's Industrial News* in 1898 (probably at the behest of Clementina Black), Ford attacked the philanthropic attempts of middle-class women managers of girls' clubs to form obedient 'morally satisfactory citizens' from the raw material of factory girls. Such women 'behave as if submission was the only virtue necessary for the poor to practice, and they unconsciously mix together in a hopeless confusion the will of God and the will of the employer':

> If a working woman is taught this kind of thing in her political associations, and in her religious and general moral elevation classes, how can we ever expect her to grasp the inner meaning of Trade Unionism which is resistance to evil, resistance to convention, in order to obtain a decent life for herself and others.[17]

It was clear to Ford, who had experienced the 'constant daily, weekly grind year after year, of keeping the girls in the Unions in anything like satisfactory numbers', that a party was needed which would couple parliamentary campaigns for labour reform with a commitment to this wider 'revolution'.[18] The development of trade unionism in tandem with the ILP, Ford suggested, offered a model of a future state in which autonomous individuality could be nurtured within a collective and thus abolish divisions of sex and class.

---

[15] Isabella O. Ford, 'Why Women should be Socialists: The New Vision in Politics', *Labour Leader* (1 May 1913), 10.

[16] Ibid. See E. P. Thompson, 'Homage to Tom Maguire', in Briggs and Saville (eds.), *Essays in Labour History*, i. 299–301.

[17] Miss Isabella O. Ford, 'An Unsatisfactory Citizen', *Women's Industrial News* (3 March 1898), 29–32 (p. 30). The *WIN* was the publication of the Women's Industrial Council and Clementina Black was the hon. sec. of the Investigation Committee of the WIC.

[18] Ibid. 29.

As numerous historians have observed, the ethical emphasis of the ILP, founded at a national conference in Bradford in 1893, married the aim of 'making socialists' within the Labour movement with the lingering sentiments of religious non-conformism.[19] Such an approach to socialism through idealist ethics and trade unionism alienated the new party from the leadership of the Marxist Social Democratic Federation in London. Explaining this hostility to his audience at the ILP annual conference in 1896 John Bruce Glasier characteristically couched ideological distinctions in the rhetoric of religious conflict:

> the ways of the SDF are not our ways. If I may say so, the ways of the SDF are more doctrinaire, more Calvinistic, more aggressively sectarian than the ILP. The SDF has failed to touch the hearts of the people. Its strange disregard of the religious, moral and aesthetic sentiments of the people is an overwhelming defect.[20]

This neat dismissal of Marxist theory as an alien imposition (without even mentioning Marx) obscured the local cooperation of the SDF and the ILP, a cooperation particularly evident in the North-West of England, where Robert Blatchford's pluralist Clarion movement held sway during the 1890s.[21] Although the leadership of the ILP developed constructive relationships with continental Marxists and Social Democrats through the Second International in 1896, resistance to theory continued to act as a marker of the 'authentic' national roots of the ILP in a native radical tradition in much of its official literature.[22] The frank self-definition of the ILP as a party of feeling—and of particularly aesthetic sentiments—was undoubtedly part of its broad appeal in the North of England during the 1890s: an appeal that was also notable for the clutch of middle-class women platform speakers who broadcast its aims.[23]

---

[19] Tony Jowitt, 'Religion and the Independent Labour Party', in Keith Laybourn and David James (eds.), *The Rising Sun of Socialism: The ILP in the Textile District of the West Riding of Yorkshire between 1890 and 1914* (Bradford: West Yorkshire Archive Service, 1991), pp. 121–34; Pierson, *British Socialists*, pp. 35–58; Lawrence Thompson, *The Enthusiasts: A Biography of John and Katherine Bruce Glasier* (London: Victor Gollancz, 1971), pp. 72–80.

[20] John Bruce Glasier, cit. Martin Crick, 'A Call to Arms: The Struggle for Socialist Unity in Britain', in David James, Tony Jowitt, and Keith Laybourn (eds.), *The Centennial History of the Independent Labour Party* (Halifax: Ryburn, 1992), pp. 181–204 (p. 185).

[21] See Crick, 'Call to Arms', pp. 181–5; Jeffrey Hill, 'The ILP in Lancashire and the North West', in James *et al.* (eds.), *Centennial History*, pp. 43–62.

[22] See, for example, J. Ramsay MacDonald, *The History of the ILP with Notes for Class Leaders* ([n.pl.]: ILP Information Committee, 1921), p. 3. As Crick points out, this self-definition has a visible legacy in the 20th-cent. history of the Labour Party. See also Pierson, *British Socialists*, pp. 35–58.

[23] June Hannam, 'Women and the ILP, 1890–1914', in James *et al.* (eds.), *Centennial History*, pp. 205–28. There is considerable historiographical debate concerning the place of women

Katherine St John Conway (later Bruce Glasier), who, like her fellow ILP campaigner Enid Stacy, had previously lectured for the Fabian Society, saw the foundation of the new party as nothing less than the birth of 'a child of the spirit of Liberty':

> [The ILP] claims every song she has sung—in whatever land—as a glorious heritage. Life, love, liberty and labour make liquid music . . . The socialist creed of 'One Body' is a declaration that liberty grows with love, and there-fore that life is love's child . . . To all who are in league with life—who believe in full fruition, beauty, and joy possible for each only as they are possible for all—to all true members of the ILP, every blade of grass, every living thing is sacred.[24]

Like Grace Black and Olive Schreiner, Conway drew on the vitalist thought of her mentor Edward Carpenter to blur the lines between reproductive labour and the political force of Labour. Although the ILP agenda included a commitment to the collective ownership of the means of pro-duction, distribution, and exchange, the hope for the new life of beauty was to effect the alteration in humanity that needed to accompany the socialist state. It was a thoroughly feminized trope of social change: a new life in which the infant child socialism was nurtured by love and beauty. Class struggle and revolution had little place in the rhetoric of the Bruce Glasiers, Keir Hardie, Philip Snowden, and Ramsay MacDonald. The young Alfred Orage claimed that it was precisely this emphasis on feeling and the power of human imagination that led him to join the ILP in Leeds.

> Do you suppose a young man weighs the probable results of his falling in love, or even thinks anything about its results before he falls? . . . As touch is the primary material sense, whence all others spring, so the primary mental sense, of which thought, imagination, reason are mere modifications is Feeling. After all, you cannot be an optimist with a sluggish liver, nor a philosopher with the toothache. I joined the ILP because I felt it the right thing for me to do: I continue in the ILP because I know it is. The feeling, however, came first, and the reasons, in plenty, came afterwards.[25]

---

and the woman question within the ILP in comparison to the SDF: see June Hannam and Karen Hunt, *Socialist Women: Britain 1880s to 1920s* (London: Routledge, 2002), pp. 14–17; Carolyn Steedman, *Childhood, Culture and Class in Britain: Margaret McMillan, 1860–1931* (London: Virago, 1990), pp. 131–5; Karen Hunt, *Equivocal Feminists: The Social Democratic Federation and the Woman Question, 1884–1911* (Cambridge: Cambridge University Press, 1996), pp. 7–15; Christine Collette, 'Socialism and Scandal', *History Workshop Journal*, 23 (1987), 102–11.

[24] Katherine St John Conway (Bruce Glasier), cit. Thompson, *Enthusiasts*, p. 75.

[25] Alfred Orage, in J. Clayton (ed.), *Why I Joined the ILP: Some Plain Statements* (Leeds, [1897]), cit. Steele, *Orage*, p. 30.

Orage's emphasis on the feeling self within socialism is markedly different from that of other contributors to the propaganda pamphlet *Why I Joined the ILP*, such as Isabella Ford, who examined the wider social questions addressed by the new party. Orage plays out his points with a style and argument clearly indebted to the aestheticism of the 1890s. Whereas collective aesthetic sentiment was an innate part of the ILP for Conway and Bruce Glasier, Orage provocatively inverts its appeal to a matter of individual desire.

In retrospect, Orage decided that his beliefs had been unduly coloured by Walter Pater and Oscar Wilde during the 1890s; a period in which 'we were very particular . . . what company we kept in the dictionary; and very promiscuous, as I now see, what ideas we entertained'.[26] Despite Orage's later unerring tendency to slide homophobic references into his criticism of Pater and Wilde in the *New Age*, Orage's journalism during the 1890s retained a distinct flavour of aestheticism well after the Wilde trial of 1895.[27] Orage and his generation of young men of letters believed, he recalled, that 'Pater had written "Marius the Epicurean" for us', and accordingly Orage's literary columns in Keir Hardie's *Labour Leader* shuffle a Paterian interest in the passing shades of the individual mind with the collective demands of the future socialist state.[28]

> Under a state of Socialism, men will be instinctively desirous of knowing more of their fellow men. Nothing will interest them so much as the human mind and its expression and capabilities. Autobiography . . . self-revelation, egotism, these will all be found in abundance. Whitman and Carpenter have begun: all the writers of democracy will continue. 'Let us have nothing but self'. It is the human mind which is of permanent interest in this world of migratory shades.[29]

Orage's explicit references might be to the established socialist canon of Carpenter and Whitman. It is, however, high aestheticism—the aestheticism of Pater's *Marius*, and its transformation of the *Bildungsroman* into a history of subjective sensation and ideas; of Wilde's 'The Soul of Man under Socialism' with its insistence on individualism and aesthetic autonomy—that is the shaping force of Orage's argument. As we have seen, Wilde's 'Soul of Man' had relatively little influence upon the well-established metropolitan community of socialist aestheticians upon its publication in 1891.

---

[26] 'R.H.C.' (Alfred Orage), 'Readers and Writers', *New Age,* 13 (12 June 1913), 177–8.

[27] On the 'ghosting' of Wilde in socialist periodicals see Ann Ardis, 'Oscar Wilde's Legacies to *Clarion* and *New Age* Socialist Aestheticism', in Joseph Bristow (ed.), *Wilde Writings: Contextual Conditions* (Toronto: University of Toronto Press, 2003), pp. 275–93.

[28] 'R.H.C.', 'Readers and Writers', pp. 177–8.

[29] 'A.R.O.', 'A Bookish Causerie', *Labour Leader* (12 June 1897), 194.

For Orage and other socialists of a younger generation, however, Wilde's dialectic of intense aesthetic individualism and communal politics seemed to provide an alternative to the resistance to modernity and high art in the works of Morris and his followers. During the early years of the ILP, the organization's emphasis on engaging individual aesthetic sentiments as part of the process of 'making socialists' provided Orage with the political correlative to his aesthetic interests.

For Orage's co-worker, Isabella Ford, however, it was not so much ideal-ism and the politics of feeling which drew her in to the Leeds ILP as its demonstrable commitment to equality. A few pages before Orage's own entry in the leaflet of 'plain statements', *Why I Joined the ILP*, Ford recalled a visit to a Labour Club in Colne Valley during which her 'last doubts were removed' about the new party. The men of the club 'had been giving a tea party to the women' and had performed all the work involved, including the washing up 'without any feminine help'. A party 'that included the educa-tion of men' in domestic labour as well as 'the education of women . . . [to] wider and truer views of life, was the party for me I felt, and so I joined it'.[30] Like several prominent members of the ILP, including Ramsay MacDonald, Ford could draw a constructive contrast between the new party and the experience of being a member of the Fellowship of the New Life during the 1880s. The tender nostalgia with which Ford frames the ineffective drawing-room socialists of the previous decade in her novel, *On the Threshold* (1895), is perhaps a mark of her conviction that, by contrast, the ILP offered a real chance for both socialism and sexual equality. Rather than the ill-defined collectivist sentiments of the Fellowship, the ILP represented a political movement in which men acknowledged domestic labour as labour and middle-class socialists could forge solidarity with trade unionists.

Ford was not only Orage's co-worker in the ILP propaganda in Yorkshire, but also, with her sister Bessie, rented and decorated the central ILP club in Leeds. It is thus not too surprising that Orage's review of *On the Threshold* in the *Labour Leader* was a friendly one despite their differing political motivations.[31] With a nod to the pervasive journalistic preoccupation of 1895, the 'New Woman', Orage titled his review 'Pre-Neo-Womanhood' and suggested that 'Democracy at last touches life' in Ford's novel. It would thus 'help many young women to cross the threshold of "stucco and window squirt" and enter the world of reality and high endeav-our'.[32] *On the Threshold*, Orage concluded, had the unusual merit of being

---

[30] Isabella O. Ford, in *Why I Joined the ILP*, cit. June Hannam, *Isabella Ford* (Oxford: Blackwell, 1989), p. 54.

[31] Hannam, *Isabella Ford*, p. 55.

[32] 'A.R.O.', 'Pre-Neo-Womanhood', *Labour Leader* (16 Nov. 1895), p. 5.

'a book of women, for men and women'.[33] Such a positive response to a novel which, as we have seen, provides a caustic analysis of the complicity of male socialists with sexual inequality and exploitation was not out of place in the *Labour Leader* during the mid-1890s. From 1894 to 1898, and thus during the foundational years of the ILP, the *Labour Leader* provided an unusual degree of support for and coverage of the woman question, thanks to the (frequently controversial) woman's column, 'Matrons and Maidens' contributed by 'Lily Bell' (Isabella Bream Pearce).[34] As June Hannam and Karen Hunt suggest, such a platform for feminist criticism was available during the 1890s precisely because the woman question 'had few immediate political implications' at the time.[35] After 1905, when the actions of the ILP members Emmeline and Christabel Pankhurst were matched by a renewed non-militant campaign for women's suffrage, women's columnists in the socialist press were obliged to become more circumspect. Isabella Ford, who had founded the Leeds Women's Suffrage Society with her sister Bessie in 1890, was one among many members of the ILP to be caught up in this later struggle.

Even by the late 1890s the political strategy of the ILP leadership started to displace the feminized ethical imperative of 'making socialists' which had drawn many women members to prominence on the platform. A new emphasis on national electoral politics led to an interest in alliances with trade unions as a means of securing victory at the polls for ILP candidates. For Ford, at least, the ideal (if not always the existing forms) of socialist trade unionism represented a 'peaceful revolution' and she insisted that the 'presence and influence of women is absolutely essential' within that movement.[36] Women everywhere, she argued, 'have even greater cause to cry vengeance than men have'.[37] Other leading women members of the ILP, such as Katherine Bruce Glasier and Margaret McMillan, were less enthusiastic about the new focus on electoral alliances with the trade union movement, believing that it would increase the marginalization of women.[38] During the mid-1890s the cheery man-to-man chat of Robert Blatchford's *Clarion* newspaper began to be mixed with contributions from women ILP activists addressing the difficulty of recruiting women to socialism if the movement

[33] Ibid.
[34] For a discussion of 'Lily Bell' see June Hannam and Karen Hunt, 'Propagandising as Socialist Women: The Case of the Women's Columns in British Socialist Newspapers, 1884–1914', in Bertrand Taithe and Tim Thornton (eds.), *Propaganda* (Stroud: Sutton, 1999), pp. 167–82 (pp. 171–3).
[35] Ibid. 179.
[36] Ibid. 180; Isabella Ford, *Leeds Forward* (Dec. 1898), cit. Hannam, *Isabella Ford*, p. 72.
[37] Ibid.
[38] Hannam and Hunt, 'Propagandising', p. 180.

concentrated on the workplace, the union, and the club.[39] Whilst the *Clarion* itself, with its caricatures, titbits, and sporting news seemed designed to be passed around working-men's clubs, 'Fabienne' argued that men needed to take the paper home with them and read it with their wives as a form of 'permeation in the kitchen'.[40] A few months later, Margaret McMillan urged women already active in the movement to act as 'intellectual mothers' of socialism and encourage the wives of men attending labour clubs to do the same.[41] McMillan characteristically teases out an acute analysis of the shortcomings of the ILP and the Clarion movement from a sentimental anecdote of a joiner's wife who brought her knitting along to a Labour Club meeting: a 'thrilling picture' she concluded, of what might be.[42]

Part of the appeal of Robert Blatchford's immensely popular *Merrie England* (1894) within the ILP was its simple criticism of material and spiritual 'ugliness' of the contemporary 'factory system' of society which prevented the people from becoming their own actors, artists, and musicians.[43] The numerous Clarion clubs and choirs that sprang up across the North-West of England during the early 1890s attest to the belief within the ILP and allied socialist groups that collective aesthetic experience could help forge political consciousness beyond the workplace. Towards the end of the decade the Ford sisters continued to combine 'making socialists' through aesthetic responsiveness with labour organization by establishing a Women's Trade Union Club in Leeds. An observer from the *Women's Trade Union Review* noted down the details of the interior of this 'bureau for labour information', half club, half tea room, with its own library:

> The whole place is painted white, and has yellow walls and a matting dado, and a wall paper covered with yellow daffodils or sweet peas—something

---

[39] On the masculinity of the *Clarion* see Martin Wright, 'Robert Blatchford, the Clarion Movement and the Crucial Years of British Socialism, 1891–1900', in Tony Brown (ed.), *Edward Carpenter and Late Victorian Radicalism* (London: Frank Cass, 1990), pp. 74–99.

[40] 'Fabienne', 'Permeation in the Kitchen', *Clarion* (27 Jan. 1894), 8.

[41] Margaret McMillan, 'The Women of the ILP', *Clarion* (10 March 1894), 3. For the significance of McMillan's idea of 'intellectual motherhood' see Carolyn Steedman, *Childhood, Culture and Class in Britain: Margaret McMillan, 1860–1931* (London: Virago, 1990), pp. 133–5.

[42] On McMillan as a journalist see Steedman, *Margaret McMillan*, pp. 141–55, 126–7.

[43] 'Numquam', *Merrie England: A Series of Letters on the Labour Problem addressed to John Smith of Oldham, a hard-headed workman fond of facts* (London: Clarion, [1894]), p. 19. As Steedman has shown, McMillan went beyond this boiled down Ruskinianism to develop her theories of creative imagination and child development: Steedman, *Margaret McMillan*, pp. 42–8.

nice. Beauty of all sorts is excluded from so many of our girls' lives, that it shall not be excluded from their club.[44]

The very feminine domesticity of the club's modish aesthetic interior is, however, in its way a corollary to the increasing sidelining of political aesthetics within the ILP at the turn of the century. Ann Ardis has suggested that Blatchford's *Clarion* began to relegate what she terms 'life-style aestheticism'—in other words, the display of taste in consumer goods that I term the aesthetic movement—to its 'Woman's Column' during this period.[45] Beauty itself thus became marginalized and feminized as a supplementary site to socialism in the form of the women's club, rather than the factory, the women's column rather than the leader page. Morris and his circle had formulated a political aesthetic in which contemporary tastes were a marker of the limitations of capitalism and the future rediscovery of beauty was contingent upon revolutionary socialism and communal production. The ILP's emphasis upon 'making' individual socialists through aesthetic responsiveness, and on economic redistribution through parliamentary means, rather than reorganizing the basis of production increasingly relegated the aesthetic to an ideological means rather than an end in itself. As the century drew to a close, the political aesthetics of the 1880s were unhitched from the socialist movement. No longer a tool in the analysis of capitalist production, aesthetic argument and education became a sentimental feminine palliative, whilst the aestheticism that captivated the young Alfred Orage formed the basis of a new interest in individualism among socialist thinkers.

II

In February 1897 Orage used his supposedly literary column in the *Labour Leader* to launch an attack on the ideological shortcomings of the ILP. As a complement to the ethical aesthetics that he claimed drew him to the party, Orage argued that the 'ILP must study economics':

> It is well to talk of ideals . . . but it is wise to remember that the present condition of things material is the organic outcome of the past, and that future conditions, while they may depend upon present ideals for their direction, will most certainly grow and branch out of the actions of today. Hence it is important that alongside of idealism, alongside the dreams which arise in the soul

---

[44] *Women's Trade Union Review* (Jan. 1897), cit. Hannam, *Isabella Ford*, p. 63.
[45] Ardis, 'Oscar Wilde's Legacies', pp. 283–4. Ardis takes her term 'life-style aestheticism' from the work of Kathy Alexis Psomiades: for a discussion of this and my distinction between aestheticism and the aesthetic movement see Ch. 1, pp. 21–2.

of man there should be science, and the thoughts which arise in the brains of man. Carpenter without Karl Marx is useless. Each is necessary to explain the other.[46]

Even as he presents Marx to his readership as a materialist alternative to Carpenter, Orage's article discloses the pervasive idealism of late nineteenth-century socialist thought and the paradoxes that structured his own later beliefs. Orage's historical materialism is evolutionary and organic rather than dialectic and material, branching out from root to twig; Marx's 'science' is no more material truth than 'thoughts which arise in the brains of man'. Ten years later, in the first of his series 'Towards Socialism' in the *New Age*, Orage had switched metaphors under the influence of the 'manly mysticism' of esoteric Buddhism, but the result is suggestive of his earlier pairing of Marx and Carpenter.[47] The world for the socialist, Orage insisted, 'is an everlasting becoming, a perpetual process of generation and regeneration, a continual mounting of life up the ladder of becoming'.[48] Socialism meant demanding 'impossible and incredible things' and being 'intolerant of anything less'. Given the current political situation, Orage anticipated that his readers might ask 'what has all this to do with the Labour Party in Parliament?' and his response at the time, as it had been with regard to the ILP and would continue over the coming years, was to reject compromise and pragmatism. 'There is', he argued, 'no inspiration in social reform, even of the most radical order, without passion for a remote end'.

It was this loss of passion for a remote end that seems to have distanced Orage from the ILP in Leeds at the end of the 1890s as it was to alienate him from the Parliamentary Labour Party a decade later. Despite trying to convince readers of the *Labour Leader* that the socialist movement could achieve unity if all its members sat down and read Marx's *Capital* properly, Orage devoted his energies for the next few years to another movement that appears the antithesis of scientific Marxism: theosophy. Orage of course was far from alone in combining such mystical interests with socialism: two of his fellow Yorkshire theosophists and later collaborators, A. W. Waddington and Arthur Penty, had been previously inspired to live the simple life in a cottage near Sheffield whilst turning out Ruskinian craft furniture.[49] Edward Carpenter's own interests led him in a similar direction in

---

[46] 'A.R.O.', 'A Bookish Causerie', *Labour Leader* (20 Feb. 1897), 58.
[47] 'R.H.C.', 'Readers and Writers', *New Age*, 14 (13 Nov. 1913), 51. Orage argued that by contrast Western Christian mysticism was 'effeminate' and nothing more than 'profound sensuality'.
[48] 'A.R.O.', 'Towards Socialism I', *New Age*, 1 (3 Oct. 1907), 361–2 (p. 361).
[49] Steele, *Orage*, p. 38.

the late 1890s, encouraged by the translation of the *Bhagavad Gita* by the leading theosophist and former Fabian, Annie Besant, in 1896. Theosophy seems to have represented a total system for such idealist socialists. By postulating a material manifestation of spiritual life and 'animal consciousness', theosophy synthesized the troubling opposition of material determinism and the autonomy of the human spirit.

Orage's critique of the ILP and his retreat to theosophy pinpoints the shifting ground of dissatisfaction with the socialist movement on the part of its aesthetic critics. The members of the Fellowship of the New Life in the 1880s had objected to the neglect of ethical ideals on the part of the Fabian Society and the SDF. But once this ethical idealism had become the animating force of the propaganda of the ILP a new form of that old opposition between individual morality and social reconstruction emerged from within the ILP itself in the 1890s. It was the work of Nietzsche and not of Marx which underpinned this systematic attack on the indeterminacy of ethical socialism by Orage and his fellow socialist writers at the turn of the century. For Hubert Bland, who had been at the founding meeting of the Fellowship of the New Life with Isabella Ford in 1883, and continued as a prominent member of the Fabian 'old gang', Nietzsche was the 'antidote to current sentimentality and to the modern tendency to carry morality into every sphere of life'. His mode of 'sparkling paradox' suggestive of 'a truth' averted the risk of entropy within the broad socialist movement: 'we are', Bland warned, 'in danger of being done to death by Ethical Societies'.[50] In a letter to the editor of the Nietzschean journal *The Eagle and the Serpent* in 1898, George Bernard Shaw was even more explicit concerning the possible remedy to the failures of ethical socialism. After a brief and partial account of the formation of the Fellowship of the New Life and the Fabian Society and their respective degrees of influence ('practically [none] at all' in the case of the former) Shaw suggests how and why Nietzsche became important to such self-consciously modern socialist thinkers.

> There was nothing to be learned from [the Fellowship of the New Life] that had not already been learned from the best of the Unitarians. Like them, it sought to free social and personal ideas and duties from superstition; but it laid an even greater stress on the sacredness of the ideals and duties than the comparatively easy going superstitious people did. It was not until after 1889, when Ibsen and Nietzsche began to make themselves felt, that the really new idea of challenging the validity of idealism and duty, and bringing Individualism round again on a higher plane, shewed [sic] signs of being able to rally to it men beneath the rank of geniuses who had been feeling their way

---

[50] Hubert Bland, *Fabian News*, 7 (July 1898), 17, cit. David S. Thatcher, *Nietzsche in England, 1890–1914: The Growth of a Reputation* (Toronto: University of Toronto Press, 1970), p. 223.

towards it for two centuries. Had the New Fellowship started with any glimmering of this conception, their history might be different. As it is, it seems to me quite possible that a Nietzsche Society might hit the target that the Fellows of the New Life missed, and might repeat on the ethical plane the success of the Fabian Society on the political one.[51]

When, in 1900, Alfred Orage was introduced to Nietzsche's *Thus Spake Zarathustra* by the Fabian Holbrook Jackson, the result of their mutual enthusiasm was, of course, another new society.[52] Contrary to Shaw's prediction, however, the group was directed at aesthetics rather than ethics.

In 1903 Orage and Jackson founded the Leeds Arts Club with the object 'to affirm the mutual dependence of Art and Ideas'.[53] The membership fee of 10s. 6d. necessarily limited membership to the professional classes in the city in contrast to Orage's earlier involvement in the ILP. This did not prevent Isabella Ford and her sisters Emily and Bessie from supporting the club as a welcome change from political agitation.[54] Emily had been one of the founder members of the original men and women's club in London whilst an art student in 1879 and the Leeds Arts Club complemented her role as vice-president of the Yorkshire Union of Artists and her old friendship with the aestheticist critic Vernon Lee.[55] Isabella Ford's literary reputation in addition to her status as a local activist and benefactor ensured her a place as one of the three women members of the management committee of the club. Ford's presence, Tom Steele asserts, rather too optimistically given his own evidence, was 'an antidote to any potentially resurgent masculinism' in Jackson and Orage's covert mission to 'reduce Leeds to Nietzscheism' through the club.[56]

Over the next three years the Saturday night meetings at the club's central premises provided an assortment of visiting luminaries who might have stepped out of a programme of socialist lectures from the 1880s: George Bernard Shaw, Edward Carpenter, T. J. Cobden-Sanderson, Isabella Ford. Mixed in amongst these were the ongoing efforts of Orage, Jackson, and A. W. Waddington to develop a distinct agenda of cultural politics among club members. The collective title of the series delivered by these three lecturers in 1905, 'Imaginary Portraits of Beyond-Men', reveals the unexpected marriage of Pater and Nietzsche that brought forth this shift in political aesthetics in the early twentieth century. Whilst Waddington's

---

[51] George Bernard Shaw, *Eagle and Serpent*, 2 (15 April 1898), 21, cit. Thatcher, *Nietzsche in England*, p. 187.
[52] See Steele, *Orage*, pp. 44–50.
[53] Leeds Arts Club manifesto, cit. Steele, *Orage*, p. 67.
[54] Hannam, *Isabella Ford*, p. 88.
[55] See Ch. 2, pp. 61–3.
[56] Steele, *Orage*, pp. 78–9; Holbrook Jackson, cit. ibid. 68.

lecture on 'Medieval Craft Guilds' made liberal use of Ruskin and Morris and Jackson's addresses on citizenship, democracy, and Shaw conformed to a Fabian norm, both speakers were adamant in insisting that collectivism was merely a means of enhancing individuality. Rather than the degraded concept of democracy, Waddington insisted that the future needed to be envisioned as a 'socialism of aristocracy in the Platonic sense'.[57] The extreme subjectivism of Paterian aestheticism gleaned from his *Imaginary Portraits* was fused to Orage's perception of Nietzsche as a mystical utopian prophet, whose superman (or 'beyond-man' in Orage's translation) would seek pleasure and pain for the sake of experience alone and who recognized that 'freedom is the will to be responsible for oneself'.[58]

This renewed interest in individuality at the Leeds Arts Club initially had some common ground with Isabella Ford's increasing activism within the women's suffrage movement in the early years of the twentieth century. In 1902 Ford accompanied a delegation of women textile workers from Yorkshire and Cheshire who were to present a mass petition for women's suffrage to a group of MPs in London.[59] Ford reminded readers of the *Labour Leader* at the time that the hostile view of many trade unionists towards women workers as 'persistent blacklegs underselling men' was in itself a consequence of such women being denied full individuality and citizenship. 'Blacklegism', Ford argued, 'is exactly one of the faults to which a class kept in a state of dependence, of political servitude, is prone'.[60] Unlike Orage, Ford's political loyalties remained firmly with the ILP and in 1903 she was elected to the party's National Administrative Council: a post she held until 1907 whereupon she was elected to the Executive Committee of the National Union of Women's Suffrage Societies (NUWSS). The report of Ford's lecture 'Women and the State', delivered to the Leeds Arts Club in 1905 with Orage in the chair, indicates the relationship between the club's aesthetics and her ethical analysis of the suffrage question as distinct from socialism. Rather than an analysis of labour such as that developed by her friend Olive Schreiner in the 1880s, Ford grounded her argument in the force of what we might now term ideology. Women's complicity with the sentimental masculine view of them as 'ministering angels', she suggested, kept them in a state of passivity and subordination and it was women who needed to divest themselves of these false beliefs.[61]

---

[57] Ibid. 70.
[58] Walter Pater, *Imaginary Portraits* (London: Macmillan, 1887); Orage, cit. Steele, *Orage*, p. 72; on Orage's intertwining of Pater, Nietzsche, and theosophy see Thatcher, *Nietzsche in England*, pp. 220–2.
[59] Hannam, *Isabella Ford*, p. 85.
[60] Isabella Ford, 'Women and the Franchise', *Labour Leader* (1 March 1902), 69.
[61] *Yorkshire Weekly Post* (28 Jan. 1905), 21, cit. Steele, *Orage*, p. 95.

The reading of Nietzsche as a moral iconoclast promoted by members of the Leeds Arts Club may have played some part in Ford's analysis of sentiment and subordination and encouraged younger feminist members such as Mary Gawthorpe and Ethel Annakin (later Snowden) to challenge social prescriptions in pursuit of suffrage.[62] Stanley Pierson suggests that Nietzsche's works led socialists to 'abandon the ascetic and altruistic values of Christianity' in the early twentieth century and this is an interpretation that makes sense of the pairing of Nietzsche with Ibsen by Shaw and other socialists of the time.[63] Unlike Orage and Waddington, however, Ford did not extend her critique of notions of duty and self-sacrifice to the ethical idealism that had first interested her in the labour movement. In the midst of the struggle for women's suffrage that had threatened to split the Labour Party, Ford argued in the *Labour Leader* (by then an official publication of the ILP) that women should be socialists on precisely those grounds. It has been said, Ford wrote in 1913, 'that "the party that has ideals is the party for women." No other parties [than the ILP] have ideals, though they have traditions.'[64] Women's participation in the ILP was of particular importance at a time when, in continental Europe,

> Socialism, on what I should call chiefly masculine lines, is being taught. Formed on narrow sex lines, it cannot have such a universal growth as here, where neither sex nor class distinction comes into our creed. Class war and sex war are poor things even if clothed in a Socialist garb, and they possess no real life.[65]

In contrast to such divisiveness abroad, Ford assured Carpenter that year that 'Comradeship, the real thing is growing fast' as a result of the simultaneous 'battles' for Irish Home Rule and women's suffrage: 'it's growing [most] amongst our sort of women & men . . . I feel like bursting with joy over it at times'.[66]

Ford's continued commitment to the ideal of collective comradeship without the boundaries of sex and class kept her loyal (but not uncritically so) to the ILP and the Labour Party for the rest of her life. Her sense that a Marxist politics of class struggle was in itself sexed as masculine and some-

[62] Gawthorpe became National Secretary of the militant WSPU and founding editor of the *Freewoman*, which in time morphed into the *Egoist* under the guidance of Ezra Pound. Annakin, Gawthorpe, and Ford worked together for the ILP and the Leeds Women's Suffrage Society during the early years of the 20th cent., but once Gawthorpe joined the Pankhursts in breaking with the ILP in 1907 she claims never to have heard from Ford again: see Hannam, *Isabella Ford*, pp. 113–23.

[63] Pierson, *British Socialists*, p. 130.

[64] Ford, 'Why Women should be Socialists', p. 10.

[65] Ibid.

[66] Isabella Ford to Edward Carpenter, 25 Aug. [1913], SCL Carpenter Collection MSS 286/220.

how foreign were beliefs that remained surprisingly durable in twentieth-century Britain. For Ford, Carpenter, and their 'sort of women & men', socialism was always to be bound up with the question of sexual equality and a desire to liberate the self from sexual prescriptions. Ford's demand for a 'revolution' thus might well have been for a revolution in the subject rather than in the material basis of society and her socialism, in that sense, remained rooted in the politics of the 1880s. But alongside fellow ethical idealists such as the Bruce Glasiers, Keir Hardie, and Margaret McMillan, Ford's coupling of the desire for a new life of beauty with a commitment to trade unionism shaped the British Labour Party well into the post-war period.

III

In December 1905 Alfred Orage took leave of his wife, his teaching post, and Leeds itself and moved into rooms in London with Arthur Penty in order to complete two books on Nietzsche and launch himself in the metropolis.[67] By the following spring, Holbrook Jackson had also left Leeds and, on his arrival in London, encouraged Orage to involve himself in a struggle within the Fabian Society. During his time as a member of the ILP Orage had dismissed Fabianism as a solution to the shortcomings of the British socialist movement, claiming that the '"Fabian Essays", useful as they are, are altogether too clever to be taken seriously'.[68] In a comically astute analysis of the metropolitan, intellectually self-conscious readership implied by Fabian publications, Orage concluded that the *Essays* were 'a sort of Socialist "Yellow Book"': a comparison which was to structure his later jibes at Ernest and Dollie Radford and their aesthetic socialist generation.[69] In 1906, however, the Radfords' friend H. G. Wells presented a paper entitled 'The Faults of the Fabian' which attacked the narrowness of the Society in the light of the far-reaching aims of socialism and provided unexpected opportunities for Orage in its aftermath.

Holbrook Jackson reported to the committee appointed to respond to Wells that the increasingly scientific focus of the Fabians had led to the

---

[67] Alfred Orage, *Nietzsche in Outline and Aphorism* (London: Foulis, 1906); Alfred Orage, *Friedrich Nietzsche: The Dionysian Spirit of the Age* (London: Foulis, 1906).

[68] For a reassessment of the relationship between the ILP and the Fabian Society see Mark Bevir, 'Fabianism, Permeation and Independent Labour', *Historical Journal*, 39 (1996), 179–96.

[69] 'A.R.O.', 'A Bookish Causerie', *Labour Leader* (20 Feb. 1897), p. 58.

neglect of 'such fruitful fields as Art and Philosophy' within the Society.[70] One consequence of such neglect was, Jackson argued, the dearth of study of the application of aesthetics within analyses of future 'social affairs as is contained in the various Handicraft Guilds resulting from the energies of Morris and his followers'.[71] The Fabian 'old gang' encouraged the formation of a series of subgroups to broaden the areas of expertise and propaganda within the Society as a result of this wave of criticism. As Jackson's statement hinted, however, these new subgroups were not to expand the Fabian basis so much as to challenge its very model of collectivism with a renewed interest in the guild system.[72] In 1907, with the blessing of Shaw and the Webbs, Jackson and Orage established the Fabian Arts Group modelled on their work in the Leeds Arts Club. This new group, like the Leeds Arts Club, disseminated a specific political philosophy through its avowed concern with the arts. If the Webbs had hoped the Arts Group would consist on lectures on typography and other craft practices by members such as Eric Gill, they were mistaken. From the outset Orage used the platform to explore the relation of craft guilds to socialism and aligned his aesthetic, anti-collectivist politics with the philosophy of Dionysian individuality in his paper 'Nietzsche contra Socialism'.[73] The arts were, after all, according to Jackson, methods of interpreting life that possessed the freedom to then be applied to life as criticism.[74]

In keeping with the Fabian interest in diversifying its output, George Bernard Shaw provided £500 for Jackson and Orage to purchase a dwindling weekly newspaper, the *New Age*, from the former Secretary of the Leeds ILP, Joseph Clayton early in 1907. By May the journal was relaunched under the joint editorship of Orage and Jackson and the banner 'An Independent Socialist Review of Politics, Literature and Art'. It was a self-consciously modern and intellectual weekly that, from the outset, scoffed at the peculiar 'fads' of an earlier generation of socialists.[75] It is hard not to read the emergence of this journal, catering to the interests of a (relatively new and insecure) urban, professional middle class, as a reaction to the unexpected success of the Parliamentary Labour Party in the general election of 1906. Orage admitted that the *New Age* 'cannot become for a long

---

[70] Ian Britain, *Fabianism and Culture: A Study in British Socialism and the Arts* (Cambridge: Cambridge University Press, 1982), p. 9.

[71] Holbrook Jackson, cit. ibid.

[72] On the part played by the Fabian Labour Research Department in developing guild socialism in this period see Margaret Cole, 'Guild Socialism and the Labour Research Department', in Briggs and Saville (eds.), *Essays in Labour History*, ii. 260–83.

[73] Britain, *Fabianism*, pp. 170–1; Steele, *Orage*, p. 137.

[74] Britain, *Fabianism*, p. 9.

[75] For the attack on faddism in the *New Age* see Ch. 4, pp. 102–3.

while, the paper of the "people"' but promised instead to be an 'organ of high practical intelligence'.[76] This distinction between the 'people' of the new mass electorate and an intellectual socialist readership ran through the current political concerns of the journal. The Parliamentary Labour Party did not offer individual memberships but instead represented the views of its component institutions: the trade unions, the ILP, and the Fabian Society. Readers of the *New Age* were in no doubt that it was the trade unions which exerted the most influence upon the party in terms of financial support and sheer numbers of affiliates. The fear of mass democracy and its effects upon cultural politics was by no means limited to Conservatives in this era.

From the outset the columns of the *New Age* contained discontented murmurings concerning the 'inveterate Liberalism' of working-class trade unionists in Parliament and the deference inculcated in them by the class system, in addition to criticism of the mere gradualist palliatives, such as old age pensions, sought by ILP leaders like Keir Hardie.[77] The trade unionist, Orage argued, 'makes the admission that labour, in the vulgar sense of work without delight, is necessary; and thereby becomes the slave of his own mind'.[78] The ILP-type of collectivist, by contrast, suffered from a poverty of imagination that makes all members of society 'masters and slaves of each' and conceives of 'Socialism as no more than the redistribution of the wages of shameful toil'. The 'main principle' of socialism for Orage was, however, 'that no man in the Socialist State shall labour without delight': anyone found guilty of the 'crime' of labour without pleasure would be sentenced 'to complete idleness for a period'.[79] Labour for Orage, like Wilde before him, was not in and of itself a source of pleasure felt through the body and the source of the aesthetic. But, like Morris, Orage argued that a revolution in the organization of the means of production could bring about a new world in which pleasure, rather than degradation, in labour was a possibility.

Orage's 1907 series, 'Towards Socialism' thus set an idiosyncratic political tone for the *New Age* from its launch which displayed a heavy debt to the aesthetic politics of the 1880s and early 1890s whilst affirming its status as 'modern' independent thought. From the title of the series, and its allusion (with a very significant substitution) to Carpenter's *Towards Democracy*, to the synthesis of the aesthetics and politics of Wilde and

---

[76] Editorial, 'To Our Readers', *New Age*, 1 (24 Oct. 1907), 408.

[77] Frank Matthews, '"The Ladder of Becoming": A. R. Orage, A. J. Penty and the Origins of Guild Socialism in England', in David Martin and David Rubinstein (eds.), *Ideology and the Labour Movement* (London: Croom Helm, 1971), pp. 147–66 (p. 162).

[78] 'A.R.O.', 'Towards Socialism IV', *New Age*, 1 (24 Oct. 1907), 407.

[79] Ibid.

Morris in the analysis of labour and pleasure, Orage wove his reaction against mass culture and democracy into the warp of a previous generation. Nowhere is this more apparent than in Orage's attempts to smooth over the long-standing belief that socialism and individualism were innately opposed to one another. Whilst Orage accepted that 'individualism' led to a society with an 'atomic structure', he argued that it was the mere 'dark shadow of the real individuality'.[80] Socialists of his sort, 'and there are many', were convinced (with a conviction bedded in theosophy mixed with Buddhism) that 'the souls of all men are so knit, so that in truth, whatever happens to oneself happens also to others'. It was thus possible for the socialist to experience both the 'unity in diversity' of solidarity and an individuality 'even more emphatic in its claims to uniqueness', which recognized that 'its uniqueness is conditional and privileged'.[81]

Wilde had snatched up the debate between individualists and socialists in the late 1880s and early 1890s and reformulated it in 'The Soul of Man under Socialism' (1891) into a dialectic in which a new individualism would emerge from socialism.[82] Orage sought an organic connection between the individual and the whole that moved further from materialism than Wilde himself had done. Wilde, for example, condemned the 'unhealthy and exaggerated altruism' of his time as a product of the 'immoral . . . use [of] private property in order to alleviate the horrible evils that result from the institution of private property'.[83] Orage, on the other hand, supplied the pithy neo-Wildean paradox 'To be altruistic from logical motives is to be as nearly devilish as a man can be', but the criticism in this case relates to the malformation of the organic relationship between individuals implied by 'logical motives'. A contemporary review of a new anthology of Wilde's writings in the *New Age* compared his 'brilliant perversities' to the 'paradoxes' of George Bernard Shaw and concluded that the current under-appreciation of Wilde's work was the result of his being 'first and foremost an artist' rather than a 'moral reformer'.[84] Yet whereas the notion of individuality of the crusading journalist Orage was invested with a spiritual autonomy from the material

---

[80] 'A.R.O.', 'Towards Socialism III', *New Age*, 1 (17 October 1907), 393–4 (p. 393).

[81] Ibid.

[82] For the topicality of Wilde's 'Soul of Man' see Josephine Guy, ' "The Soul of Man under Socialism": A (Con)Textual History', in Joseph Bristow (ed.), *Wilde Writings: Contextual Conditions* (Toronto: University of Toronto Press, 2003), pp. 61–83.

[83] Oscar Wilde, 'The Soul of Man under Socialism' (1891; repr. London: Journeyman, 1988), pp. 1, 3.

[84] Anon., 'Review: *Oscar Wilde: Art and Morality* ed. Stuart Mason', *New Age*, 2 (14 Nov. 1907), 53.

world, the artist Wilde understood individualism to be a product of the capitalist structure.[85]

By 1913 Orage had become anxious to distance his politics and aesthetics (and those of the *New Age*) from the works of Pater and Wilde. These two were decadents, Orage argued, because they elevated the part before the whole, style over content in their works. The 'poseur' Wilde was hampered by his amateur style that displayed 'not mastery of the language, but service under it as a mistress'.[86] The only part of Wilde's works that came 'within reach of manly criticism' was his 'Nietzscheism'.[87] Despite Orage's hysterical homophobia (whilst insisting that he used 'decadence' in an aesthetic, rather than a moral sense and merely pursued the critic's task of ministering to a diseased style), Wilde's discussion of aesthetic autonomy had undoubtedly informed a major shift in the policy of the *New Age* around 1911.[88] In July of that year the *New Age* included an attack on the aesthetics of H. G. Wells by the Tory journalist J. M. Kennedy and precipitated a marked turn away from the Fabian interest in realist fiction and drama exploring social questions.[89] In the autumn Orage himself produced a series of 'unedited opinions', written like Wilde's *Intentions* in the form of Socratic dialogue, which attacked the coupling of politics and aesthetics. Propagandist art, the lead debater argues, 'does not exist':

> The expression of intense feeling I can understand. An exposure of social evil is also necessary and useful. So, too, are expositions in science. But what have these to do with beauty? The sole object of a work of art is to reveal beauty and leave that beauty to affect whom it may . . . it is the nature of all spiritual things that they are above utility.[90]

It seems that Orage increasingly viewed both aesthetics and individuality as perfectly autonomous forces operating in a 'spiritual' realm. Artists, he argued, 'make a colossal error when they accept the testimony of their reason and deny the asseveration of their soul. They cease, in fact, to be artists.'[91] Seeking authority for his disaggregation of aesthetics and politics, Orage turned to Matthew Arnold's definition of poetry (and thus, Orage argued, art itself) as a criticism of life. Criticism, Orage concluded 'is a

---

[85] 'A.R.O'., 'Towards Socialism III', *New Age*, 1 (17 Oct. 1907), 393.

[86] 'R.H.C.', 'Readers and Writers', *New Age*, 13 (12 June 1913), 177–8 (p. 177).

[87] Ibid. Presumably Wilde's 'Nietzscheism' refers to his explosion of conventional pieties and the individualism of 'The Soul of Man'.

[88] 'R.H.C.', 'Readers and Writers', *New Age*, 18 (25 Nov. 1915), 85.

[89] J. M. Kennedy, 'The Last Straw', *New Age*, 9 (6 July 1911), 232–4; Martin, *New Age under Orage*, p. 112.

[90] [Alfred Orage], 'Unedited Opinions: The Limitations of Art', *New Age*, 9 (12 Oct. 1911), 562–3 (p. 562).

[91] Ibid. 563.

stronger attitude to assume towards life than mere reflection' and 'Progress in the spiritual meaning is, in short, a perpetual running away from what is called life'.[92]

Orage's reaction against the purposive realism of the Edwardian era in 1911 matched that wider shift in aesthetic interests which Virginia Woolf (with teasing hyperbole) dated as an alteration in the human spirit on or around 1910, the year of Roger Fry's first Post-Impressionist exhibition. Significant as that exhibition was for aesthetic discussions in the *New Age*, Orage's editorials were far more concerned with pressing questions of the future of socialism. The *New Age* orchestrated a campaign against Lloyd George's National Insurance Bill ('the worst Bill of modern times') in 1911 which was supported by the 'flunkey-like' Labour Party.[93] Such a bill represented yet another instance, Orage and his fellow leader writers concurred, of the misguided collectivist impulse towards redistribution of income without reorganization of the means of production. Moreover, in this instance the proposal was merely to impose a compulsory tax on the pitiful incomes of the poorest in order to force them to provide unemployment benefits and pensions for themselves. In contrast to such centralizing tendencies that did nothing to advance a real social change, Orage looked with hope towards the coming general strike as an 'alternative arm [of action] to that of the Parliamentary [Labour] Party':

> To the profound satisfaction of humanists, the working classes show signs of being prepared to stake everything—happiness, life, home and England—on their determination to improve the conditions of their class . . . Only by the most desperate courage will their class be lifted out of its present slough.[94]

The revival of mass unionism around 1910 fortified Orage's belief that the revolution could only emerge through proletarian struggle. The courage of a class was to change the material world; the humanist artist possessed of individuality was to bring about spiritual progress by running away from that life.

This separation of collectivist material politics from individualist, autonomous aesthetics forms part of a familiar narrative of the fate of ethical aesthetics in the modernist era. The radical nineteenth-century aesthetic tradition of deploying art as a critique of alienation and, as Terry Eagleton suggests, 'the ideal reconciliation of subject and object, universal and particular, freedom and necessity, theory and practice, individual and society', founders against the rationalized regime of late capitalism.[95] Orage's

---

[92] [Alfred Orage], p. 563.
[93] 'Notes of the Week', *New Age*, 9 (12 Oct. 1911), 533–5 (pp. 535, 533).
[94] Ibid. 534.
[95] Terry Eagleton, *The Ideology of the Aesthetic* (Oxford: Blackwell, 1990), p. 369.

attempts to revel in the perfect autonomy of the aesthetic—an art that was always beyond life, that was precisely and purposefully useless in all but the taste of possible freedoms it offered—are in this respect at one with the negative aesthetics of Futurism and Vorticism which Orage, as editor, offered a critical platform. Yet whilst the works of F. T. Marinetti and Wyndham Lewis blasted through traditional form, grammar, and syntax, Orage increasingly turned to tradition itself as a means of maintaining value against material determinism. Guild socialism was one such a repository of tradition for Orage and several of his followers: the disaggregated collectives of the guilds were to make new national values by reinvigorating the traditional mode of workshop production; the spiritual force of the beyond-man artist was to lead that nation beyond the common aspiration thanks to his access to the timeless freedoms of autonomous aesthetic values.

It was this constant tension between the social force of an interest group and the spiritual power of the individual that underscores the anarchistic tendencies of guild socialism.[96] The reaction against the compromises of the Parliamentary Labour Party and the collectivism of the Fabian Society led Orage and fellow former Fabian guild socialists such as Sam Hobson to insist on nothing less than a complete transformation of society to make 'man [sic] in the workplace both director of his economic and of his political destinies'.[97] Whilst self-consciously modern proponents of guild socialism such as Hobson and G. D. H. Cole developed analyses of the way out of the capitalist wage system in the *New Age*, Orage's old friend Arthur Penty insisted that only a return to medievalism would do.[98] Penty rooted his discussion of the guild system in the works of Ruskin and Morris, but his analysis of the exceptional position of the artist marks just how widespread the turn from Morris's productivist aesthetic had become by the early twentieth century. Morris had argued that after the revolution the innate pleasure of labour would reawaken somatic aesthetic susceptibilities among the men and women populating collective workshops. By 1914, Penty worried about the erasure of high art implied by this revolution and the current tendencies of Fabian collectivism.

Penty argued that the artist and the aristocrat were fellows in acknowledging their mutual superiority to the mass: 'the average man . . . being a

---

[96] Matthews, 'Ladder of Becoming', p. 162.

[97] Ibid.

[98] Sam Hobson's book *National Guilds: An Inquiry into the Wage System and the Way Out* (1914) was serialized anonymously in the *New Age* from April 1912 to Dec. 1913. On Hobson, G. D. H. Cole and guild socialism see Gary Taylor, *Orage and the New Age* (Sheffield: Sheffield Hallam University Press, 2000), pp. 48–74; M. Cole, 'Guild Socialism and the Labour Research Department', pp. 260–83.

democrat . . . will have nothing to do with' the artist, preferring 'the inferior mind'. If 'democracy took control of affairs, it would never trouble to think about the welfare of art' and, even if it did, something would be amiss as 'there is one thing the democracy cannot do, and that is to exercise discrimination'.[99] Democracy was 'impotent' and 'invariably lacks the leadership of the best and wisest' because it failed to acknowledge among artists, heroes, and aristocrats alike that the greatness of any man consists of 'a strong bias in a given direction [and] that bias is his individuality'.[100] Guild socialism for Penty and, to some extent, Orage and Hobson, was an anti-capitalist model that preserved traditional functional hierarchies of talent and specialization whilst dismantling class. Production itself was to become the task of appropriate collectives or guilds; art, taste, and the genius of leadership were to be determined by the autonomous realm of the spirit and these natural aristocrats would refresh the life of the guilds. The mass culture of collectivist democracy, by contrast, could only smother these supermen. Whereas Morris attempted to construct a somatic aesthetic in which the pleasures of the body were always a means of access to an aesthetic that only possessed relative autonomy, Penty's aesthetic returns to an Arnoldian exercise in taste, value, and discrimination.

This anti-democratic tone of the *New Age* in the pre-war period was in keeping with a wider reaction against the mass at the time. Shaw, for example, was only one among many Fabians who assimilated their own interpretations of the superman with an existing interest in specialization and the role of the expert in the future society.[101] But despite its Fabian origins the *New Age* was to play host to the writings of anti-statist and anti-democratic writers from across the political spectrum in the early twentieth century. The distinction of elite instrumentality from the masses in politics and culture was a common feature that connected attacks on the 'servile state' by Cecil Chesterton, Hilaire Belloc, and H. G. Wells with the re-evaluation of aristocracy and functional specialization by Orage, Hobson, J. M. Kennedy, Oscar Levy, and Anthony Ludovici.[102] To say that the political affiliations of these individuals were diverse would be a gross understatement.

---

[99] Arthur J. Penty, 'Art and Revolution', *New Age*, 14 (19 March 1914), 617–18 (p. 618).

[100] Ibid.

[101] Thatcher, *Nietzsche in England*, pp. 199–200, points out that Shaw's version of the superman always remained distinct from Nietzsche's (and the thought of many British Nietzscheans) as a result of his retaining an ideal of a democracy of supermen. For Shaw's philosophy of the superman see Ch. 4, pp. 119–29.

[102] On the role of the latter two writers in disseminating Nietzscheism and anti-semitism in the *New Age* see Dan Stone, *Breeding Superman: Nietzsche, Race and Eugenics in Edwardian and Interwar Britain* (Liverpool: Liverpool University Press, 2002), pp. 12–24, 33–8.

For Ernest Radford, who contributed a regular letter from Paris to the *New Age* during 1911, the stark contrast between this political diversity in pursuit of a common theme and the editorial policy of socialist journals during his own youth was too much to bear. Radford accused Orage of 'lowering' the *New Age* from its original socialist high ground and 'infect[ing] politics' with a 'hotch-potch of Nietzsche' and 'megalomaniac's notions', contained most notably in J. M. Kennedy's discussion of Tory democracy. The journal had become 'a paper in which the reader can detect neither purpose nor principle'.[103] Kennedy recommended that Radford, 'an idealist of idealists, and idealogue of idealogues', should 'go on writing verses: The *New Age* can take care of itself'. Radford's complaint was merely a sign of his dated understanding of political belief: 'when Mr Radford complains that there is "neither purpose nor principle" in the *New Age* at the present time, he means of course, that there is no idealistic purpose and no sentimental principle'.[104]

As if to underline the unsuitability of such idealism and sentiment in a thoroughly modern journal, Orage published the first of his cheerily misogynist 'Tales for Men Only' a few weeks after Radford's dishing by Kennedy. Adopting the pseudonym 'R. H. Congreve', which he was to use a few months later in his attacks on literary realism, Orage's short fictional 'Tales' constantly pit the sentimentalism, idealism, materiality, and 'flood of sex' of feminized mass culture against the masculine will to progress.[105] 'Congreve' reports on the continual siege laid by women against 'our group of men . . . intent on creating between them the collective soul or superman'.[106] In the first tale Marian thinks her degree in philosophy entitles her to join the conversation of this select Nietzschean club; her lover must be shown by Congreve that woman is always part of the great 'Maya' or illusion of life, and thus rescued from sentimental ties. A poet who brings along his girlfriend to meetings like 'a little mouse on his sleeve' is finally excluded from the homosocial 'circle closed against the mob' as he is clearly corrupted by her into idealizing femininity in his work.[107] A member's sister, with a library full of 'Shaw and Chesterton, Yeats and Synge, Wells, Kipling, Bennett, Galsworthy . . . *et hoc genus omne*' insists on the necessity of ethical purpose and realism in art against Congreve's prioritization of its

---

[103] Ernest Radford, 'A Friendly Letter', *New Age*, 9 (13 July 1911), 259.
[104] J. M. Kennedy, 'A Friendly Letter', *New Age*, 9 (20 July 1911), 284.
[105] 'R. H. Congreve', 'Another Tale for Men Only III', *New Age*, 9 (28 Sept. 1911), 517–18 (p. 518).
[106] 'R. H. Congreve', 'A Fourth Tale for Men Only I', *New Age*, 11 (2 May 1912), 13–14 (p. 13).
[107] 'R. H. Congreve', 'Another Tale for Men Only I', *New Age*, 9 (14 Sept. 1911), 469–70 (p. 469); 'Another Tale for Men Only III', *New Age*, 9 (28 Sept. 1911), 517–18 (p. 518).

inutility and 'charm'.[108] 'How like Oscar Wilde, she said', straying onto dangerous ground with Orage's alter ego, 'I do believe your attitude is only a pose—forgive me for being so rude! Isn't that in Oscar Wilde?'[109] Miss Forester's brother is only persuaded to renounce her and re-establish his rank among those who sacrifice the 'sentimentalities' of 'family ties' to follow the 'path to perfection ... paved with the arts' by an apposite Nietzscheism of Congreve's: 'The artist is the arrow, humanity is the bow. It is his aim and humanity's hope that he may be shot beyond this world.'[110]

This need to sunder the man of exceptional talent from the mass in order to achieve progress for the race cuts across the political and aesthetic interests of the *New Age* from 1911; and the mass is, almost invariably, feminized. Whereas the humour of Orage's 'Tales for Men Only' seems to reflect a masculinity in crisis, concurrent editorials on 'The Crisis in Literature' or 'Sentimentalism' were intemperate arraignments of feminized politics and aesthetics. 'Generally', one such article suggests, 'women should be disclaimed as readers by the artist whose business is with beauty and truth in literature. The patronage of women invariably results in the decline of arts.'[111] This opposition between feminized mass culture and autonomous masculine aesthetics, in Orage's phrase, 'hangs together' with the shifting attitude towards the women's movement in the *New Age* after 1911. Although the *New Age* published an even-handed supplement on women's suffrage in February of that year, as the editorials came to focus increasingly on the guild system so too they began to contest the analyses of women and labour developed by writers and activists like Isabella Ford and Olive Schreiner.

There was no natural affinity, an editorial argued in August 1912, between the women's movement and the labour movement. Even women 'wage-slaves' did not share the same desires as 'men wage-slaves':

> Olive Schreiner has recently claimed all labour for women's province equally with men. But her claim and women's claim as represented by what they do are two totally different things. Women, we may say, so far from taking all labour for their province are in industry—to the extent that they *are* in—under protest and against their will. Not only is their demand for economic emancipation feeble in comparison with that of men, but it is

---

[108] 'R. H. Congreve', 'A Third Tale for Men Only III', *New Age*, 10 (22 Feb. 1912), 397–8 (pp. 397, 398).
[109] Ibid.
[110] Ibid.
[111] 'The Crisis in Literature II', *New Age*, 9 (31 Aug. 1911), 420. See also 'Unedited Opinions: Sentimentalism', *New Age*, 11 (16 Aug. 1912), 59.

not nearly as strong as their demand, made in a thousand feminine ways, to be emancipated from the industrial system altogether.[112]

Schreiner and her peers simply did not understand that industry (and, one infers, capitalism) was a male 'invention and the whole system of it is his own contrivance' and thus whilst a man was naturally at home in it, a woman never could be. The significance of this argument for the sexual politics of guild socialism was that, with the abolition of wage-slavery, men would tend back to the pleasures of the workshop, whilst women would remain at home, and become 'more womanly, more pleasing and profitable to themselves'.[113] It was, the author admitted, 'a hard doctrine for women who have fed on the dangerous doctrines of Ibsen and Shaw'.[114] Isabella Ford herself confessed to Edward Carpenter that Schreiner's *Woman and Labour* seemed 'rather stale' by the time it was eventually published in 1911. But despite feeling 'so very very tired of Woman with a big W.' that she felt incapable of being a 'good judge' of Schreiner's work, Ford's belief in the natural affinities of the women's and labour movements remained unshaken by the arguments of the *New Age*.[115]

As Ford enthused to Carpenter about the new growth of comradeship and idealism within the labour movement as a result of the struggle for women's suffrage and Irish Home Rule in 1913, the *New Age* sharpened its attacks on the rapprochement between the Labour Party and the NUWSS. An editorial, possibly by Orage's anti-feminist contributor Beatrice Hastings, castigated 'that traitor to women, that witch (we should like to say more), Miss Olive Schreiner' for inviting women to claim all labour for their province and hence squeeze men out of the labour market and force down wages. Women, it concluded, 'can best assist men and themselves by making for home as fast as their best instincts can carry them'.[116] The idealism of the 1880s that had enabled writers like Schreiner to frame an analogy between art, labour, and biological reproduction had no purchase upon the aesthetics and politics of the *New Age*. Art was beyond the material, just as the artist was a type of the 'beyond-man'; labour was man's invention and could only be his liberation with the abolition of the wage system; biological reproduction was, once stripped of sentimentalism, women's dull material process of sustaining the mass, eternal and unchanging. It was women's revolt from nature, spurred on by Ibsen and Shaw, that had led to the deplorable 'spread of sentimentality in men' in politics and aesthetics

---

[112] 'Notes of the Week', *New Age*, 11 (22 Aug. 1912), 385–90 (p. 387).
[113] Ibid. 388.
[114] Ibid.
[115] Isabella Ford to Edward Carpenter, 17 Sept. 1911, SCL Carpenter Collection MSS 386/187.
[116] 'Notes of the Week', *New Age*, 14 (22 Jan. 1914), 356.

at the turn of the century; 'a sentimentality that can only be regarded as effeminacy'.[117]

IV

In March 1911, shortly before he began publishing his own series of 'Tales for Men Only', Orage accepted 'A Post-Impressionist Study' for the *New Age*, entitled 'The Great Talk'. Responsive as ever to the aesthetic and political currents of her metropolitan circle, the author, Dollie Radford, brought a modish narrative method and an equally timely subject into collision in the tale. The study adopts the point of view of a wife and mother playing hostess at the seaside to four 'big men' who 'hypnotised her into aloofness' with the 'spectacle' of their 'Great Talk', modulating in the course of the weekend from 'appearance and reality' to 'ethics in Art'.[118]

> After clearing away the supper, and conscientiously washing up the plates and dishes, the woman joined the men at the table and waited, meekly, to slip her little net of speech into the enchanted stream.
>
> But the stream swept along so swiftly, above her head, beneath her feet, that when she stretched out uncertain hands to stay its speed, it rushed through them with the roughness of great cables, and her hands smarted to their finger-tips.
>
> So it came to pass that, being denied expression, the woman came to be the Great Talk's only listener. (489)

Whilst the men battle it out on the 'peaks of abstract thought' the woman's 'inward vision' gives substance to the Talk itself in vivid colours and abstract forms. It seemed as if 'her own mind [was] used as a kind of chain, upon which one man after another had slipped his bead of monologue . . . then it seemed to her she had been a kind of human phonograph' (489). The visitors depart, sublimely unconscious of the subjectivity of their hostess, and she speaks, at last, to her male companion: "'Don't you hear the coast being worn away?" she asked, laughing. "Well?" "Well, the land *must* be being made up to it on the other side, mustn't it—or England wouldn't be what she is."' (489) Radford's study ends with this figure of the feminized nation, worn away by the stream of abstract male

[117] 'Notes of the Week', *New Age*, 11 (22 Aug. 1912), 388.
[118] Dolly [sic] Radford, 'The Great Talk: A Post-Impressionist Study', *New Age*, 8 (23 March 1911), 488–9.

argument on one side and shaped afresh on the other by the fragments of subjective (post-)impressionism.

Whether or not Orage's 'Tales for Men Only' were a deliberate rejoinder to Radford's study, Radford's allusion to the gendered politics of the arts and the nation spoke to an increasing concern of Orage's in the years immediately before the war. Despite Orage's own emphasis upon the need for individuality within politics and aesthetics, he was troubled by the early modernist interest in 'art as self-expression'. From this 'extreme individualism ... arise the esperantos, volapuks and private sign languages now exhibiting in studios' as the arts fractured into Post-Impressionism, primitivism, Vorticism, Cubism, Futurism, Imagism. Against this seeming fragmentation of the arts, Orage sought for a new holism in aesthetics and politics, concluding that 'to recover the spirit of Art it is necessary, I believe, to recover the spirit of the Nation'.[119] The nation, for Orage, had become the repository of aesthetic unity and a new spirit that could see an end to the effeminate 'triflers' of early modernism. Rejecting the elective principle of a commune or collective, only those groups which were embedded in traditional hierarchies, such as the workshop guild, the patriarchal family, or the nation itself now seemed to Orage to offer an alternative to the complete atomization of society. Radford's feminized England was ever-renewed in shape by the flows of history and aesthetic debate; Orage's nation was, like the family and the guild, a bulwark against the tides of commercialism and effeminacy in politics and the arts.

In a critical review of his former co-editor, Holbrook Jackson's retrospect *The Eighteen-Nineties* in 1914, Orage made clear that his resistance to the 'private sign languages' of early modernism was part of a longer story of sex, socialism, and the aesthetic culture of the nation. Identifying himself to his readers as 'both a student of Pater and an early member of the I.L.P' and 'more truly [the] embodiment [of the period] than any of the more prominent writers of those days', Orage mapped out the conflicts of his youth:

> Our social reformatory zeal was not allowed to interfere with our pursuit of personal 'moments'; nor, on the other hand, did we imagine that the latter would interfere with the former. The point, however, to observe it that it did! And melancholy was quite naturally the result for a while of one or the other choice. There were those, for example, who in the choice between personal and social idealism chose the former; there were those likewise who chose the latter; I am thankful to say that I was one of them. Of the first set the end was in almost every instance one of melancholy, of decadence, of suicide, or premature death. They had cut themselves off from society hoping to blossom on

---

[119] 'R.H.C.', 'Readers and Writers', *New Age*, 14 (16 April 1914), 754–5 (p. 755).

a stem cut off from the trunk of the tree; and they withered away. Of the second set it is not for me to speak. These things, however, can be said of them, that they thrust hedonism behind them, abjured Pater and his whole school, and plunged into the waters of what Mr Kennedy superciliously calls democracy. It remains to be seen whether, after this cleansing elemental bath, this return to simple truths, simple words, and simple life, we shall, as I hope, recover an art at once national and individual.[120]

By June 1914, the war itself seemed to hold the promise of such another 'cleansing, elemental bath' for Orage. War offered a welcome return of 'spiritual sanities' through its destruction of decadence and cultivation of nationalism where democracy had faltered.[121] The war demanded action in the world of art and, as for Ezra Pound and his fellow Imagists, 'can they produce a poem to match a rifle, or even parallel in their verse the discipline of the goosestep?'[122] Orage could only hope that 'they may all perish in the war' as a result of their precious solipsism.

Even as he maps out the diverse directions of the aesthetic politics of his youth, Orage elides the continuing influence of Pater and Wilde in the *New Age*. Orage's rejection of the ethical imperative of realism, his insistence on the spiritual autonomy of the aesthetic (and the artist) and repugnance at the massification of collectivism indicate the extent to which his politics and aesthetics continued to grow from, rather than abjure, aestheticism. By diagnosing both aestheticism and the 'sentimental' socialist aesthetics of the fin de siècle as part of a pathology of effeminacy, Orage ruled out the pluralist reflections on labour, selfhood, and sex that had preoccupied his early comrades, Edward Carpenter and Isabella Ford. It was, Orage noted, no coincidence that Oscar Wilde rose to fame on the London stage the same year that the ILP was founded in Bradford. On the eve of the First World War, these two phenomena of 1894 represented to Orage distinct choices: personal radicalism, aestheticism, and death; or social revolution, politics, and life. Politics and aesthetics were no longer, even for socialists, a simple both/and: for Orage, at least, contemporary aesthetics were either symptoms of political malady or a surgical tool in the hand of the critic. That sense of an aesthetic democracy, lying latent and waiting for the call to a future of hope had gone with the hope for democracy itself.

---

[120] 'R.H.C.', 'Readers and Writers', *New Age*, 14 (13 Nov. 1913), 50–2 (p. 50).
[121] Taylor, *Orage and the New Age*, pp. 90–1.
[122] 'R.H.C.', Readers and Writers', *New Age*, 15 (8 Oct. 1914), 548–9 (p. 549).

7

Legacies: Socialism, Aesthetics, and the Modernist Generation

> We've been sitting in the Park and listening to the Band and having a terrific argument about Shaw. Leonard says that we owe a great deal to Shaw. I say that he only influenced the outer fringe of morality. Leonard says that the shop girls wouldn't be listening to the Band with their young men if it weren't for Shaw. I say the human heart is touched only by the poets. Leonard says rot, I say damn. Then we go home. Leonard says I'm narrow. I say he's stunted. But don't you agree with me that the Edwardians, from 1895 to 1914, made a pretty poor show. By the Edwardians I mean Shaw, Wells, Galsworthy, the Webbs, Arnold Bennett. We Georgians have our work cut out for us, you see. There's not a single living writer (English) I respect: so you see, I have to read Russian: but here I must stop. I just throw this out for you to think about, under the trees. How does one come by one's morality? Surely by reading the poets. And we've got no poets. Does that throw light upon anything? Consider the Webbs—That woman has the impertinence to say that I'm a-moral: the truth being that if Mrs Webb had been a good woman, Mrs Woolf would have been a better. Orphans is what I say we are—we Georgians—but I must stop.[1]

In 1922 Virginia Woolf playfully killed off her Edwardian elders and thus, in a familiar manoeuvre in her works, left herself a Georgian orphan, self-tutored in her art. For Woolf, George Bernard Shaw and Beatrice Webb had come to stand as types of a generation lacking aesthetic content, whose members sought to change the world and its citizens through pragmatic material reforms and a high-realist practice of representation. This supposedly Edwardian habit of conceiving the world and the self through material externalities alone was subjected to a more detailed and rather more famous attack on the grounds of aesthetics in Woolf's essay 'Mr Bennett and Mrs Brown' a year or so after she wrote this letter. In this instance, however, the active Fabian researcher and campaigner Leonard Woolf was present to defend Shaw and his early mentors, the Webbs, against the political content

---

[1] *The Letters of Virginia Woolf*, ed. Nigel Nicholson, 6 vols. (London: Hogarth, 1975–80; hereafter *LVW*), ii. 529. Virginia Woolf to Janet Case, 21 May 1922.

of the onslaught.[2] For Leonard (according to Virginia, at least), the social reforms propagandized by Shaw and the Webbs over the past twenty-five years made it possible for working-class girls to approach a full and rich social subjectivity in 1922. Young women not only have time off, he responds, but can also choose to listen to the band in the municipal park during that period of leisure. For Virginia Woolf this is merely 'stunted' work at the fringes. Morality—and here it seems Woolf is talking about her own rather than that of the shopgirls in the park—can come only from the purely aesthetic realm of the poets, and thus the unaesthetic Edwardians have left her generation of Georgians orphaned. If Woolf is amoral (or apolitical) as Beatrice Webb judged, then that is because Webb herself was not 'good'. Webb's virtue is not judged by ethics but rather by aesthetics: she lacked the aesthetic value that could have made Woolf moral.

In Woolf's experimental novella *Jacob's Room*, published in the same year that she wrote this letter, young Jacob Flanders escapes from lunch in Cambridge with his tutor, Mr Plumer, sometime in the first decade of the twentieth century. Mr Plumer receives his students in a room lined with books 'by Wells and Shaw; on the table serious sixpenny weeklies written by pale men in muddy boots—the weekly creak and screech of brains rinsed in cold water and wrung dry—melancholy papers'.[3] Mrs Plumer taps the weeklies with 'her bare red hand' and tells Jacob she feels she can only know the truth about anything after she has read these papers. Jacob can take no more; he rushes into the street to find his own truth: ' "Bloody beastly!" he said, scanning the street for lilac or bicycle—anything to restore his sense of freedom' (33). Freedom and truth for Jacob Flanders, that young Edwardian who never makes it past Woolf's end point of 1914 to become a Georgian, lies in individual aesthetic responsiveness, in flashes of being, not these 'scrubbing and demolishing . . . elderly people'(33).

For the chief culprit of this Edwardian scrubbing and demolishing, George Bernard Shaw, the separation of political and rationalist truth from aesthetic value and responsiveness—the need to leave the subject alone with his or her own desires—was a means of the socialist movement embracing modernity. Such modernity required a definitive break from the generation of Victorians who had devoted themselves to the political aesthetics of the religion of socialism in the 1880s; a generation notably absent from Woolf's account of politics and aesthetics in the twentieth century, and one which was even more out of joint with her resolutely anti-sentimental aesthetic. In his preface to *Major Barbara* of 1905, Shaw teased out the distinctions between material politics and affective aesthetics. William Morris and

---

[2] See Duncan Wilson, *Leonard Woolf: A Political Biography* (London: Hogarth, 1987).
[3] Virginia Woolf, *Jacob's Room* (London: Grafton, 1976), p. 32.

other socialist poet-agitators from the 1880s failed, he argued, because the poor 'do not share their tastes nor understand their art criticisms. They do not want the simple life, nor the aesthetic life . . . What they do dislike and despise and are ashamed of is poverty.'

> The difference between a stockbroker's cheap and dirty starched white shirt and collar and the comparatively costly and carefully dyed blue shirt of William Morris is a difference so disgraceful to Morris in their eyes that if they fought on the subject at all they would fight in defence of the starch.[4]

Shaw's preface, written nine years after the death of Morris, confirms the death of the ideal of aesthetic democracy within the Fabian socialist mainstream in the early twentieth century. Although Ian Britain's work has done much to correct the popular notion of the Fabian Society as a group of ascetic abstainers who found pleasure only in filing systems, he also makes it clear that specialization played an increasingly important part in Fabian political thought at the turn of the century.[5] In the Fabian socialist future, the needs of the social organism would determine an increasing differentiation of various types of labour.[6] Talents and tastes for 'hand' and 'brain' labour, including art itself, simply were not distributed democratically by nature. Whilst an affective response to the lack of beauty under capitalism thus would never inspire a revolution among the masses, the expert municipal provision of basic cultural goods in the form of libraries, free concerts, theatres, galleries, and gymnasiums could educate the people.[7]

It is this reduction of aesthetics to a functional social good by Shaw's Edwardian Fabian generation that Woolf dramatizes as the cause of her orphaned, amorality. This utilitarian approach to aesthetics on the part of the Fabian 'old gang' was, as we have seen, also the subject of considerable consternation on the part of Alfred Orage and his fellow guild socialist contributors to the *New Age*. But unlike Orage, Woolf's exorcism of Edwardian politics and literature elides the continuing influence of writers and activists who had embraced the religion of socialism during the 1880s and for whom poetics, ethics, and politics were intimately related. This Victorian generation offered a political aesthetic that was, for reasons we shall see shortly, potentially more problematic for Woolf than the Edwardian high realists and political pragmatists she dismissed in the 1920s. That Woolf was aware

---

[4] Shaw, preface to *Major Barbara* (1905) in George Bernard Shaw, *Collected Prefaces* (London: Odhams, 1938), pp. 121–2.
[5] Ian Britain, *Fabianism and Culture: A Study in British Socialism and the Arts, 1884–1918* (Cambridge: Cambridge University Press, 1982), pp. 143, 226–9.
[6] Peter Beilharz, *Labour's Utopias* (London: Routledge, 1992), pp. 51–90.
[7] Chris Waters, *British Socialists and the Politics of Popular Culture 1884–1914* (Manchester: Manchester University Press, 1990), pp. 131–45.

Figure 7. Photograph of (l. to r.) Noel Olivier, Maitland Radford, Virginia Stephen, Rupert Brooke, 1911. National Portrait Gallery x13124.

of the productivist political aesthetics of this generation is, however, indicated by a photograph of her on holiday on Dartmoor in 1911. The right-hand side of this image may be familiar to readers of Hermione Lee's biography of Virginia Woolf in which it appears as a cropped inset image. Such an expedient excision is understandable: the right-hand side, after all, captures two of those who have shaped the literary history of the earlier twentieth century as a contrast to all that is signified by 'Victorian'. There sits Virginia Stephen, a year before her marriage to Leonard Woolf, experimenting with headscarves and the simple life alongside the poet Rupert Brooke.

If we widen the angle of vision on that photograph slightly, and look, appropriately enough, to the left, the full picture reveals continuities that survived that convenient killing off of Woolf's Edwardians. Sitting to the left of this camp of what Woolf termed 'Neo-Pagan' simple lifers, are Noel Olivier, daughter of the Fabian socialist colonial administrator, Sydney Olivier, and Maitland Radford, the son of Dollie and Ernest Radford, whose socialist commitments continued into the twentieth century. As we have seen, in 1893 Dollie Radford had affirmed that she wanted to teach her children 'to be socialists' and believed that such a commitment could not come through didacticism but a feeling of belonging with 'the struggling ones' alone.[8] For Radford, the imaginative act of sympathy with an exploited proletariat was a necessary part of material politics. In this she was allied to Sydney Olivier, who became increasingly marginalized from the Fabian mainstream at the turn of the century as he continued to insist upon an ethical and internationalist dimension of socialist democracy. In 1899 Olivier worried to Edward Pease that the Fabians were losing their commitment to being 'better in elementary force' than the common run of politicians.[9] This ongoing emphasis upon the importance of feeling within politics and of politics in the arts struggled on into the moment of literary modernism and inflected modernist debates as a second generation reinterpreted the ethical idealism and communal aesthetics of the 1880s.[10]

---

[8] William Andrews Clark Memorial Library, UCLA, MSS R126, Dollie Radford Diary, 3 April 1893.

[9] Sydney Olivier to Edward Pease, 20 Oct. 1899, cit. Norman and Jeanne MacKenzie, *The First Fabians* (London: Weidenfeld & Nicolson, 1977), p. 271.

[10] For a discussion of Woolf's ambivalence towards democracy, and affection for the generation inspired by Whitman and Thoreau, in the context of the role of the public intellectual see Melba Cuddy-Keane, *Virginia Woolf: The Intellectual and the Public Sphere* (Cambridge: Cambridge University Press, 2003), pp. 40–58.

I

In the early 1890s a collection of socialists who had met in clubs and discussion groups in Bloomsbury in the previous decade began to move out of
London and cluster together on the North Downs near the Kent and Surrey
border. The vegetarian simple-lifers Kate and Henry Salt had moved from
Tilford to Crockham Hill in the late 1880s and, on his return from serving
as Colonial Secretary in British Honduras in 1891, Sydney Olivier settled his
family in nearby Limpsfield Chart.[11] Edward Pease, who had been one of the
founders of the Fellowship of the New Life and subsequently secretary of
the Fabian Society, moved with his wife Marjorie to live a few fields away
from the Oliviers' 'mansion'.[12] By early 1892, Henry Salt wrote to Edward
Carpenter to tell him that he was looking about the neighbourhood for a
'cottage for the Kropotkines [sic]' and concluded that the time was ripe 'to
get a few unrespectable people in the neighbourhood; a Prince who does his
own work would be a healthy tonic to the debilitated gentility of Oxted &
Limpsfield'.[13] Shortly after Constance Black left her post of librarian at the
People's Palace in London's East End to marry Edward Garnett in August
1889, the couple also began to experiment with Surrey life in a rented
cottage near Dorking.[14] The cottage at Henshurst Cross became a regular
retreat for radical émigrés, such as Constance's Russian mentor Sergei
Stepniak, and London labour activists. Constance's sister, Clementina
Black, joked with Richard Garnett that the constant singing of the nightin-
gales outside the cottage 'distressed my peace as a labour agitator' on her
holiday there 'by toiling at their vocation for twenty hours out of the
twenty-four'.[15]

By 1895, Constance's growing reputation as a translator of Russian
literature and Edward's increasing income as a publisher's reader enabled

---

[11] N. and J. MacKenzie, *First Fabians*, pp. 99–100. Henry Salt confided to Edward Carpenter
that the Oliviers' house 'Champions' was rather a 'mansion', but Sydney Olivier's self-defence
to the simple lifers was 'that their children being so noisy and troublesome . . . must be stowed
away at as great a remoteness as possible'. Salt suggested 'doses of bromide' as an alternative
treatment. Henry Salt to Edward Carpenter, 29 Feb. 1892, SCL Carpenter Collection 356/9.

[12] Marjorie Pease went on to play a major role local politics for many years: surely a unique
instance of a Surrey parish council dominated by socialists. Richard Garnett, *Constance
Garnett: A Heroic Life* (London: Sinclair Stevenson, 1991), p. 147.

[13] Henry Salt to Edward Carpenter, 29 Feb. 1892, SCL Carpenter Collection 356/9.

[14] Richard Garnett suggests that Constance left her post (and precipitated her marriage) due
to a pregnancy that subsequently miscarried. Garnett, *Constance Garnett*, p. 67. See also
George Jefferson, *Edward Garnett: A Life in Literature* (London: Jonathan Cape, 1982),
pp. 15–39.

[15] Clementina Black to Richard Garnett, 2 June 1890, Harry Ransom HRC, cit. Garnett,
Constance Garnett, p. 66.

them to commission the architect William Harrison Cowlishaw to build a house for them and their young son David among the Fabians at Limpsfield Chart.[16] On a return visit from Ceylon that year Constance's younger sister Grace Human (née Black) took time out from her new leaning towards theosophy to arrange the purchase of some adjacent land.[17] In due course Cowlishaw built 'Gracie's Cottage' which housed a series of aesthetic tenants at the turn of the century including Ford Madox Hueffer, whom Edward Garnett introduced to Joseph Conrad, and who, in return, introduced D. H. Lawrence, then a young schoolteacher in nearby Croydon, to the Garnetts and hence the Radfords.[18]

Despite joining the Fabian Society in 1893 and standing for its executive in 1894, Constance Garnett's immersion in contemporary Russian literature gave her political beliefs a distinctly pacifistic and internationalist slant in the last decade of the nineteenth century.[19] Writing to Natalie Duddington in the aftermath of the October Revolution in Russia, Garnett claimed that 'International Socialism' was what she cared for more than anything else: 'for twenty years or more [it] seemed the hope of the world' to her and was 'after all my religion'.[20] Garnett's spiritual and anti-bureaucratic interpretation of socialism led to her resigning from the Fabian Society in 1897, but the Fabian response to the Boer War in 1899 ensured that Garnett and other followers of the 'religion of socialism' made a decisive and permanent break from the organization.[21] George Bernard Shaw's first reaction to the outbreak of the war in South Africa in October 1899 was to write to Edward Pease arguing that it would be 'too silly' to split the Fabian Society

---

[16] Cowlishaw was to become a popular Arts and Crafts architect and marry Edward's sister Lucy. See Garnett, *Constance Garnett*, p. 146.

[17] Ibid. 158; Contance Garnett's sister-in-law Olive Garnett commented that 'Gracie has become a model wife & will not do any thing without consulting her husband. Marriage has changed her views considerably', 29 Dec. 1893, in Barry C. Johnston (ed.), *Olive and Stepniak: The Bloomsbury Diary of Olive Garnett, 1893–1895* (Birmingham: Barletts Press, 1993), p. 20.

[18] David Garnett, *The Golden Echo* (London: Chatto & Windus, 1953), pp. 35–6. Conrad subsequently moved into Ford's farm at Hythe in Kent, displacing the previous tenant, Walter Crane: Garnett, *Constance Garnett*, pp. 170, 268–9.

[19] See Rebecca Beasley, 'Russia and the Invention of the Modernist Intelligentsia', in Peter Brooker and Andrew Thacker (eds.), *Geographies of Modernism* (London: Routledge, 2005), pp. 19–30.

[20] Constance Garnett to Natalie Duddington, 26 Nov. 1917, cit Garnett, *Constance Garnett*, p. 299.

[21] David Garnett attributed his mother's resignation to the fact that 'Constance and . . . Clementina cordially detested the Potter sisters and particularly hated the brand of State Socialism which owed so much to the efforts of Mr and Mrs Sidney Webb. This aversion led Constance readily to abandon her Socialist beliefs in later life'. Garnett, *Golden Echo*, p. 8.

'by declaring ourselves on a non-socialist point of policy'.[22] The Fabians had not formulated an official line on the issue of Irish Home Rule and Shaw believed that such neutrality preserved the Fabian focus on the permeation of the domestic policy of the nation state.

Divisive as the Home Rule question had been, however, the British involvement in the Boer War seemed to many socialists—not least Olive Schreiner—to be the epitome of the aggrandizing force of modern international capitalism. Despite his position as a civil servant in the Colonial Office, Sydney Olivier had little compunction about sharing his anger at the contents of a draft ultimatum to be sent by Joseph Chamberlain to the Transvaal Republic in the summer of 1899. Constance's son David recalled Olivier marching through the woods at Limpsfield to rouse the opposition of his neighbours. The Garnetts and the Oliviers were in consensus: 'such a war was to the advantage of the shareholders of the Johannesburg gold mines and Kimberley diamond mines but were our soldiers' lives and the Boers' liberties to be sacrificed for them?'[23] The following November the Fabians held a ballot to decide whether or not to make an official pronouncement on the war. Hubert Bland was chief among the Fabian 'old gang' in insisting that neutrality should be accompanied by attempts to permeate the new imperialism with Fabian tenets of efficiency and welfarism and in this he had the support of Shaw and the Webbs. Bland's argument won the ballot by a narrow margin and led to the resignation of 18 members, of whom many, such as Ramsay MacDonald, Henry Salt, and Walter Crane, had embraced socialism during the 1880s as an ethical and aesthetic religion.[24] The Boer War was no less divisive for the wider socialist movement. Robert Blatchford, who had opposed colonial expansion in the past, declared in the *Clarion* that 'I cannot go with those Socialists whose sympathies are with the enemy', whilst John Burns was subjected to attacks by jingoists for holding out the opposite view.[25]

In the autumn of 1899, Olivier was posted to Jamaica as Colonial Secretary and his opposition to the emerging Fabian stance on Empire was thus muted. The next year Shaw's pamphlet *Fabianism and the Empire* cemented an official position on the matter by arguing that Fabian doctrines of national efficiency were the natural complement to Britain's imperial destiny: both, Norman and Jeanne MacKenzie observe, consisted of 'an elite offering salvation to the poor'.[26] Whilst young David 'Bunny' Garnett

---

[22] Shaw, cit. N. and J. MacKenzie, *First Fabians*, p. 268.
[23] Garnett, *Golden Echo*, p. 55.
[24] N. and J. MacKenzie, *First Fabians*, pp. 272–4.
[25] Ibid. 269.
[26] Ibid. 278.

responded by joining Noel Olivier and her sisters in burning Joseph Chamberlain in effigy on Guy Fawkes Night, his mother pursued the cause of free speech and internationalism in time of war.[27] Garnett complained to Felix Volkhovsky that they would 'soon need a Society of Friends of English Freedom' to match the Russian equivalent through which she had gained her own literary interests in the early 1890s: 'we have practically no liberty of the Press or of speech just now. If one speaks one's opinions, one is called a traitor and enemy of the country and no one can get a hearing.'[28] It was with this in mind that both the Garnetts offered their support to Olive Schreiner's husband S. C. Cronwright-Schreiner when he visited Britain on a lecture tour sponsored by their Limpsfield neighbour, the economist J. A. Hobson.[29] In the pro-Boer cause at least, Schreiner was at one with her husband and their joint notoriety led to violent jingoist riots at Cronwright-Schreiner's meetings.[30] Cronwright-Schreiner was forced to write to Edward Carpenter cancelling a lecture tour near Millthorpe, amid the outburst of jingoist opinion that followed the relief of Mafeking, and returned straight back to Limpsfield from a visit to Keir Hardie.[31]

The divisions within the socialist movement surrounding the Boer War presaged the even more bitter debates and schisms of 1914–18. For twenty years the 'religion of socialism' in Britain had just managed to hold together internationalists and prophets of imperialist national efficiency, the inheritors of radical utilitarianism and the 'sentimental' socialists of an extended Gladstonian Liberalism. By the turn of the century such cohesiveness was no longer possible. The Garnetts, the Oliviers, and the Radfords immersed their children in the ethical ideals of their generation, selecting new progressive educational establishments like Abbotsholme and Bedales that emerged from the Fellowship of the New Life and emphasized the values of heterosocial comradeship and the simple life.[32] But the sense that such

---

[27] Garnett, *Golden Echo*, p. 59.

[28] Constance Garnett to Felix Volkhovsky, n.d., cit Garnett, *Constance Garnett*, p. 179.

[29] On Hobson's response to the culture of jingoism see Paula Krebs, *Gender, Race and the Writing of Empire: Public Discourse and the Boer War* (Cambridge: Cambridge University Press, 1999), pp. 1–31.

[30] On the problematics of Schreiner's pro-Boer propaganda, ibid. 109–42.

[31] S. C. Cronwright-Schreiner to Edward Carpenter, 22 May 1900, SCL Carpenter MSS 360/4.

[32] Cecil Reddie, a member of the Fellowship of the New Life, founded Abbotsholme with funding from Edward Carpenter and advertised extensively in the FNL journal *Seed-time*. The school hymn was adapted from Whitman's 'The Love of Comrades'. J. H. Badley, who had been in the circle of Roger Fry and Goldsworthy Lowes Dickinson at Trinity, Cambridge, opened Bedales as a coeducational school in 1893. Noel Olivier and Jacques Raverat were both pupils at the school in its first decade and the school's ethos formed a significant factor in the neo-pagan interest in outdoor pursuits and the simple life of comradeship. See Paul Delany, *The Neo-Pagans: Friendship and Love in the Rupert Brooke Circle* (London: Hamish Hamilton, 1987), pp. 12–15.

ethical commitments were an intimate part of an imminent great change in the political organization of society was in abeyance. If nothing else, the mass jingoism and demonstrations of working-class Tory patriotism during the Boer War did much to mute the hope that the workers were on the verge of revolution, full of desire for a new and beautiful life of socialism.

When Virginia Woolf started to read contemporary Russian fiction in despair at the state of Edwardian English literature ten years later, the translations she had to hand were almost certainly the work of Constance Garnett. Indeed, in her essay 'Mr Bennett and Mrs Brown' (1923) Woolf argued 'Constance Garnett's translations were a crucial influence on the novel' at the turn of the century, 'for after reading *Crime and Punishment* and *The Idiot*, how could any young novelist believe in characters as the Victorians painted them?'[33] For Garnett these literary efforts to which, Katherine Mansfield assured her, the modernist generation owed so much, were inseparable from politics.[34] Inspired to learn Russian in the early 1890s by Stepniak and comrades in the Society of Friends of Russian Freedom, Garnett's lifelong anti-militarism was grounded in her encounter with Tolstoy. Tolstoyan aesthetics were, as we shall see shortly, to play a significant part in stimulating the aesthetics of the Bloomsbury Group, in the form of Roger Fry's reaction against *What is Art?* in his *Vision and Design* (1920). Garnett's Tolstoyan politics were also to have a material influence on the shape of the Bloomsbury circle during the First World War, if only, once again, by reaction. In 1916 David Garnett joined his lover, the painter Duncan Grant, in appealing against conscription into active service. Garnett urged the Tribunal to consider that he had been raised as a pacifist and socialist as a result of his mother's visit to Tolstoy shortly after his birth. The chairman was, however, under the impression that Tolstoy was a town in Russia and, as a result of the appeal which followed, Garnett, Grant, and Woolf's sister, Vanessa Bell, set up home in Charleston, East Sussex, where the former two could fulfil non-combatant service requirements as agricultural labourers.[35] Within a few years, Charleston itself had become a site in which the relationship between art and life was rethought and sketched out around the domestic interior, whilst the birth of a daughter to Vanessa Bell and Duncan Grant in 1918 confirmed a new phase of experiments in family life. When David Garnett married Grant and Bell's daughter Angelica in 1942 (much to her parents' horror), he merely formalized the intermingling of Bloomsbury and Limpsfield, aesthetic autonomy

---

[33] Virginia Woolf, 'Mr Bennett and Mrs Brown', *Nation*, 34 (1923), 342.
[34] Garnett, *Constance Garnett*, pp. 308–9.
[35] Ibid. 294–5.

and ethical idealism, that took place during the first four decades of the twentieth century.[36]

Although Peter Stansky concludes from a survey of Woolf's reading that William Morris was 'a presence in [her] life', Woolf's encounter with the afterlife of 1880s socialism came primarily through her friendship with Rupert Brooke and his fellow neo-pagans in the first decade of the twentieth century.[37] The group was drawn from a rather younger generation than that of Woolf's Bloomsbury and was formed from several overlapping circles: former pupils of Bedales school, such as Noel Olivier and Jacques Raverat; young Cambridge graduates and Fabians, like Brooke; the children of the simple-lifers of Limpsfield.[38] The group's favoured garb of socks and sandals, emphasis on fellowship, vegetarianism, camping, and mixed nude bathing indicates the continuing influence of simple life advocates of the 1880s like Edward Carpenter and Henry Salt. This progeny of late nineteenth-century socialist faddism displayed some characteristics that alienated older Fabians and which suggest the way in which the simple life was interpreted by a new generation. Physical desire, which had served as a transcendent force for generating a new and healthy social body for Edward Carpenter, seems to have been reduced to the 'natural' and indomitable force of heterosexual attraction by Brooke and his peers. This retraction of the pluralism of the original simple-lifers was also matched by the racist and anti-semitic tendencies of the new generation: the natural, desiring body that could transform society was now of a rather more specific type and race.[39] That embrace of manliness and healthy virility which had formed a reaction against high capitalism and bourgeois existence in the 1880s socialist movement was recuperated in the 1910s as an exclusive mark of social

[36] Vanessa Bell's son Quentin also married into the second generation of 1880s socialism (twice over) in 1952 by wedding Anne Olivier Popham, the daughter of Brynhild Olivier (daughter of Sydney and sister of Noel) and Arthur Ewart 'Hugh' Popham (son of Arthur Popham and Florence Radford Popham, m. 1912). The Pophams senior had attended the original men and women's club in 1881. Florence Radford Popham was the sister of Ernest Radford and Ada Wallas. The Pophams and Radfords were cousins who shared material interests in the family drapers firm, Popham & Radford, in Mannamead, Plymouth.

[37] Peter Stansky, *William Morris and Bloomsbury*, The Bloomsbury Heritage Series (London: Cecil Woolf, 1997), p. 7.

[38] Delany sums up the relationship of the neo-pagans to Fabianism succinctly: 'being Neo-Pagan was something that Young Fabians did when they were not being Fabians, or that the children of Fabians did as a way of not following in their parents' footsteps'. Delany, *Neo-Pagans*, p. 42.

[39] Lee, *Virginia Woolf*, p. 293. For a detailed study of Brooke's figuring of Jewishness as a negotiation of national and sexual identity see Roger Ebbatson, *An Imaginary England: Nation, Landscape and Literature, 1840–1920* (Aldershot: Ashgate, 2005), pp. 149–55.

distinction. Followers of the religion of socialism had turned from Judaeo-Christian ethics and sought a replacement in an aesthetic politics. The neo-pagans, as the name suggests, rejected the claim of conventional morals altogether, opting for a spirit more Hellenic than Hebraic.

Drawing, perhaps, on her experience of the rambunctious behaviour of Brooke and his peers at Fabian Summer Schools, Beatrice Webb deplored the new spirit animating Cambridge radicals in the early twentieth century. Writing to her sister, Kate Courtney, in 1911 she commented:

> there is a pernicious set [at Cambridge] presided over by [Goldsworthy] Lowes Dickinson, which makes a sort of ideal of anarchic ways in sexual questions—we have, for a long time, been aware of its bad influence on our young Fabians. The intellectual star is the metaphysical George Moore with his *Principia Ethica*—a book they all talk of as 'The Truth'! I can never see anything in it, except a metaphysical justification for doing what you like and what other people disapprove of! So far as I can understand the philosophy it is a denial of the scientific method and religion—as a rule, that is the net result on the minds of young men—it seems to disintegrate their intellects and their characters.[40]

Whilst Webb's account of Moore's *Principia Ethica* is, as Paul Levy observes, 'a grotesque misunderstanding' of the work, the attitudes of which she disapproves do 'bear some relationship to what some of Moore's followers—and later, [the Bloomsbury Group]—made' of his philosophy.[41] Moore's rejection of Kantian idealism and displacement of notions of mystic organic unity with a philosophy grounded in individuated responsiveness certainly shaped the aesthetic and ethical beliefs of fellow members of the Cambridge Apostles at the turn of the century such as Lytton Strachey, Leonard Woolf, and Roger Fry.[42] Unlike the latter, however, Brooke combined membership of the Apostles with that of the Fabian Society during his years as an undergraduate and seems to have clung on to the aesthetic democracy of William Morris, whilst showing willing to embrace a little sexual anarchy in the school of Moore.[43] Whatever effect Moore's 'Ideal Utilitarianism' had upon the ethics of the young poet, in 1908 Brooke insisted that the Cambridge Fabians needed more, not less of the ethical ide-

---

[40] Beatrice Webb to Kate Courtney, 18 Sept. 1911, cit. Paul Levy, *G. E. Moore and the Cambridge Apostles* (London: Weidenfeld & Nicolson, 1979), p. 5.

[41] Levy, *G. E. Moore*, p. 5.

[42] Ibid. 7; Lee, *Virginia Woolf*, p. 302; Tom Regan, *Bloomsbury's Prophet: G. E. Moore and the Development of his Moral Philosophy* (Philadelphia: Temple University Press, 1986), pp. 3–28; S. P. Rosenbaum, 'Preface to a Literary History of the Bloomsbury Group', *New Literary History*, 12 (1981), 329–44 (p. 337).

[43] See W. C. Lubenow, *The Cambridge Apostles, 1820–1914: Liberalism, Imagination and Friendship in British Intellectual and Professional Life* (Cambridge: Cambridge University Press, 1998).

alism and aesthetic interests of an earlier socialist generation. These young politicians were of a rather selfish sort, he thought, and lacked the requisite ethical idealism to bring a new life of socialist beauty into being.[44] Brooke's lecture 'Democracy and the Arts', delivered to the Cambridge University Fabian Society three years later, exhibits his continued attempts to negotiate the inheritance of William Morris and what he termed 'the Morrisites'.[45] For all Brooke's attempts to distance himself from Morrisite notions of a communal craft aesthetic, Ian Britain concludes that this paper contains echoes of Morris's *Signs of Change* in its endorsement of a democracy of taste, if not of aesthetic gifts.[46]

To Noel Olivier, at least, the lines of social and cultural distinction between Virginia Woolf's distinguished family and those of the Limpsfield socialists and neo-pagans remained all too palpable. Writing to Brooke in May 1912, Olivier anticipated that her forthcoming visit to the newly wed Virginia at Asheham would merely prove to her hosts that 'I'm too common & much of a dunce to associate with these folks', but the visit was paid and repeated nevertheless.[47] The aesthetics of the 1880s simple-lifers and their emphasis on heterosocial fellowship caught and held Woolf's interest during the years in which her own craft as a writer and the social experiments of Bloomsbury took shape. Despite Woolf's retrospective revisions, then, it is clear that the pragmatic Edwardian socialism of Shaw and the Webbs in the early twentieth century was counterbalanced by the afterlife of the aesthetic politics of the 1880s: a politics in which desire for the beautiful and the affect of poetry was part of the process of social change. Woolf's early twentieth-century Bloomsbury thus overlay an earlier Bloomsbury of the mid-1880s like a palimpsest. Like the members of the Fellowship of the New Life, which had numbered Sydney Olivier among its early members, Woolf's experiments in collective living at Gordon Square 'were full of experiments and reforms . . . Everything was going to be new; everything was going to be different. Everything was on trial.'[48] As Stansky suggests, both groups of innovators 'recognized the supreme importance of the domestic and its radical implications', but the political disjunction between the two also made for some important distinctions.[49]

---

[44] Rupert Brooke, 1908, in *The Letters of Rupert Brooke*, ed. Geoffrey Keynes (London: Faber & Faber, 1968).

[45] Britain, *Fabianism*, pp. 266–70 (p. 266).

[46] Ibid. 267.

[47] Noel Olivier to Rupert Brooke, 13 May 1912, in *Song of Love: The Letters of Rupert Brooke and Noel Olivier*, ed. Pippa Harris (London: Bloomsbury, 1991), p. 174.

[48] Virginia Woolf, 'Old Bloomsbury', in *Moments of Being*, ed. Jeanne Schulkind (repr. London: Pimlico, 2002), p. 47.

[49] Stansky, *William Morris and Bloomsbury*, p. 24.

In characterizing the politics of Bloomsbury, Raymond Williams has suggested that the group's emphasis upon the 'civilized individual', which encompassed free and frank intellectual discussion of the anomalous position of women (and, we might now add, homosexuality), defines them as a 'fraction' of the existing English upper class.[50] Despite their self-definition against the 'stupidity' of the ruling class, the members of the Bloomsbury Group were, Williams contends, merely prefiguring a later development of that class. Nowhere, Williams suggests, is this more evident than in their critiques of capitalist society, always expressed as 'a matter of conscience' felt by the individual or the group towards the working class as helpless victims, rather than as solidarity.[51] It is not insignificant in this context that, unlike Constance Garnett and her sisters Clementina and Grace two decades earlier, for example, it was unthinkable for Woolf to go so far as to live without servants. For Leonard Woolf, who returned from Ceylon to join this trial of a new life in 1911, and Roger Fry, who reacquainted himself with the Stephen sisters in 1910, the political traces of this earlier Bloomsbury were more perceptible. Fry had been at Cambridge during the mid-1880s when his fellow Apostles were wrestling with a sense of social duty, the new excitements of socialism in London and philosophical enquiries into the limits of idealism. Whilst Fry worked through the aesthetics and ethics of the 1880s in his essays of the early twentieth century, Leonard Woolf pursued a more practical interest in Fabian politics in tandem with the artistic innovations of his fellows.

For Virginia Woolf, however, the surviving traces of the political aesthetics of 1880s Bloomsbury were in many ways more problematic than the pragmatics of Shaw and the Webbs because they threatened her tentative steps towards forming an individualist and autonomous radical aesthetic. If the mainstream Fabian Society represented, as Williams argues, another example of the cool 'social conscience' of a fraction of the ruling class, then the ethical idealism that characterized the Fellows of the New Life and members of the early Independent Labour Party represented something rather different: a radical sympathy that sought to elide the individual in the name of solidarity. This self-deadness was in sharp contra-distinction to Woolf's interests in the aesthetics of subjective individuality and it was troublingly close to the nineteenth-century association of womanhood with self-sacrifice and altruism. Christine Froula has recently reframed Woolf's engagement with social questions and suggested

---

[50] Raymond Williams, 'The Bloomsbury Fraction', in *Problems in Materialism and Culture* (London: Verso, 1980), pp. 148–69.
[51] Ibid. 155, 156.

that Williams's argument undervalues the collective significance of 'civil-ization' in Bloomsbury, in which 'community's interest in disinterestedness is continually proposed, if never perfectly enacted; and where the work of art calls people not to see as one but to see differently and then seek to "persuade each other" in arduous negotiation of an always changing *sensus communis*, or common understanding'.[52] Attentive and illuminating as Froula's work is, it brings to the fore the very stark difference between the Bloomsbury Group's Enlightenment emphasis on rational civic consensus and the affirmation of art as a place of collective unity through feeling, rather than by understanding, by the ethical idealist socialists of the 1880s. In order to achieve civilization through Bloomsbury's modernism, one must effect a Kantian detachment of sentiment from judgement. Woolf's works thus consistently deconstruct the affect of sympathy in pursuit of free, civilized individuality for a woman, and hence retreat from the ethical aesthetics of 1880s socialism.

II

These contrasts between the political aesthetics of the 1880s and of Bloomsbury are perhaps most visible in Woolf's writings concerning the Women's Co-operative Guild. Virginia Woolf's old acquaintance Margaret Llewelyn Davies had been active in the organization since the mid-1880s and by the early twentieth century she was not only national secretary of the Guild but also had overseen the massive expansion of its membership and sphere of action.[53] The Women's Co-operative Guild had been founded with the simple aim of fostering working-class women's involvement in the co-operative movement by encouraging them to save and shop using their local branch store. By the early twentieth century however, Llewellyn Davies, like Clementina Black, believed that the co-operative movement helped to advance the 'control of industry by the people for the people' and that the Guild represented an unprecedented opportunity for working women to make their voices heard.[54] When Virginia introduced Leonard Woolf to Llewelyn Davies in 1912, she unwittingly laid the foundation for his future

---

[52] Christine Froula, *Virginia Woolf and the Bloomsbury Avant-Garde: War, Civilization, Modernity* (New York: Columbia University Press, 2005), p. 3.
[53] Gillian Scott, *Feminism and the Politics of Working Women: The Women's Co-operative Guild, 1880s to the Second World War* (London: UCL Press, 1998), pp. 35–66.
[54] Editor's Note, *Life as we have Known it*, ed. Margaret Llewelyn Davies (London: Hogarth, 1931), p. ix.

career with the Fabian Society.[55] Leonard had recently been converted to socialism as a result of visiting the poor in the East End under the auspices of the Charity Organisation Society and finding the individualist doctrines of 'character' formation promoted by the COS insufficient to solve the problems at hand. With an unexpected echo of Beatrice and Sidney Webb's courtship and partnership, the Woolfs were prompted by Llewelyn Davies to embark on a fact-finding tour of northern manufacturing towns in the spring of 1913 which culminated in them attending the annual conference of the Women's Co-operative Guild in Newcastle.[56] It was Leonard's subsequent work promoting the Women's Co-operative Guild that first brought him to the attention of the Webbs later that year.[57]

Shortly after Woolf had submitted the typescript of her first novel, *The Voyage Out*, to the publishing house of her half-brother Gerald Duckworth, she thus joined Leonard in visiting jam factories in Manchester and girls' clubs in Salford; whilst Edward Garnett drafted an enthusiastic report on her novel in Limpsfield.[58] For Leonard, at least, the experience of seeing a series of working-class women stand up and address the Guild congress on current political subjects was, he wrote to Llewelyn Davies, 'simply absorbing': 'Virginia is so enthusiastic that she will not rest until she is sent again some day as a delegate'. Virginia added in her own hand 'this is quite true about both of us. Being ignorant does not mean that one cant [sic] at least appreciate (however being ignorant only applies to me)'.[59] Leonard's account of Virginia's response—of her absorption, enthusiasm, and desire to be one of these women speaking for fellow working women—sits oddly with Virginia's anxious overstatement of veracity and more distanced condition of ignorant appreciation. If Leonard thinks Virginia wants to be one of the delegates, then Virginia tries to appreciate these women; to evaluate them in the terms of Paterian aesthetic criticism; to know them as they really are by the impression they make on her, whilst knowing nothing of their material history.[60]

These contrasting states—knowledge and appreciation, absorption and detachment—led to some tension between Woolf and Llewelyn

[55] See Sybil Oldfield, 'Margaret Llewelyn Davies and Leonard Woolf', in Wayne Chapman and Janet Manson (eds.), *Women in the Milieu of Leonard and Virginia Woolf: Peace, Politics and Education* (New York: Pace University Press, 1998), pp. 3–32.

[56] Lee, *Virginia Woolf*, pp. 327–9.

[57] Leonard Woolf, *Beginning Again* (London: Hogarth Press, 1964), pp. 105, 111.

[58] Lee, *Virginia Woolf*, p. 329; Jefferson, *Edward Garnett*, pp. 186–7.

[59] Leonard Woolf to Margaret Llewelyn Davies, 13 June 1913. *The Letters of Leonard Woolf*, ed. Frederick Spotts (London: Weidenfield & Nicolson, 1989), p. 381.

[60] Walter Pater, *Appreciations: With an Essay on Style* (London: Macmillan, 1889). See Perry Meisel, *The Absent Father: Virginia Woolf and Walter Pater* (New Haven: Yale University Press, 1980); on Woolf's debt to Victorian aesthetic prose writers more generally see Michael

Davies when she returned to the subject of the conference nearly twenty years later in her preface to the collection of memoirs of working-class Guildswomen, *Life as we have Known it* (1931).[61] But at the time Woolf's response to the congress was one of expression rather than of absorption. Writing to her friend, the simple-lifer and neo-pagan, Ka Cox, Woolf was thrilled by the prospect of individual power labour activism offered women of her generation.

> I see at a glance that nothing—except perhaps novel writing—can compare with the excitement of controlling the masses. The letters you'd get! The jobs you would be sent on—and then people would always be telling you things, and if you could move them you would feel like a God. I see now where Margaret [Llewelyn Davies] and even Mary McArthur get their Imperial tread. The mistake I've made is in mixing up what they do with philanthropy. Why don't you force yourself into some post when you get back—in 6 months time you'd be driving about 6,000 helpless women in front of you.[62]

The 'mistake' Woolf made of mixing the work of Llewelyn Davies and Mary McArthur with philanthropy is not, in this case, that of blurring political categories. Woolf does not experience a sudden realization that socialism represents an *analysis* in absolute opposition to the sort of Victorian philanthropy practised by her mother, Julia Stephen, and half-sister, Stella Duckworth. She is, rather, correcting the assumption that such activism depends upon the feminized qualities of self-abnegation and self-sacrifice that made nineteenth-century philanthropy the necessary corollary of liberal individualism. Think of Mrs Ramsay's self-cancelled self in *To the Lighthouse*: a life fully absorbed into others, visiting 'this widow, or that struggling wife in person with a bag on her arm, and a notebook and pencil with which she wrote down in columns carefully ruled for the purpose wages and spendings, employment and unemployment, in the hope that thus she would cease to be a private woman'.[63] Suddenly the organization of labour seems to present a means by which a woman can become a great public self, even one worthy of an entry in the *Dictionary of National Biography*. Three weeks before her first novel was accepted

---

Whitworth, 'Virginia Woolf and Modernism', in Sue Roe and Susan Sellers (eds.), *The Cambridge Companion to Virginia Woolf* (Cambridge: Cambridge University Press, 2000), pp. 150–3.

[61] Llewelyn Davies objected to Woolf's focus on the aesthetic limitations of working-class women and her original conclusion (published in the *Yale Review* in 1930) that it would be unlikely that any such women would ever prove a poet in the near future. Lee, *Virginia Woolf*, p. 359.

[62] Virginia Woolf to Ka Cox, 18 March 1913. *LVW*, ii. 19.

[63] Virginia Woolf, *To the Lighthouse* (London: Folio Society, 1988), p. 8.

for publication, Woolf considered the alternative of being a labour leader and wielding power in a manner that matched her art at the time: controlling the masses as a novelist controls her characters.

By 1931, when she came to write her preface to *Life as we have Known it* for the Guild, such will to individual power by swaying the masses with affective rhetoric had been worked too far through into the fabric of fascism for Woolf to want to claim it again. Her introductory letter instead rewrites the Guild congress of 1913 as 'a revelation and a disillusionment' that 'humiliated and enraged' her. Woolf's letter to Ka Cox at the time maintained an analogy—deeply problematic as it was—between the woman artist and the labour leader: both could take the stories and desires of the mass and craft it into some kind of history, some tangible social effects. But by 1931, the art of the novelist and the politics of the collective were radically out of joint. Woolf cannot even affirm that the work she prefaces is a book, nor that her preface is a preface. The preface is rather, Woolf insists, a letter addressed to a single old friend about the many letters that follow it. Woolf's text is thus troubled by the aesthetic status of this book made up of the autobiographical recollections of working-class women. *Life as we have Known it* is a book that in its very title affirms the collective as the site of knowledge and experience; a book which contains this experience of the material world within the hard covers of the Woolfs' Hogarth Press, a publishing house better known for works of high art.

Woolf's negation of the collective as a site of aesthetic experience is worked through the text in terms that indicate her intimate familiarity with, and resistance to, late nineteenth-century structures of feeling. She recalls her experiences of the women of the Guild at the 1913 conference and notes that they wanted material goods like 'baths and money':

> To expect us, whose minds, such as they are, fly free at the end of a short length of capital to tie ourselves down to that narrow plot of acquisitiveness and desire is impossible. We have baths and we have money. Therefore, however much we had sympathised, our sympathy was largely fictitious. It was aesthetic sympathy, the sympathy of the eye and of the imagination, not of the heart and of the nerves; and such sympathy is always physically uncomfortable.[64]

Sympathy of the heart and the nerves—that life blood of nineteenth-century sentiment and affect—simply no longer functions alongside the aesthetic sympathy of the artist's imagination in the modernist era. Woolf stages her attempts to achieve such wholeness at the meeting by jumping into 'the person of Mrs Giles of Durham', a miner's wife (p. xx). But

---

[64] *Life as we have Known it*, p. xxvi.

after all, Woolf concludes 'the imagination is largely the child of the flesh' and her own body (and mind) is too supple to inhabit Mrs Giles: it lacks the stiffness, the density, the rawness of these women 'stamped' with slow-moving determination and labour (p. xxi).

> One could not be Mrs Giles of Durham because one's body had never stood at the washtub; one's hands had never wrung and scrubbed and chopped up whatever meat it may be that makes a miner's supper. The picture was therefore always letting in irrelevancies. One sat in an armchair or read a book. One saw landscapes and seascapes, perhaps Greece or Italy, where Mrs Giles . . . must have seen slag heaps and row upon row of slate-roofed houses. (p. xxi)

Woolf's experience and imagination are composed of what the Bloomsbury interpretation of Moore's philosophy construed as 'reality': ideas, art, the 'good'.[65] Mrs Giles of Durham, on the other hand, is confined to the 'phenomenal' materiality of cheap meat, raw red hands, and slag heaps. Woolf's sympathy must therefore remain 'thin spread and moon coloured' with 'no life blood or urgency about it' (p. xviii).

Hermione Lee observes, quite rightly, that Woolf's feminist programme is 'above all a literary one . . . inextricably bound up with her desire to "revolutionise biography"'.[66] It would be easy to assume that the opportunity of writing the preface to *Life as we have Known it* offered a glorious piece of serendipity for Woolf in this respect. Just as Woolf was refining the lecture that was to become her feminist essay, *A Room of One's Own,* with its imaginative leap into the untold story of Shakespeare's sister, here was an opportunity to reflect on another revolution in biography; that of working-class women writing their own life stories. But it simply doesn't happen like that. Woolf hoped that by reading the memoirs of Guild members sent to her by Llewelyn Davies these working women would 'cease to be symbols and would become instead individuals'. Yet Woolf's judgement on these testaments remains, at the end, a purely aesthetic judgement of their shortcomings. The texts 'threw some light upon the old curiosities' that had made the congress 'so thick with unanswered questions' for Woolf, but the matter of working-class women's lives 'lacked variety and play of feature. Here are no reflections, [a literary critic] might object, no view of life as a whole, no attempt to enter into the lives of other people.'[67] 'Indigenous and rooted to one spot', these working-class women cannot exercise the free play of aesthetic judgement, and thus cannot be individuals for Woolf, as their

---

[65] Lee, *Virginia Woolf*, p. 302.
[66] Ibid. 13.
[67] *Life as we have Known it*, p. xxxvii.

desires are limited to things, like baths and money, that are means to an end
(p. xxii). Biographies made up of baths and money (or, indeed, great public
appointments and knighthoods) were precisely those testaments to the
material self—the outer rather than the inner life—that Woolf was seeking
to make impossible and irrelevant in her era.

In part Woolf's unease with the collective stories of the Women's Co-
operative Guild is a result of what Kate Flint identifies as 'an anxiety, even
an uncontrollable physical repulsion' felt by Woolf when 'confronted with
the working classes *en masse*'.[68] In this case, however, Woolf's emphasis
on the problem of sympathy indicates a more studied disavowal of a
nineteenth-century representational tradition in which women writers used
their feminine powers of feeling to imagine the lives of the poor for a
middle-class audience. Woolf's discussion of how she simply cannot be Mrs
Giles of Durham acknowledges a sense of difference in a way that Mrs
Gaskell never could. It is, of course, no surprise that as a self-conscious
modernist, Woolf's anti-sentimental aesthetic involves the rejection of the
feminized and derided Victorian pleasure of feeling with the struggling
ones. Yet such aesthetic radicalism also strikes out the ethical idealism that
had underpinned the religion of socialism in the 1880s and 1890s. The
world of ideas and books, trips to Greece, and Impressionist painting will
never be accessible to Mrs Giles of Durham, just as Mrs Woolf of
Bloomsbury cannot feel the anger and tiredness of a life of scrubbing and
wringing. This, it seems, is because there is no longer a noumenal realm of
organic unity which we can all feel together, united by common sense of
aesthetic responsiveness.

A few years before the Woolfs attended the Guild conference, Gerald
Duckworth published *The Makers of our Clothes*, a report on workers and
working conditions in the London tailoring and dressmaking trades written
by Clementina Black and Mrs Carl Meyer.[69] The study emerged from a
combination of the labour movement campaign for a minimum wage and a
long-standing philanthropic interest in sweated trades which had flourished
around the *Daily News* Anti-Sweating Exhibition in 1906. The text itself
displays this nineteenth-century marriage of philanthropy, sympathy, and a
more material politics of representation. Black declares in her introduction
that nearly all the impoverished home-workers she encountered in the
course of the survey were 'good citizens who deserve well of their country,
and who mostly receive, in return for prolonged and patient labour, a very

---

[68] Kate Flint, 'Virginia Woolf and the General Strike', *Essays in Criticism*, 36 (1986), 319–35
(p. 323).
[69] Mrs Carl Meyer and Clementina Black, *The Makers of our Clothes: A Case for Trade
Boards* (London: Duckworth, 1909).

small share in the joys, the comforts or the beauties of life'.[70] The democratic language of citizenship and material entitlement is welded here to the
ideal that all desire and respond to the beauty of life. Black employs characteristic skill in transforming the survey's tabulated data and interview
notes into narrative accounts of working-class women's lives. These are narratives that are tied to those things like baths and money that for Woolf prevent working-class women's entry into the aesthetic. Take, for instance, the
case of the young girl 'who presses trousers . . . and whose work . . . is paid
only 7s. a week':

> She works in the same room with two young men pressers and is of [the] opin-
> ion that she presses trousers quite as well as they do. She does not know their
> wages but feels sure that they are not getting less than 18s. She began work at
> 2s. 6d. in this factory, four years ago and has risen by degrees, but had, to use
> her own phrase, 'a lot of trouble' to get her last rise of 1s. a week. She and her
> parents are, justly, much dissatisfied with her present wage, and are also dis-
> pleased that the employer has not kept a promise that she should learn
> machining. That a young girl should spend four years of her life wielding
> heavy pressing irons in a hot, ill-ventilating room, and attain at the end no
> higher payment than 7s. a week, seems indeed a cruel state of things.[71]

Virginia Woolf's response to these sorts of cases at the Guild conference in
1913 had been, she recalls (with some personal anachronism), to feel irri-
tated and depressed that these were narratives which could go nowhere as
women did not have the vote. By the early twentieth century, Clementina
Black had come to a similar realization that women's suffrage was a necessary part of her labour activism.[72] But alongside her activities for the
National Union of Women's Suffrage Societies and editorship of the suffrage journal, the *Common Cause*, Black seems to have attempted to
reshape another form of representation for working-class women.

   Black's rendering of the interview with the trouser presser marks a distinctive turn away from the vein of philanthropic representations of the
poor in the nineteenth century. The propagandist turn to sympathy for this
'cruel state of things' does not reduce the girl to a mute object of pity. As

---

[70] Ibid. 11.
[71] Meyer and Black, *Makers of our Clothes*, p. 50.
[72] See Clementina Black 'The Year's Progress in the Women's Suffrage Movement', *The
Englishwoman*, 4 (1910), 255–60. Black, like Isabella Ford, resisted attempts by the 'People's
Suffrage Federation' to fold the question of women's suffrage into a broader campaign for
adult suffrage for all men and women alike, arguing that although this was her eventual goal,
it would delay the establishment of votes for women on the same terms currently existing for
men. On adult versus women's suffrage in the socialist movement during this period see June
Hannam and Karen Hunt, *Socialist Women: Britain 1880s–1920s* (London: Routledge, 2002),
pp. 108–11.

Emma Francis argues, the 'snapshots' of women workers in Black's industrial investigations imagine 'a full, autonomous and dignified subjectivity for the working-class woman, as both woman and worker'.[73] The presser remains an agent in a community well aware of its rights and bargaining powers. She is an individual with plans and strategies, and just enough liberty to know that the value of her work is the same as that of men. In this construction of agency, this sense that stories of lives dominated by baths and money were stories that needed to be self-represented in the age of democracy, Black's works for the Women's Industrial Council anticipate Llewelyn Davies's later editions for the Women's Co-operative Guild. Neither Black nor Llewelyn Davies were concerned with the aesthetic value of these stories as stories, but they both emerged from a nineteenth-century world of purposive literary realism in which reading of others remote from the self could develop a wider ethical sensibility: the act of representation was, in part at least, a necessary means of escaping the narrow lot of individualism.

By 1931 Woolf's aesthetic was no longer about marshalling six or 6,000 characters to walk in her authorial step, or constructing a web of sympathy between characters and the implied reader, but flashing light out through the desires and imaginations of her subjects in order to explore individuation. In the middle section of Woolf's *To the Lighthouse* (1927), titled 'Time Passes', a radical rejection of nineteenth-century sentimental narrative and temporal structure is paired with the sturdy constant of the charlady, Mrs McNab. The death of Mrs Ramsay, whose consciousness has been the dominant point of view for the first part of the book, is bracketed off as an aside in this section, imploding the nineteenth-century literary convention of the deathbed scene: '[Mr Ramsay stumbling along a passage stretched his arms out one dark morning, but, Mrs Ramsay having died rather suddenly the night before, he stretched his arms out. They remained empty]'.[74] This brilliant subversion of realism is sustained throughout the passage in which 'history' and 'events' (the First World War, deaths, and worldly achievements) are relegated to brief addenda to the subjective passage of time in the consciousness of the abandoned house.

Only Mrs McNab remains a resolute object in this internalized world as she stumps and 'leers' her way through the dusting:

> Visions of joy there must have been at the wash-tub . . . Some cleavage of the dark there must have been, some channel in the depths of obscurity through which light enough issued to twist her face grinning in the glass and make her,

[73] Emma Francis, 'Why wasn't Amy Levy More of a Socialist?', in N. Valman and N. Hetherington (eds.), *Critical Essays on Amy Levy* (Athens, Ohio: Ohio University Press, forthcoming).
[74] Woolf, *To the Lighthouse*, p. 118.

turning to her job again, mumble out the old music hall song. Meanwhile the
mystic, the visionary, walked the beach, stirred a puddle, looked at a stone,
and asked themselves 'What am I?' 'What is this?' and suddenly an answer
was vouchsafed them (what it was they could not say): so that they were warm
in the frost and had comfort in the desert. But Mrs McNab continued to drink
and gossip as before.[75]

The passage is at once an account of irreconcilable difference, between the
mystic living in the 'reality' of ideas and the charlady made of material phenomena, and at the same time full of subtle ironies that undermine such a
limited reading. The radiant enlightenment of the mystic on the beach is
contrasted with the dense obscurity of Mrs McNab and neither the chink of
light that makes the latter sing, nor the answers to the great questions posed
by the former can ever meet in shaping a world. Kate Flint concludes that
'class positions are [thus] hierarchically reaffirmed' at the end of 'Time
Passes'.[76] Yet the gentle mockery of that ungendered self, freed by a length
of capital to ask 'What am I?', is unmistakable in the parenthesis '(what it
was they could not say)' as it is the bathos of Mrs McNab's world persist-
ing as ever in a solid community of drink and gossip. Woolf's radical aesthetic needed to claim a space for this androgynous 'mystic', the writer, as
an autonomous individual whose life and thought, unlike that of Mrs
Ramsay (or Julia Stephen), was freed from thinking through Mrs McNab;
free from prioritizing ethical obligations over the aesthetic.[77] Woolf's aesthetic is in part a refusal of the woman writer's assimilation in a nineteenth-
century tradition of feminine sympathy and, more broadly, the absorption
of the upper middle-class woman into a life of duties towards others. But
Woolf's very knowingness in playing with this tradition acknowledges, as in
this passage, a sense of loss: the loss of an aesthetic realm of the ideal that
could shape the world for more than one individual alone in the desert of
modern life.

Woolf's evaluation of working-class women's contributions to *Life as we
have Known it* is couched in the same language of density and darkness that
shapes Mrs McNab's mind, impenetrable to the rays of narrative consciousness in *To The Lighthouse*. 'These lives', Woolf concludes regarding
the autobiographical fragments, 'are still half hidden in profound obscurity.
To express even what is expressed here has been a work of labour and

---

[75] Ibid. 120.
[76] Flint, 'Virginia Woolf and the General Strike', p. 332.
[77] In a contiguous passage in the 'Time Passes' section, Mrs McNab recalls Mrs Ramsay
as inhabiting a self-obscuring 'grey cloak' of good works, bound to think through the feelings
of her charlady: '"Good evening, Mrs McNab," she said, and told cook to keep a plate of milk
soup for her—quite thought she wanted it, carrying that heavy basket all the way from town'.
Woolf, *To the Lighthouse*, p. 125.

difficulty' (p. xxxvii). For the generation of socialists inspired by William Morris, art and labour had been part of the same somatic aesthetic tradition: a natural bodily pleasure derived from crafting beauty from nature. For Woolf, labour can only ever detract from art and both exist in entirely different realms: phenomena and reality. Floundering a little regarding what might be gained by those like herself from a closer unity with working-class women (the odd word subsisting in their vocabularies) Woolf concludes brightly, 'we have as much to give them as they to give us—wit and detachment, learning and poetry, and all those good gifts which those who have never answered bells or minded machines enjoy by right' (p. xxviii).

The belief in a democracy of aesthetic responsiveness shared by Clementina Black and so many socialists of the 1880s embraced feeling and hope for others not as philanthropic sentiment, but as a radicalizing site of collective unity. In her preface for the Guild, if not in her fiction, Woolf returns to the language of nineteenth-century aesthetic philanthropy: the aesthetic is the rightful gift of the privileged and they may choose to share it with the less fortunate. It is neither a common capacity of desire nor a force for social transformation, but a means by which the individual freed by capital can effect her detachment from the world of material phenomena and write herself as an autonomous being.

III

If Woolf's works thus implicitly rewrite the ethical concerns with representation, individuation, and sympathy shared by many women socialists of the 1880s, then her good friend and fellow Bloomsbury aesthetician, Roger Fry, was drawn to address the legacy of Morris's era in more explicit terms. Fry went up to Cambridge in 1885, a few months after the resurgence of socialist societies and debates in London. Whilst the young Virginia Stephen was confined to the nurseries of Kensington in these years of political enthusiasm, two of Roger Fry's closest friends at University, Goldsworthy Lowes Dickinson and C. R. Ashbee, went so far as to attend a lecture at Kelmscott House for the Hammersmith Branch of the Socialist League.[78] For Ashbee this encounter with William Morris shaped his future career, leading him to live at Toynbee Hall in the East End and establish the Guild of Handicraft, committed to the communal production of Arts and

---

[78] Frances Spalding, *Roger Fry: Art and Life* (London: Granada, 1980), p. 23. E. M. Forster, *Goldsworthy Lowes Dickinson* (London: Edward Arnold, 1934), pp. 84–91 suggests that his subject also remained fairly conservative throughout the turmoil of the 1880s.

Crafts goods.[79] His friends' excitement at the prospect of socialist reform unsettled some of Fry's received opinions, but did not bounce him into a wholehearted enthusiasm for a new life after the revolution. Writing to his mother in the aftermath of the Trafalgar Square demonstration and riots of 1887, he hoped 'that it won't come to much because then one would have to make up one's mind what position to take up, which of all things is objectionable to me'.[80] Whilst all his 'friends were already convinced that social service of some kind was the only end worth pursuing in life' Fry alone, as he recalled to Shaw years later, 'cherished as a guilty secret a profound scepticism about all political activity and even progress itself and had begun to think of art as somehow my only possible job'.[81]

When she came to write his biography in the late 1930s Woolf was sure, however, that one meeting that resulted from Fry's tangential relations with the socialist movement in the 1880s had a profound effect on his thinking. In July 1886 Edward Carpenter visited Cambridge and, Woolf concludes, turned Fry's thoughts 'to democracy and the future of England'.[82] Fry himself was to rewrite Carpenter's democratic aesthetics of somatic response in the early twentieth century, but Carpenter, unlike other socialist notables Fry met at the time, at least gave beauty and art a central place in his ideal of democracy. Fry recalled that Shaw had 'dazzled' him with wit and worldly experience at a Cambridge lunch party around the same time, but the latter 'explained incidentally that [he] had "gone into" the subject of art and there was nothing in it. It was all hocus pocus.'[83] Brilliant as Shaw's display was, it thus had little purchase on the idealism of Fry, Lowes Dickinson, and Ashbee and had no chance against the worship inspired by Carpenter. C. R. Ashbee noted in his journal, 'It is as if we had a hero among us . . . We are knit together by a presence.'[84] Carpenter's celebration of fellowship and the virile love of comrades across classes as the foundation of a new democracy certainly resonated with this generation of young men blurring the lines between homosocial intellectual excitement and homosexual love. Carpenter's own route from

---

[79] On Ashbee's relationship with Morris see Peter Stansky, *William Morris, C. R. Ashbee and the Arts and Crafts* (London: Nine Elms Press, 1984), pp. 11–14. Stansky comments that Ashbee was a socialist 'in a fairly superficial sense' (p. 4); for an excellent discussion of Ashbee's sexual politics of philanthropy at Toynbee Hall and after see Seth Koven, *Slumming: Sexual and Social Politics in Victorian London* (Princeton: Princeton University Press, 2004), pp. 264–8, 278–9.

[80] Virginia Woolf, *Roger Fry: A Biography* (1940; repr. London: Vintage, 2003), p. 47.

[81] Draft letter, Roger Fry to George Bernard Shaw [*c.*1928] in *The Letters of Roger Fry*, ed. Denys Sutton, 2 vols. (London: Chatto & Windus, 1972), ii.

[82] Woolf, *Roger Fry*, p. 47.

[83] Ibid. 56.

[84] Ashbee, cit Spalding, *Roger Fry*, p. 23.

Figure 8. Roger Fry, *Edward Carpenter*, 1894. National Portrait Gallery 2447.

Cambridge, to a philanthropic curacy and his experiment in smallholding at Millthorpe, seemed to unite their several interests: a critical reaction against the establishment; a desire for social service; the pursuit of truth and beauty; a language in which homosexual love could speak its name as a positive force for social and cultural transformation.

Fry somewhat disingenuously described Carpenter to his parents as 'one of F. D. Maurice's curates once' but reassured them that he was 'agreeably disappointed' on meeting him; having expected to find Carpenter 'a rampant and sensational Bohemian', Fry was greeted by 'a most delightful man ... absolutely free from all affectation'.[85] A visit to Millthorpe with Lowes Dickinson the following Easter confirmed to Fry that Carpenter was 'quite one of the best men I have ever met, although he has given up so much for an ideal'.[86] A year later it seemed to Fry's rather conservative parents that their son was making a similar sacrifice by passing over an academic career in science for an uncertain future as an artist. Fry moved back into the parental home to study art under Francis Bate in Hammersmith and a rare moment of paternal approval seems to have related to Fry's choice of footwear. Writing to Carpenter to thank him for a gift of a pair of his sandals, Fry added that his father was thinking of ordering a pair: 'a Lord Justice in sandals will be a landmark in the process of civil ... I mean decivilisation'.[87]

The most visible aesthetic legacy of this friendship remains Fry's 1894 portrait of Carpenter, which the artist bequeathed to the National Portrait Gallery in London on Carpenter's death in 1929. The painting, like Fry's first major critical study, *Giovanni Bellini* (1899), displays his debt to fin-de-siècle aestheticism. The muted palette of greys and browns and the full-length pose of the subject in a composition of strong vertical and horizontal lines is as suggestive of Whistler's contemporary portraits as Fry's monograph is of that other Ruskin-baiter, Walter Pater.[88] Yet Diana Maltz argues that Fry's grasp of the distinctions between such high aestheticism and Carpenter's own insistence on a democracy of collective feeling can be read in this work: the sitter's muted dress, back turned to the mirror, repudiates the self-reflection and display of the decadent dandy.[89] Fry's early enthusiasm for Ruskin had begun to wane during his travels in Italy in the early 1890s and by the turn of the century his own theory of individual sensuous response to the significance of form in a work of art began to take shape under the influence

[85] Fry, cit. ibid. 24.
[86] Fry, cit. Woolf, *Roger Fry*, p. 47.
[87] Spalding, *Roger Fry*, p. 24.
[88] Ibid. 64.
[89] Diana Maltz, private communication to the author.

of the American art critic Bernard Berenson.[90] But even in Fry's highly influential collection of essays on modernist aesthetics, *Vision and Design* (1920), it is possible to see how Fry clings on to the Carpenterian idea of a democracy of aesthetic responsiveness. As carefully as he rewrites the legacies of Morris and Ruskin, Fry remains bound up with a desire to reconcile aesthetic autonomy with communal production and the latent *sensus communis* that constructs a bond between the artist and the untutored observer. In the teeth of Clive Bell and Virginia Woolf's counter-arguments, eventually published as Bell's *Civilization* (1928), Fry strives for an aesthetics of democracy.[91]

In 1909 Fry published 'An Essay in Aesthetics' in the *New Quarterly* and marked out his rejection of the ethical aesthetics that had underpinned his friends' enthusiasm for the 'religion of socialism' in the 1880s. The 'view taken by Ruskin' that 'the imaginative life' subserves morality was in itself, Fry argued, a morally dubious self-deception.[92] For Fry, the realm of art was absolutely autonomous from 'actual life': art expressed and stimulated an imaginative life in which responsive action and moral responsibility were absent (14). Ruskinian and Tolstoyan aesthetics, in which art was valued through its contribution to an ethical affect, denuded art of its rightful status as a site of 'greater purity and freedom of . . . emotion' than morally responsive 'actual life' (16). Fry's rejection of conventional mimetic theories of art is in many ways reminiscent of Wilde's critical writings over a decade earlier. 'It might even be', Fry argues, 'that . . . we should rather justify actual life by its relation to the imaginative, justify nature by its likeness to art' (15). Yet this legacy of the playful, purposive aestheticism of the 1890s is hitched rather oddly in Fry's essay to a far more earnest inheritance of nineteenth-century cultural thought.

Fry insists that art exists as a means of expressing the emotions but in order to fulfil this function art must be 'adapted to that disinterested intensity of contemplation, which we have found to be the result of cutting off the responsive action' (19). The freedom and autonomy of the aesthetic emotion thus lies for Fry in that same quality of 'disinterestedness' that Matthew Arnold argued was the ideal state of the critic and of culture itself in 'The Function of Criticism at the Present Time' (1865). Like Arnold, Fry perceives the very weakness of Ruskinian aesthetics to lie in its prioritization of material history and contemporary ethics over the autonomous development of art itself. Fry honed his criticism quite pointedly in the

---

[90] Spalding, *Roger Fry*, pp. 64–70.

[91] On Leonard and Virginia's divergent responses to *Civilization* see Flint, 'Virginia Woolf and the General Strike', p. 325.

[92] Roger Fry, 'An Essay in Aesthetics' (1909); repr. in *Vision and Design* (London: Chatto & Windus, 1920), p. 14.

direction of the political aesthetics of 1880s socialism when he was invited to give a lecture to the Fabian Society in 1917. The very title of the lecture, 'Art and Life', alludes to Ruskin's dictum 'there is no wealth but life' and Morris's own lectures 'The Aims of Art' and 'How we Live and How we might Live'.[93]

Although Fry names neither writer in his address, his assertion that 'the forms of Gothic architecture were merely the answer to certain engineering problems which had long occupied the inventive ingenuity of twelfth century architects' is a calculated blow to the political aesthetics of both.[94] The veneration of the medieval craftsman and guild system that arose from Ruskin's 'The Nature of Gothic' and was developed by Morris and his followers is thus squashed as a dangerous and naïve acceptance of 'the general atmosphere—the ethos, which the works of art of a certain period exhale' (2). For Fry, aesthetic development is entirely autonomous from material history. Art simply does not correspond to life, and moments like the emergence of the Gothic merely underscore that whereas 'in life the direction of movement was sharply bent backwards, in art the direction followed on in a continuous straight line' (3).

Fry's modernist assertion of the absolute autonomy of the aesthetic may well have pleased some of his audience in the Fabian Society at the time. The year 1917 marked a fresh start for the Society after six years of internecine conflict between a new generation of members, such as G. D. H. Cole and Sam Hobson, who favoured guild socialism and claimed Morris as their inspiration, and the 'old gang' of the Webbs and Shaw.[95] But Fry himself had been happy to invoke Morris's aim of bringing art and everyday life into closer conjunction through communal labour a few years earlier in 1912, when he established the Omega Workshops.[96] In a letter soliciting support for his venture from George Bernard Shaw, Fry argued that 'since the complete decadence of the Morris movement nothing has been done in England but pastiche and more or less unscrupulous imitation of old work'. A collective of artists 'working together with mutual assistance instead of each insisting on the singularity of his personal gifts' could bring new value to

---

[93] John Ruskin, *Unto This Last* (1860) in *The Complete Works of John Ruskin*, ed. E. T. Cook and Alexander Wedderburn, 39 vols. (London: George Allen, 1903–12), xvii. 105.

[94] Roger Fry, 'Art and Life' (1917); repr. in *Vision and Design* (London: Chatto & Windus, 1920), p. 3.

[95] Betty Vernon, 'Beatrice Webb and Margaret Cole: Fabian Politics and Pacifism', in *Women in Milieu of Leonard and Virginia Woolf*, pp. 145–69 (p. 147).

[96] For an account of Fry as the natural successor of Morris see Stansky, *William Morris and Bloomsbury*, pp. 21–5.

'decorative work' and the domestic interior: 'co-operation', Fry concluded, 'is a first necessity' in this sphere of work.[97]

Both Fiona MacCarthy and Frances Spalding are careful to emphasize the differences between the Omega collective—whose members included Vanessa Bell, Duncan Grant, Henri Gaudier-Brzeska, and Wyndham Lewis—and the earlier workshop experiments of the British Arts and Crafts movement.[98] Unlike his friend C. R. Ashbee and Morris himself, for example, Fry was little interested in perfecting durable craft objects and bought in ready-made plain pieces of furniture for the artists to decorate with the free play of aesthetic creativity. The Omega provided a steady income for artists ready to apply their talents to everyday objects of luxury interiors and did not seek to dismantle the division between the chair-maker in High Wycombe and the Slade graduate running a studio. As Stansky points out, however, the essay in which Fry first gave shape to his idea of reforming the domestic arts appeared in a context that was in direct conversation with the political concerns of Arts and Crafts socialists of the 1880s.[99] In 1912 Fry contributed an essay he later titled 'Art and Socialism' to a book edited by H. G. Wells on the future of the nation, *Socialism and the Great State*.[100] Although Fry explicitly stated that he was not a socialist himself, he argues that Wells's proposition for an anti-authoritarian (and anti-Fabian) 'Great State' promises a hopeful future for the arts as 'the greatest art has always been communal, the expression—in highly individualised ways, no doubt—of common aspirations and ideals'.[101] There are distinct echoes of Morris's *Signs of Change* and *News from Nowhere* in Fry's discussion of the relation between the 'high' and 'lesser' arts in a socialist future:

> Supposing, then, that under the Great State it was found impossible, at all events at first, to stimulate and organise the abstract creative power of the pure artist, the balance might after all be in favour of the new order if the whole practice of applied art could once more become rational and purposeful. In a world where the objects of daily use and ornament were made with practical common sense, the aesthetic sense would need far less to seek consolation and repose in works of pure art. (50)

[97] Roger Fry to George Bernard Shaw, 11 Dec. 1912, BL Add. Mss. 50534.

[98] Spalding, *Roger Fry*, p. 178; Fiona MacCarthy, 'Roger Fry and the Omega Ideal', *The Omega Workshops, 1912–1919: Decorative Arts of Bloomsbury* (London: Crafts Council, 1983), pp. 9–13.

[99] Stansky, *William Morris and Bloomsbury*, p. 23.

[100] H. G. Wells, Countess Warwick, and G. R. S. Taylor (eds.), *Socialism and the Great State: Essays in Construction* (New York: Harper Brothers, 1912).

[101] Fry, 'Art and Socialism', in *Vision and Design*, p. 40.

The 'present unreality' of art imbued with 'false values' as a result of 'its symbolising of social status' would be purified by this contact with craft practice (49, 51). When the disorderly tat of an everyday station waiting room—much like the 'miserable wreckage' of Morris's 'aesthetic drawing room'—has been swept away by the socialist state along with inequitable social conditions, then 'people would develop some more immediate reaction to the work of art than they can at present achieve' (49).

The qualitative difference between Morris and Fry is that 'the people' in the latter's account are not part of a productive aesthetic continuum, but responsive consumers exercising 'collective artistic judgement' (51). The aesthetic emotion may well be a capacity available to all for Fry, but it remains remote from the labour of 'actual life and its practical utilities'. In his later writing, Fry couched the separation in terms that invoke Moore's idealism: those fortunate enough to experience the artist's effort 'to bend our emotional understanding' properly 'feel it to have a peculiar quality of "reality" which makes it a matter of infinite importance in their lives' (199). For Fry, rather like Wilde, socialism will free the artist from the material world of phenomena to dwell in the 'reality' of ideas and a newly tasteful collective of consumers may even make its 'poets and painters and philosophers and deep investigators . . . a new kind of kings' (51).

Wyndham Lewis was quick to identify this parallel between the philosophy of the Omega and 1890s aestheticism in the attack on Fry that accompanied his secession from the organization in 1913. As to the Omega's tendencies in art, he wrote in an open letter to interested parties,

> they alone would be sufficient to make it very difficult for any vigorous art-instinct to long remain under that roof. The Idol is still Prettiness, with its mid-Victorian languish of the neck, and its skin of 'greenery-yallery', despite the Post-What-Not fashionableness of its draperies. This family party of strayed and Dissenting Aesthetes, however, were compelled to call in as much modern talent as they could find, to do the rough and masculine work without which they knew their efforts would not rise above the level of a pleasant tea-party, or command more attention.[102]

The 'rough and masculine work' of Wyndham Lewis's virile modernism must break away from the effeminate aestheticism of the Omega which seeks merely to decorate and obscure the products of the machine age. As Morris reacted against the decorative aestheticism of the 1880s and 1890s by returning to an ideal of the manly labour of handicraft, so too Lewis 'wanted to . . . incorporate the power' of the virile productive process 'into

---

[102] Wyndham Lewis, cit. Spalding, *Roger Fry*, pp. 186–7.

his own pictorial vocabulary'.[103] Yet as Richard Cork makes clear, Lewis's Vorticist secession embraced the machine, rather than the labourer, as the source of production and modernity.[104] An aesthetic of virile production in the modernist era involved stripping away the sensuous realm of the feeling body: that very realm which had first drawn Fry towards the aesthetics of democracy through his friendship with Edward Carpenter.

IV

The Bloomsbury Group and the collection of socialist writers and artists who moved through the Fellowship of the New Life and the ILP shared a belief that aesthetics and the future of society were intertwined. Yet the insistence within the Bloomsbury Group that disinterestedness was both the grounds of civilization and of aesthetic judgement irrevocably divided its political interventions from those of the socialists of the 1880s; a division that somehow seems a priori to more easily captured differences between analyses of class or economic determinism. Nowhere is this division more clear than in the contrast between Woolf's interventions in the cause of women and peace, and efforts in the same field by her predecessors. In 1938 Virginia Woolf published her polemical essay, *Three Guineas*, exploring the relationship between patriarchal institutions, women's subordination, and the tyranny of war. The evolution of the essay had been almost as protracted and full of variation as Olive Schreiner's efforts with her 'sex book', *Woman and Labour*, which had finally reached the press in 1911 after over twenty years of restructuring and enforced rewriting as a consequence of the destruction of a manuscript during the Boer War. Whilst Schreiner's attempts to address the 'Woman Question' led to the irruption of aesthetic allegories into her prose argument, Woolf's struggle to bring together the questions of professions for women and the culture of masculine militarism across a hundred years of British history led her to a short-lived experiment with a new hybrid, the 'novel-essay'.[105] Schreiner predicted, in a chapter entitled 'Woman and War', that the extinction of war itself 'will not be delayed much longer' once 'Mother nature' was appointed umpire in the struggle of women to achieve 'free trade' in their labour and hence take part

---

[103] Richard Cork, *Vorticism and Abstract Art in the First Machine Age*, 2 vols. (London: Gordon Fraser, 1976), i. 87.

[104] Ibid. 85–101.

[105] See Charles G. Hoffman, 'Virginia Woolf's Manuscript Revisions of The Years', *PMLA*, 84 (1969), 79–89; Virginia Woolf, *The Pargiters: The Novel-Essay Portion of 'The Years'*, ed. Mitchell A. Leaska (New York: New York Public Library, 1977).

in national government.[106] Disclaiming any innate moral superiority on the part of women, Schreiner argued that women have an 'intimate, personal, and indissoluble' relation to war: 'we have in all ages produced, at enormous cost, the primal munition of war' in the shape of men's bodies.[107] When Woolf published *Three Guineas* on the eve of another world war, she too predicated an end to war upon women's participation in governing institutions. As Schreiner claimed that women would be immune to the 'tinsel of trumpets and flags' that seduced men with glory, so too Woolf argued that 'the daughters of educated men' schooled by subordination would be 'free from unreal loyalties' like 'patriotism'.[108]

War in *Three Guineas*, however, as Susan Pedersen argues 'appears purely psychological in origin, a consequence of the misguided valorization of those quintessentially masculine attributes of competition and aggression'.[109] The 'daughters of educated men working in their own class—how indeed can they work in any other'—Woolf suggests should form an 'Outsiders Society' to meet appeals to these 'sex instincts' of patriotism and war with 'complete indifference'.[110] Woolf's weapon of indifference is the ethical application of her argument for women's access to the hitherto masculine realm of 'disinterested' culture. Woolf's essay strives to make the 'daughters of educated men' the epitome of the nineteenth-century liberal subject: rational and disinterested individuals who dismiss appeals to romantic ideals of particularity with an assertion of the universal; 'As a woman my country is the whole world' (234). It is as if for Woolf the absolute autonomy of the aesthetic was a model of the state scarce imaginable in the nineteenth century: a state in which women (or daughters) could be in themselves autonomous and disinterested beings rather than purely relative creatures.

---

[106] Olive Schreiner, *Woman and Labour* (London: Fisher Unwin, 1911), pp. 178, 166–7.

[107] Ibid. 169.

[108] Ibid. 171; Virginia Woolf, *A Room of One's Own and Three Guineas*, ed. Michèle Barrett (Harmondsworth: Penguin, 1993), p. 203.

[109] Susan Pederson, *Women's Stake in Democracy: Eleanor Rathbone's Answer to Virginia Woolf* (Austin, Tex.: Harry Ransom Humanities Research Centre, 2000), p. 23.

[110] Woolf, *Three Guineas*, pp. 234–5. Woolf's own footnote to her statement on class is worth quoting here: 'In the nineteenth century much valuable work was done for the working class by educated men's daughters in the only way that was then open to them . . . If [women who now have educations of their own] . . . renounce the very qualities which education should have bought—reason, tolerance, knowledge—and play at belonging to the working class and adopting its cause, they merely expose that cause to the ridicule of the educated class, and do nothing to improve their own.' Woolf recommends that her readers discover the unglamorous nature of working-class women's lives from *Life as we have Known it*. Woolf, *Three Guineas*, p. 310.

Romantic appeals to the 'Teutonic' race, if not nation, were of course the staple of Schreiner's argument in 'Woman and War' and a staple that, by the 1930s, connoted the fascism that Woolf was writing against in *Three Guineas*. It is precisely women's interestedness, their particular contribution to the production of life that, for Schreiner, will ensure that their labours in the field of government will bring an end to war. Schreiner's claim that 'men's bodies are our woman's work of art' speaks simultaneously of a politics and aesthetics of production and engagement in the material world.[111] Schreiner's feminism of 'virile' womanhood sought to insert women into a history of communal labour; Woolf's symbolic cremation of the word 'feminist' in *Three Guineas* aimed to do away with the 'obsolete' and partial demand of women of the right to earn a living and replace it with the freedom to stand outside history, beyond the reach of 'sex instincts'.[112] For George Bernard Shaw, who had been ostracized by many for abandoning his former position of neutrality during the First World War, this aspiration towards disinterestedness was in itself morally culpable. In *Heartbreak House* (1919), Shaw rewrote for the post-war period the Chekhovian drama—made familiar by Constance Garnett's translations—of the leisured household oblivious to the forces of history pressing upon it. In his preface, Shaw arraigned a generation of upper-middle-class writers possessed of 'social opportunities of contact with our politicians, administrators, and newspaper proprietors' but who failed to bring their cultural knowledge to bear on these individuals.[113]

> They hated politics. They did not wish to realize Utopia for the common people: they wished to realize their favourite fictions and poems in their own lives; and, when they could, they lived without scruple on incomes which they did nothing to earn . . . They took the only part of our society in which there was leisure for high culture, and made it an economic, political, and, as far as practicable, a moral vacuum; and as Nature, abhorring the vacuum, immediately filled it up with sex and with all sorts of refined pleasures, it was a very delightful place to be.[114]

The palpable, satiric anger Shaw's text directs at the 'vacuum' of autonomous aesthetics in the Bloomsbury era is an oddly appropriate

---

[111] Schreiner *Woman and Labour*, p. 174.
[112] Woolf, *Three Guineas*, pp. 227, 234.
[113] Shaw, preface to *Heartbreak House* (1919) *Collected Prefaces*, p. 378.
[114] Ibid. 378–9.

counterpart to Woolf's Swiftian attack on the unreal pomp of patriarchal institutions twenty years later.[115]

If Shaw held the individualizing autonomous aesthetic of Bloomsbury responsible for abandoning collective, cultural engagement—for not speaking of the aesthetic as a symbol of morality—Woolf held the material pragmatism of Shaw and the Webbs responsible for her amorality. The Fabian emphasis on material security and collective ownership as a means of securing 'absolute individualism' and increasing specialization was a complement to Bloomsbury's own aesthetic specialization. As fractions which distinguished themselves from the ruling class, but were, in so many ways, an immediate part of it by this time, both groups developed what Williams terms 'a social conscience' that aimed 'in the end to protect the private consciousness'.[116] Shaw's intellectual 'superman' provided the brains of social engineering; Woolf's visionary artist ensured that aesthetic development continued on in its straight line of autonomy, perceptible to those individuals freed by capital to see it. Romantic radical appeals to a historicized, productive aesthetic of the people were, of course, still in existence in the early twentieth century. But by the 1920s, at least, it was not the socialist movement that sought to knit together politics and aesthetics in this manner. A year before Woolf published *Three Guineas*, Arthur Penty, the former guild socialist and Morrisite art critic of the *New Age*, concluded that fascism was the natural reaction to the poison and ugliness of modernism and Bolshevism. Fascism, he argued, appreciated the 'strong sense of reality' imbued in 'traditional things' and thus offered the only hope of knitting together the people with a politics of collective, productive art.[117]

---

[115] Jane Marcus, '"No More Horses": Virginia Woolf on Art and Propaganda', *Women's Studies*, 4 (1977), 265–90 (p. 273); Brenda R. Silver, 'The Authority of Anger: *Three Guineas* as a Case Study', *Signs*, 16 (1991), 340–70.

[116] Williams, 'Bloomsbury Fraction', p. 167.

[117] A. J. Penty, *Tradition and Modernism in Politics* (London: Sheed & Ward, 1937), p. 58.

Index